Longman Dictionary of Art

Judy Martin

Longman Dictionary of Art

A handbook of terms, techniques, materials, equipment and processes

Longman

About the author

Judy Martin has a Diploma in Art and Design and an MFA (Master of Fine Art). She has lectured in drawing, painting, design and modern art history, since when she has concentrated on writing and editing, particularly publications in art techniques and art history. She lives in London.

Longman Group Limited,
Longman House, Burnt Mill, Harlow,
Essex CM20 2JE, England
and Associated Companies throughout the world.

First published 1986

British Library Cataloguing in Publication Data

Martin, Frances Judy
Dictionary of art.
1. Art—Dictionaries
I. Title
703'.21 N33

Set in Linotron Bembo and Gill
by MCL Dataset Ltd, Ruislip, Middlesex
Printed in Great Britain
by Butler & Tanner Ltd., Frome, Somerset.

ISBN 0-582-89229 5

Introduction

The *Dictionary of Art* is a reference work for practising artists. Primarily, it is intended to be of use to school and college students specializing in art, to the many people involved with various art forms through evening classes and other part-time courses, and to the interested amateur working at home without access to formal tuition. The *Dictionary* provides information on techniques, processes, equipment and materials used in major art disciplines and some specialized design areas. It covers a wide range of detail. Cross-references are included where appropriate to identify related items that will enlarge upon the context of a given definition.

The main categories included in the *Dictionary* are painting, drawing, sculpture, printmaking and ceramics. The *Dictionary of Art* covers many traditional and commonly used modern terms which have specific meanings in the context of any or all of the basic categories described. It does not cover areas related to some aspects of art, eg electronics, photography, video, which have their own technical vocabularies. The value of this reference work is intended to be in the assembly of all these terms within a concise and accessible form.

Historical detail is noted only where it is appropriate to the full definition of a technical or practical term. Artists' biographies and explanations of schools and movements in art history are already well documented in dictionary and glossary form. However, some terms have been included here which deal with recent developments in form and style, such as Conceptual Art, Land Art and Performance Art, because these often depart emphatically from the use of traditional materials and equipment and in this sense have a bearing on the increasing range of techniques and activities which are generally defined as art.

Since the words which refer to the techniques, tools and materials of art relate directly to studio practice, it frequently happens that one term belongs to more than one discipline or has acquired more than one meaning, or a term is used with different shades of meaning according to the context. Variations in usage are explained wherever identifiable and some thought has gone into attempting to define in words the subtlety of qualities that are basically visual or tactile.

A real understanding of tools, materials and processes in art is gained essentially through practice. The practice of an art or craft is a highly pleasurable activity. I hope that this book will increase that pleasure by removing some of the perplexity about the language of art.

Judy Martin

Abbreviations used in the dictionary

abb	abbreviation
adj	adjective
adv	adverb
n	noun
pl	plural
prep	preposition
vb	verb

Fr	French
Ge	German
Gr	Greek
It	Italian
Lat	Latin
US	United States

a

abozzo *n* (*It* sketch, outline)
1 (*painting*) The first stage of a painting when the image is roughly sketched in outline or as a monochrome underpainting.
2 (*sculpture*) The term is also used, less commonly, to refer to the rough shaping of material in the initial stages of carving or modelling.

abrade *vb*
1 To shape a form by ABRADING.
2 To apply an ABRASIVE tool or material to a surface. **abraded** *adj*.

abrading *n*
The technique of shaping a rigid material, especially stone, by rubbing it with abrasive tools and substances that gradually wear down the surface. It is a laborious, lengthy process but the end result is characteristically different from sculpture carved with cutting tools, abraded forms typically having shallow curves and a uniform surface texture.

abrasion *n*
1 The process of using an abrasive.
2 The effect of an abrasive tool or material applied to a surface.

abrasive *n*
A substance sufficiently hard and resistant to grind, smooth or polish the surface of a rigid material by friction. An abrasive may be used in the form of powder, grit or granules, as a coating on paper, fabric or a solid base, or itself in solid form. Abrasives commonly used in sculpture vary from coarse to very fine and include EMERY, PUMICE, SILICON CARBIDE.

absorbed *adj*
The quality of oil paint that has dried with a dull finish due to the oil vehicle of the paint sinking into the support or ground.

absorbency *n*
The capacity of a material to take up a liquid or take in moisture from the surrounding atmosphere.

absorbent ground *n*
A porous ground for painting which absorbs some of the liquid

content of the paint. It is used to speed drying and encourage a matt effect in the finished surface. Gesso is an absorbent ground, as is any composition with a high content of chalk or plaster. The absorbent quality can be an advantage, but with oil paint there is the danger that the ground will soak up the oil too quickly, leaving an uneven paint texture in which the pigments are unstable.

abstract *adj*
The description of an art form or object which is primarily an arrangement of basic visual elements, eg colour, line and contour, mass, shape and texture. An abstract image exists largely within its own terms of reference; purely abstract art is not intended to be representational of the real world in any sense, but the term is also applied to pictorial and symbolic images which may be loosely derived from natural or man-made forms but are described in terms of independent formal elements. See also NON-OBJECTIVE.

academic *adj*
The description of any style or technique in art that conforms to conventional principles such as those taught in academies of art. It is often used to imply an unfavourable judgement of work connected to outmoded or conservative traditions, but in a stricter sense describes work which shows evidence of formal study of theory and practice in a particular discipline.

academy *n*
An institution set up to promote particular standards in art, provide training in theory and practice of fine art disciplines and establish a body of members who will assist with or participate in these aims. The first academies were set up by artists and patrons to give their work influential professional status, superseding the medieval guild system. In various countries the academies gradually acquired the status of national institutions with considerable influence in dictating principles and practice in art. This influence is now less marked, owing to the more widespread provision of art education in various forms, but established academies retain their status as important schools and exhibition centres.

academy board *n*
A prepared support for oil painting consisting of good quality pasteboard coated on one side with a white oil-based ground. Boards are available in a variety of sizes and in some types the ground has an impressed texture simulating canvas weave.

academy figure *n*
A painting or drawing of a human figure at half life-size, made as

an exercise in the course of studying human form and posture. In such works, the pose of the figure is often based on a classical sculpture or traditional figure composition.

acanthus *n*
A traditional sculptural decoration applied to architectural forms, a stylized motif based on the serrated, deeply cut foliage of the acanthus plant.

accelerator *n*
An additive which speeds the chemical change in another substance. Specially formulated chemical accelerators are added to polyester resins to promote curing; a simpler example is common salt, which can speed the hardening of plaster.

accidental colour *n*
1 Colour reflected on an object from its surroundings or from neighbouring objects. Also called reflected colour. Compare LOCAL COLOUR.
2 An optical effect which occurs when a person stares fixedly at a patch of bright colour and then looks away. He or she will temporarily perceive a patch of colour in the same rough shape as the first, but in its complementary colour: ie if the original shape is red, the apparent shape is green.

accidental light *n*
Any source of light depicted in a painting other than daylight. The light from candles, a fire, the moon or an artificial source may be introduced for dramatic effect, eg to create specific points of focus and contrasts of tone and colour.

accidental point *n*
A VANISHING POINT in a pictorial composition which does not lie on the HORIZON LINE.

acetate *n*
See CELLULOSE ACETATE.

acetone *n*
A strong liquid solvent capable of dissolving hardened resins, dried films of oil paint and oil varnishes.

acetylene *n*
A colourless, flammable hydrocarbon gas used to fuel an OXYACETYLENE TORCH.

achromatic colours *n pl*
Black, white and grey, as distinct from all the hues of the colour circle which are known as chromatic colours.

acid bath *n*
A tray or dish containing acid solution in which a metal plate is immersed during the etching process. The type of acid and strength of solution used depend upon the metal of the plate and the qualities required in the etched surface. Acids commonly used are nitric, hydrochloric and ferric chloride.

acid-resist *n*
A substance which withstands the corrosive effect of acid, such as those used to protect non-printing areas of an etching plate. See HARD GROUND, SOFT GROUND, STOPPING OUT VARNISH.

acrolith *n* (*Gr* high stone)
A statue consisting of a wooden trunk with stone head and limbs attached, originally a primitive Greek form. The body might be overlaid with gold or draped with fabric for decoration.

acrylic paint *n*
Paint consisting of pigment evenly dispersed in an emulsion binder which is a liquid form of synthetic acrylic resin. The paint is quick-drying, whether applied thickly or thinly, and forms a tough, flexible, waterproof film in which colours retain their brilliance. The majority of acrylic paints are thinned and mixed with water and synthetic mediums are available which correspond to the chemical composition of the paint, but certain types are also produced that are used with turpentine or a spirit solvent. Acrylic paints are available as thick pastes or viscous fluids, packaged in tubes or jars. Alternatively, it is possible to buy constituent elements -- emulsion base, liquid pigments, diluents or thickeners -- which enable the painter to mix colours according to individual requirements.

acrylic plastics *n pl*
A range of rigid, lightweight, synthetic plastics used as sculpture materials, available in the form of sheets, rods, blocks or tubes which may be colourless and transparent, coloured and translucent or completely opaque. They can be shaped by cutting and abrading. As thermoplastic materials which soften under heat, they can be stretched and shaped into forms which are retained as the material cools and recovers rigidity.

acrylic polymer emulsion *n*
1 A synthetic, resinous PRIMER used to prepare a support for application of acrylic paints. It consists basically of a polymer emulsion mixed with white pigment and is dense, free-flowing and brilliantly white, drying to a tough, flexible, waterproof film.

2 Any of various synthetic emulsions used as diluents or mediums for acrylic paints.

acrylics *n pl*
1 *abb* ACRYLIC PAINTS.
2 *abb* ACRYLIC PLASTICS.

additive *n*
Any substance which is added to another to alter its properties.

adherence *n*
The ability of a paint to cling to the support and form a permanent, stable surface. The properties affecting the paint's adherence are the adhesive quality of the BINDER or VEHICLE, the elasticity of the paint when dry, and its resistance to atmospheric conditions and chemical change. It also depends upon the nature of the support: eg oil paint adheres well to a properly primed canvas but is not stable when applied to either a polished or highly absorbent support.

adsorption *n*
The strong bonding of a thin layer of one substance to the surface of another due to the cohesion of its molecular structure.

adulterant *n*
An inert substance added to paint simply to increase the bulk. This is an economy measure used in the manufacture of inexpensive paint ranges.

advancing colour *n*
A colour which the viewer perceives as apparently coming forward from a picture surface, by comparison with other hues and tones in the painting. In general, pure, intense and warm colours (red, orange, yellow) tend to advance by comparison with cool hues or devalued tones. This property can be used to contribute to an illusion of spatial depth. See also RETREATING COLOUR.

adze *n*
A heavy wood carving tool used for roughing out a form. It has a thick metal blade, curved or angled downwards from the top of a wooden handle, so the cutting edge of the blade is at right angles to the handle.

aerial perspective *n*
See ATMOSPHERIC PERSPECTIVE.

aerugo *n*
See VERDIGRIS.

aesthetic[1] *adj*
The description of a work that is judged to meet broadly held standards of beauty or good taste. Originally this was directly related to the formal theory of AESTHETICS but is now more generally applied, and not only to art objects, as an evaluation of visual character.

aesthetic[2] *n*
A system of evaluation related to a particular theory of the practice and function of art and appreciation of its products.

aesthetics *n*
The philosophy of art with regard to criteria of beauty and the ways in which beauty can be perceived in art.

affiche originale *n* (*Fr* original poster)
A poster or other advertisement designed by a named artist, either hand-drawn or printed as a LIMITED EDITION.

after —— *prep*
When followed by the name of an artist, this term indicates that the work on which it appears is a copy or reproduction based on an original work by that artist. It appears on engravings to indicate a work engraved and printed by someone other than the originator of the image. On a painting or drawing, it denotes a copy or pastiche.

agate *n*
1 A stone which is an impure, variegated form of quartz, characteristically banded with layers of different colours and textures.
2 *abb* AGATE BURNISHER.

agate burnisher *n*
A hand tool used to rub down and burnish gold leaf. The agate tip is set in a handle and may be cylindrical, pointed or hooked. There are different versions of this tool for broad or detailed work and they vary in weight and thickness.

agate ware *n*
Decorative ceramic ware made from different coloured clays rolled and beaten together to form a body with a streaky, layered colour effect similar to the appearance of agate.

aggregate *n*
An inert granular material mixed with cement to make concrete, commonly sand (fine) or gravel (coarse) or a combination of the two. The aggregate supplies body and texture to the mixture.

airbrush[1] *n*
A mechanical painting tool which emits a fine spray of liquid paint or ink. It is fed with a supply of the medium from an attached reservoir and, separately, with compressed air from an external source. The paint combines with the air jet at the tip of the tool to form the spray. In sophisticated models with an adjustable nozzle, the paint can be directed as a broad spray or a line as sharp as a pencil mark, but the airbrush itself does not make contact with the support as does a paintbrush or drawing tool. See also COMPRESSOR.

airbrush[2] *vb*
To apply a liquid medium to a support using an airbrush. **airbrushed** *adj*.

airbrushing *n*
The technique of painting with an AIRBRUSH.

air eraser *n*
A tool similar to an AIRBRUSH, designed to emit a pressurized spray of fine abrasive powder which will erase a thin film of paint from a support.

alabaster *n*
A soft stone of metamorphic origin, used in stone carving. It is naturally translucent, found in a range of pale colours including pure white and pink, and sometimes heavily veined. It is relatively easy to carve and can be brought to a highly polished finish.

à la poupée *n* (*Fr* with a dolly)
A technique of inking an intaglio plate with different colours. A coloured ink is applied with a DOLLY to the appropriate area of the plate. The ink is pushed into the intaglio marks and the plate wiped in preparation for printing. This process is repeated until every area of the plate is coloured. See also INTAGLIO PRINTING.

albumen *n*
A water-soluble protein found in egg yolk and white. When diluted with water and spread as a thin layer, it dries on exposure to light and air, forming a tough, practically insoluble film. This property is exploited in TEMPERA painting, with the use of egg as a BINDER for pigments.

alizarin *n*
A synthetic dye derived from coal tar, used in the manufacture of permanent LAKE PIGMENTS. It was originally developed as alizarin crimson, a less expensive substitute for natural rose

madder dyes, and is now the basis of a range of red, brown and purple hues.

alkyd *n*
A synthetic resin used as a VEHICLE for paints. The term is a derivation of 'alcid', originally used to describe a compound of acid and alcohol, but alkyd resins used in paints are modified with oil. The paints may be applied by the same techniques used in oil painting, but they have the distinctive property that all the colours have similar drying rates and dry more quickly than oil colours.

alla prima *adv* (*It* at first)
The technique of painting directly on a primed support to produce a finished work in one session. The term originally referred to painting in oils, when the colours were applied with immediate reference to their finished effect, by contrast with the gradual process of modifying tones and colours in successive layers of underpainting and glazes. Also known as direct painting and *au premier coup* (Fr).

alligator cracks *n pl*
A pattern of cracks in a layer of oil paint or varnish, usually due to upper layers drying more quickly than those beneath, with a subsequent movement in the paint surface as drying continues. The sharp-edged cracks are often in only one film of paint or varnish, but can penetrate different layers.

all-over painting *n*
A covering term for various forms of abstract painting in which all areas of the picture surface are treated as having equal value in the image, and there is no focal point or dominant feature. It may also imply that the picture area is not framed by the dimensions of the support: the image appears cut off at the edges rather than described within the given format.

alloy *n*
A metal which is the end product of a combination of two or more metals.

altarpiece *n*
A work of art placed on, above or behind the altar of a Christian church. It may be a painting or sculpture, typically relief sculpture, and often consists of two or more parts fixed or hinged together. A winged altarpiece is one in which a central image is flanked by hinged panels which can be opened for display or closed to conceal the image, depending on the occasion. The subject matter is religious, usually relating to the Holy Family or

a patron saint, and more complex images may include a number of narrative scenes depicting the life of the subject or stories from the Bible. See also ANCONA, POLYPTYCH, PREDELLA, REREDOS, RETABLE.

alto rilievo *n* (*It*)
HIGH RELIEF.

alumina *n*
Aluminium oxide, in the form of a lightweight, white, crystalline powder. It is a refractory substance, used as an ingredient of clay bodies and ceramic glazes. Alumina hydrate, or hydrated aluminium oxide, is the form used as an inert base for the preparation of LAKE PIGMENTs.

amasette *n*
A spatula made of horn or ivory formerly used in grinding and mixing oil colours, now replaced by the PALETTE KNIFE.

amorino *n* **amorini** *pl* (*It* little love)
A small winged cherub representing the infant Cupid, often included as a symbolic or decorative element in Renaissance paintings and sculptures.

anaglyph *n*
An image carved in low relief.

analagous colours *n pl*
Colours that are close together or run in sequence on the colour circle, which are therefore related and harmonious, eg blue and a successive range of blue-greens.

anamorphosis *n*
A two-dimensional image designed and executed in such a way that from a frontal viewpoint it appears completely distorted, to the point of being unrecognizable, and can only be seen in correct shape and proportion when viewed from a particular angle, through a special lens, or reflected in a curved mirror.

anastatic printing *n*
See RELIEF ETCHING.

ancona *n*
A large altarpiece consisting of a number of panels mounted together within a frame in a fixed relation, ie not hinged.

aniline colours *n pl*
A range of synthetic dyes made from aniline, a liquid derived from coal tar. They are used in the preparation of LAKE PIGMENTs

and form the colouring agents for various paints, inks and commercial dyestuffs.

animal size *n*
A solution of glue made from the bones or skins of animals.

anneal *vb*
To soften a metal by ANNEALING. **annealed** *adj*.

annealing *n*
The process of heating and cooling a metal to soften it and relieve internal stresses in the material, after which it is more responsive to cutting and shaping processes. The hardness of a metal is directly related to the temperature to which it has previously been heated and the rate at which it has cooled: thus the process of annealing is judged according to the properties of the metal and the work for which it is required.

anti-cerne *n* (*Fr* negative ring)
The method of forming outlines around areas of colour in a painting by leaving an unpainted line between one colour and the next. On a white ground or support this effectively shows as a white outline.

antimony *n*
A metallic element at one time used in various forms to make pigments, eg antimony white, antimony yellow, now all obsolete.

applied arts *n*
Art and craft disciplines applied to the design and decoration of functional objects, ranging from pottery, textiles and furniture to industrial products involving complex engineering. The aesthetic values of the object and its functional capacity have equal importance in the design.

aquafortis *n* (*Lat* strong water)
A once common term, now generally discarded, for the nitric acid solution used for biting the image into an etching plate.

aquarelle *n* (*Fr* watercolour)
1 The technique of watercolour painting in which the paint is applied in transparent washes of colour, without use of opaque colour for emphasis or highlighting.
2 A painting executed in this way.
3 By extension, the term may also be used to refer to a monochrome print or drawing hand-coloured with watercolour washes.

aquatint *n*

1 A technique in etching which produces areas of even texture on the metal plate, giving a printed effect of flat tones similar to those produced by ink or watercolour washes. The term covers various processes by which this can be achieved, the basic method being to coat the plate with an even layer of acid-resistant resin which is fixed on the plate by heat action. The plate is then immersed in acid which bites into the tiny spaces between the resin particles. When the resin is removed with a solvent, the plate is pitted with tiny holes which will retain printing ink. A variety of tone is achieved by coating areas of the plate with stopping out varnish before immersion in acid: areas to print white are stopped out before any biting, then the lightest grey, and so on; the darkest tones occur in the areas exposed longest to the acid. Aquatint is often applied over etched lines to produce a combination of line and tone in the finished print. See also DUST BOX, INTAGLIO PRINTING, ROUGH AQUATINT, STOPPING OUT.
2 A print taken from a plate bearing an image produced by this process.

aqueous *adj*

The description of a substance made with, containing or resembling water.

arabesque *n*

A decorative pattern composed of flowing curved and interlaced lines, usually including plant forms such as leaves, flowers and tendrils, and sometimes also animal motifs. It may be carved as a surface decoration, painted, drawn or printed, depending upon the application.

architectonic *adj*

1 Strictly, the description of something relating to architecture or having architectural properties.
2 As applied to an art object, it implies that the work has an inherent stability and balance, in which parts are logically ordered, in relation to each other and to the overall structure and the space it occupies.

armature *n*

In sculpture, the basic framework over which a malleable modelling material is applied. It becomes the internal support of the sculpture and allows modelling of extended forms in materials that lack tensile strength. A small armature can be constructed from strong wire, a larger one from metal rod or piping, and the skeletal framework can be given bulk by the addition of lightweight materials such as wooden laths, polystyrene blocks or crushed wire netting.

Armenian bole *n*
See BOLE.

arriccio, arricciato *n* (*It* wrinkle)
A layer of plaster laid on a wall to form the basic support for FRESCO painting. It may be applied to a roughcast coating and is itself relatively coarse. The composition is drawn out on the arriccio which is then covered gradually as the INTONACO is applied. See also SINOPIA.

art *n*
1 A technique or method used in the deliberate creation of an image or object.
2 Collectively, the various techniques and methods by which images and objects can be created.
3 An activity or process in which acquired skills or knowledge are applied to presenting an idea in visible form.
4 Any or all of the products resulting from such techniques, methods or activities.

artefact, artifact *n*
A man-made object, whether produced for artistic or utilitarian purposes, particularly one which is hand-crafted.

artist's proof *n*
A print made by any printmaking process which is a final state kept or sold by the artist personally. It is signed and marked AP or Artist's proof and may acquire a higher value than the numbered EDITION prints.

artwork *n*
1 A diagram or illustration designed to be printed by commercial reproduction methods.
2 Diagrams, illustrations, photographs or typography, or any combination of these elements, assembled in a form suitable for printing by commercial reproduction methods.

asbestine *n*
A form of TALC sometimes used as an inert pigment.

asphaltum *n*
See BITUMEN.

assemblage *n*
1 A three-dimensional work constructed from or including objects and materials not typically associated with sculpture. These components may be manufactured or natural materials. A found object, or group of objects, is typically the starting point for the work.
2 The process of creating a work of this kind.

asymmetrical *adj*
The description of a form or composition which, assuming a central axis through the form, displays a varied arrangement of components around or on either side of the axis. The arrangement is not necessarily out of balance, but the balance does not depend upon similarity between the component parts and their relative positions within the overall structure. Compare SYMMETRICAL.

atelier *n* (*Fr* studio)
1 An artist's private studio where the artist personally works or gives tuition to students.
2 A workshop in which a particular art or craft is carried out, eg a printmaker's workshop.

atelier libre *n* (*Fr* open studio)
A large studio where artists and students can work on payment of a small entrance fee. The fee covers hiring of a model for life drawing and painting, but no formal tuition is included.

atlantes *n pl*
Statues of male figures, nude or clothed, used as architectural supports, ie in place of columns, the male counterparts of caryatids. They are named after the Greek legend of Atlas, who was made to carry the sky on his shoulders.

atmospheric perspective *n*
The method of creating an illusion of distance in a painting by representing distant objects and landscape with less emphasis in outline, detail, tonal contrast and colour intensity than applied to objects in the foreground. This corresponds to the natural loss of clarity in a view over a considerable distance, due to atmospheric effects. In addition, colours may seem to acquire a bluish tinge as they recede and this effect is also imitated. Also called aerial perspective and, less accurately, colour perspective.

attribute *vb*
To give ATTRIBUTION to an unsigned work of art. **attributed** *adj*.

attribution *n*
The designation of a work of art as having been executed by a particular artist, although the work itself is unsigned. It may be attributed to the artist on grounds of characteristic style, subject matter, manipulation of materials etc. There are further grounds for attribution if documentary evidence exists that the artist conceived and may have executed such a work.

auger *n*
A drilling tool used to bore deep holes in wood, consisting of a long metal shaft with a spiralled tip. A wooden handle is set horizontally across the top of the shaft and is turned rapidly by hand to rotate the drilling tip.

au premier coup *adv* (*Fr* at the first stroke)
See ALLA PRIMA.

aureole *n*
In Christian art, the depiction of a circle of light surrounding the head or body of a sacred figure.

autograph *n*
The term applied to a work thought to have been executed entirely by a known artist, not contributed to or carried out by pupils or studio assistants under the artist's supervision.

autolithograph *n*
A lithographic print made from an original image drawn directly on a plate or stone by the artist.

automatism *n*
The practice of allowing a drawing or painting to be formed without conscious direction, eg by an artist manipulating a pencil or brush without looking at the image it is creating. The idea of tapping subconscious creative powers has been given particular importance in certain styles and techniques of painting, though in a practical sense it is difficult to identify separate states of conscious or subconscious motivation.

aux trois crayons *adv* (*Fr* with three crayons)
The technique of drawing with white, red and black chalks on a tinted paper. The variations of tone that can be achieved in this way allow a subtle modelling of forms.

avant-garde¹ *n* (*Fr* vanguard)
An identifiable group of artists producing work in which the concepts and techniques are experimental and innovatory, or in any way beyond the mainstream of ideas contributing to the art of a particular period. The term has less application now than in the past because of the range of work acceptably encompassed in contemporary art.

avant-garde² *adj*
The description of an artist or group of artists, or work produced by such artists, identified as belonging to the avant-garde.

awl *n*
A hand tool consisting of a metal point set in a wooden handle. The point may be narrow and needle-like or relatively thick and strong. The tool has various uses, eg for piercing soft sheet materials or starting holes in wood for insertion of nails or screws.

axis *n*
An imaginary line through the centre of a form or composition around which the elements are disposed with a degree of balance or symmetry.

azo pigment *n*
A type of synthetic organic pigment derived from coal-tar and petroleum distillates. Azo colours are in the range red, yellow and brown; they are reliable and permanent pigments.

azurite *n*
A natural mineral substance, basically copper carbonate, used as a light blue pigment suitable for water-based paints, eg in fresco and tempera painting. It is permanent but rare and relatively expensive and has been superseded by artificial equivalents. The substance is a gemstone also used for ornamentation.

b

bachiru *n*
A Japanese technique of ivory carving in which the surface of the ivory is coloured with pigments and a design is carved or incised to show the original pale tone of the material.

back-glass painting *n*
A method of painting on a sheet of glass by a working process which is the reverse of painting on the surface of an opaque support. The details and finishing strokes are applied first to the glass: the artist then works over these gradually laying in tones and colours that form the broad masses of light and shade and the background to the image. The painted side of the glass is then sealed with a protective backing and the painting is viewed from the other side, through the thickness of the glass.

background *n*
1 The area in an image which lies behind or recedes from objects

or figures in close view.
2 The area in an image which surrounds the main forms or motifs.

backing *n*
1 Any form of protective covering laid across the back of a painting or framed picture to strengthen the support against warping or to seal the back of the picture against dust, moisture etc.
2 A non-adhesive paper layer attached to the adhesive side of MASKING FILM, which is peeled away as the film is laid on a support.

back iron *n*
A rigid support to which an armature can be attached, but which itself remains outside the form of the completed sculpture. A common type of back iron is a metal rod set vertically in a base board and bent at an angle of 90° to form a horizontal arm that supports the armature. The horizontal support may otherwise be a separate unit threaded onto a vertical rod, adjustable by means of a wing nut that secures it at the required height.

badger blender *n*
A large brush used to blend colours on a support, not suitable for the initial application of paint. Traditionally it is made of badger hair, though it may now be of synthetic bristle; the bristles are all of the same length, packed tightly in a round ferrule to produce a head which is rounded, slightly splayed and flattened across the tip.

balance *n*
The visual impression of order and internal logic in a composition in which the characteristics of different elements, eg colour, direction, shape, scale, texture, tone, apparent weight, are successfully integrated as a coherent image.

ball clay *n*
A highly plastic secondary clay used as an ingredient in various clay bodies. In the raw state, ball clay may be stained blue or dark grey by the presence of vegetable matter, but this is driven off in firing and the fired clay is white or cream.

ballpeen hammer *n*
A hammer with the head flattened at one end to form a striking face, the other end being rounded for use in beating metal, flattening rivets etc.

balsam *n*
A term applied to any of a number of natural OLEORESINS.

bandsaw *n*
A mechanical power-driven saw consisting of a circular band of metal toothed along one edge which is continuously cycled through heavy machinery on a fixed track, used for curved ashaped cuts in wood, metal or rigid plastics.

banker *n*
A heavy wooden workbench used to support a block of stone or wood for carving, or a work being modelled. Typically the top is square, set on a frame of thick timber. A turntable may be fitted so the sculpture can be rotated while work is in progress.

barbotine *n* (from *Fr barboter* = to daub, splash)
Decoration of ceramic ware created by TRAILING coloured slips over the surface.

baren *n*
The tool traditionally used for rubbing down paper over an inked wood block when hand-printing a woodcut, a circular pad made of bamboo fibres covered with a bamboo sheath. It is rubbed over the back of the paper in a circling motion to apply even pressure over the image area.

basalt *n*
A fine-grained, dark-coloured igneous rock sometimes used as a material for stone carving. Like granite, it is extremely hard and requires specially strengthened carving tools. The surface takes a high polish and some types of basalt have a naturally glassy texture.

basalt ware *n*
Ceramic ware made from a stoneware body stained black with mineral colourings, which when fired resembles basalt rock. There is no natural clay formed directly from the rock.

base *n*
1 (*sculpture*) A plinth, podium or other construction on which a sculpture is displayed, or the lower part of the sculpture itself on which its weight rests.
2 (*painting*) The liquid ingredient of a paint, the vehicle for the pigments.
3 (*painting*) The inert pigment used to absorb dyes in the manufacture of LAKE PIGMENTS.
4 (*printmaking*) A wood block on which a metal printing plate or lino block can be mounted to bring it to type height.

base metal *n*
A general term referring to any common metal, eg copper, tin,

zinc, as distinct from the precious metals gold, platinum and silver.

bas relief *n* (*Fr*)
LOW RELIEF.

basse taille *n* (*Fr* low cut)
An enamelling process in which a design is cut into a metal base and the whole piece is then covered with transparent enamel. When the enamel is fired it flows evenly, filling the cavities and leaving a thin layer on the raised areas; its transparency emphasizes the light and shade in the relief surface.

basso rilievo *n* (*It*)
LOW RELIEF.

bat, batt *n*
A flat slab of material used as a supportive surface on which clay is worked, dried out or fired. Bats used as shelving in a kiln must be made of refractory material. Plaster, being porous, is the material commonly used to make bats on which clay is worked and left to dry.

battle-piece *n*
Any painting, sculpture or other form of art depicting a battle scene or some specific aspect of wartime conflict. One of the primary functions of this type of art has been to record and celebrate victories in war, but there has been a more general tradition of attempting to convey the atmosphere of battle without reference to a specific event, and the genre also includes works made in protest against the horrors of war.

bat wash *n*
A liquid containing refractory material, painted on kiln shelves to prevent clay bodies or melting glaze from sticking to the shelves during firing. A mixture of flint and water is commonly used.

beaux arts *n* (*Fr* fine arts)
1 A general term for fine art disciplines and the techniques and processes involved in them.
2 The term is also used more specifically to refer to the traditions of the Ecole des Beaux Arts in Paris.

bed *n*
The flat, horizontal area of a printing press on which the block, plate or stone is held in place while a print is taken. The bed may be immoveable and subject to pressure applied from above, or may mechanically travel to the point where it becomes subject to pressure.

bench hook *n*
A device designed to provide stable support for fine work carried out at a bench or table. It consists of two sections of wood fixed together at right angles. One is placed horizontally on the work surface and the other laps over the side, hooked to the edge of the bench. A lip of wood on the upper section forms a stop against which a solid material or object can be held steady. It has various uses, eg in the cutting or engraving of a wood block, in shaping of fine metalwork etc.

bentonite *n*
A fine, highly plastic clay of volcanic origin. It may be used as an ingredient in a clay body, to improve its plasticity for ceramic work, or in a glaze where it encourages suspension of other materials. In powder form it can be converted to a malleable paste when mixed with water and has various uses as a binding material, eg in making soft pastels.

bestiary *n*
An illustrated book containing a catalogue of real, mythical or invented animals and birds. In medieval times hand-drawn books of this kind included moral texts as an important feature, but the imagery was often a more influential aspect, providing sources of motifs for carvings and manuscript ILLUMINATION.

bevel[1] *n*
A surface plane meeting another surface at an angle other than a right angle.

bevel[2] *vb*
To cut a bevel in a block or thick sheet of solid material, ie to create a plane at an angle to the original surface or surfaces.
bevelled *adj*

bevelling *n*
The process of filing or scraping the edges of an INTAGLIO PRINTING plate at an angle of 45° to the flat surface. This is done to eliminate sharp edges which may cut the paper covering the surface of the plate when a print is taken.

bibelot *n* (*Fr* trinket, curio)
A small ornament or decorated object for personal use, highly crafted and typically worked in precious metals and stones.

bidri *n*
A form of surface decoration on metal in which a zinc alloy is used as the base material on which a design is incised. The incisions are filled with silver and the alloy is stained black with a

chemical paste, so the silver design is clearly traced on the dark background.

binder *n*
1 The ingredient of a paint that holds together the particles of pigment and fixes them in a continuous film as the paint dries. This may be the basic medium or vehicle in the paint, eg oil or gum, or a substance added to the vehicle to ensure cohesion of the pigments in handling and drying.
2 More generally, any fluid or paste-like ingredient added to a material or combination of materials to contribute an adhesive property.

biomorphic *adj*
The term describing a type of imagery used in certain forms of abstract art, in which the abstract shapes and motifs are derived from the forms of living organisms, typically having irregular, curving shapes.

birka *n*
A type of chisel used in ivory carving, consisting of a short metal shaft set in a wooden handle and honed to a cutting edge at the tip.

biscuit *n*
Ceramic ware which has been fired once without a glaze. In this condition it may be porous, but the clay has become insoluble. Also called bisque, bisquit.

biscuit firing *n*
The preliminary firing of ceramic ware before a glaze is applied.

bisque, bisquit *n*
Alternative terms for unglazed ceramic ware, more commonly called BISCUIT.

bistre *n*
A brown pigment with a yellow tone, made from the soot obtained in burning beechwood. Bistre was at one time popular for creating transparent tonal effects in watercolours and wash drawings, but being impermanent, it has since been superseded by more reliable pigments.

bite[1] *vb*
To corrode metal by exposing it to acid, primarily referring to treatment of a metal plate in ETCHING. **bitten** *adj*.

bite[2] *n*
The result of the corrosive action of acid on metal. The bite varies

according to the strength of acid solution and the length of time during which the metal is exposed.

biting, biting in *n*
The process of etching an image or design on a metal plate by exposing it to the corrosive action of acid.

bitumen *n*
A brown mineral pigment at one time widely used in tinted grounds and underpainting, now discarded as a paint pigment because of its various disadvantages: it bleeds through other colours, has a slow drying rate which can cause severe cracking in paint layers, and it tends to darken and become more opaque with age. The principal use of bitumen now is as an ingredient of acid-resistant materials used in etching. Also called asphaltum. **bituminous** *adj*. See also HARD GROUND, SOFT GROUND, STOPPING OUT VARNISH.

black-figure *n*
A style of decoration applied to early Greek pottery in which an image was painted in black glaze on a ground of natural red clay, interior details of the forms being incised through the black coating to show as red lines. See also RED-FIGURE.

black mirror *n*
See CLAUDE GLASS.

blanc fixe *n* (*Fr* fixed white)
Artificially produced barium sulphate in the form of a fine white powder, an inert pigment used as an extender or filler for paints and grounds and also as a base for opaque LAKE PIGMENTS.

blank *n*
1 A metal component, eg of a constructed metal sculpture or other form of metalwork, which requires further shaping or preparation.
2 A flat piece of metal cut to a required shape on which a design is applied by ENAMELLING.

blanket *n*
1 (*etching*) A piece of thick felt trimmed to fit the bed of an etching press, which covers plate and paper to spread pressure evenly and cushion the plate as an impression is taken. Two or three layers are usually used.
2 (*offset printing*) The thick sheet of rubber that covers the impression cylinder of an offset press. The blanket picks up the image from the inked plate and carries it to the paper.

bleeding *n*
1 A spread of oil from an oil-based paint or printing ink as it seeps

into the ground or support. This may be seen as a discoloured area surrounding a brushmark or printed line: if the oil is a vehicle for a strong pigment, the bleeding may be tinged with colour.
2 The merging of one colour with another on the support when paint is applied in a dilute or liquid form.
3 See BLEEDING THROUGH.
4 The practice of printing an image so that it spreads to the cut edge of a page, eg in a book or magazine, rather than being contained within the page margins.

bleeding through *n*
The appearance of an underlayer of paint through the surface layers, particularly in oil painting. This may be due to a strong pigment which gradually works its way through overlying colours, or it may occur as the surface layers become more transparent with age, gradually revealing forms and colours which were originally overpainted.

blend^1 *vb*
1 To merge two or more colours on a support.
2 To mix two or more substances to form a compound. **blended** *adj.*

blend^2 *n*
A compound substance in which the ingredients are evenly mixed.

blender *n*
A brush designed for softening and spreading colours on a support, not used for the initial application of paint. See BADGER BLENDER, FAN BLENDER.

blending *n*
Any technique of merging two or more paint colours on a support, so the point of transition from one to another is inexact. This may be done by softening the edges of painted areas with a brush, fingers, rag or sponge and may produce an actual mixture of tones and hues or an area of textured colour rather than hard-edged contours.

blind mould *n*
A mould in two or more pieces which, when assembled, gives no access to the interior space. This may be used to make a hollow cast, the mould interior being coated with casting material before it is fully assembled.

blind printing *n*
A method of producing an embossed design on paper by pressing the paper over an uninked relief block or intaglio plate, with

sufficient pressure to mould the design as a raised and textured image on the paper. Also called *gauffrage* (*Fr*).

blind tracery *n*
See TRACERY.

blisters *n*
Swellings or ridges appearing on the surface of a painted canvas or panel. The swelling may be in the paint layers only or may indicate that the ground has also lifted from the support. This can be due to poor adherence of the paint or dampness attacking the painting through the back of the support.

bloating *n*
The appearance of blisters in a clay form when it is fired. This may be due to the clay boiling when fired too fiercely or air pockets in the clay blowing out when heated.

block *n*
1 (*sculpture*) A solid mass of material for carving.
2 (*printmaking*) A flat-surfaced, usually rectangular piece of material on which an image or design is cut for RELIEF PRINTING.

block book *n*
A form of illustrated book produced by relief printing from hand-cut wood blocks. Each page is printed from a single block which carries both text and illustrations.

blocking in *n*
In painting, the process of laying in the basic form of a composition with areas of tone and colour, indicating the broad masses of the forms without detail or outline.

block printing *n*
Relief printing from a block of material, commonly wood or linoleum. See LINOCUT, WOODCUT, WOOD ENGRAVING. See also COLLOGRAPH.

bloom *n*
1 (*painting*) An opaque veil that develops in the surface layer of a varnished painting, caused by dampness penetrating the varnish either when it is applied or later, if the painting is kept in a cold, damp atmosphere. The bloom is at first a misty grey or blue-white, but may turn yellow and then black, becoming increasingly opaque, if conditions are not corrected. Also known as chill.
2 (*sculpture*) A cloudy film on the surface of concrete cast in a plaster mould. This is due to interaction between the materials in which the concrete picks up a fine layer of plaster from inside the

mould. The effect may be deliberately contrived by omitting use of a PARTING AGENT when casting.

blot drawing *n*
The process of developing an image from an accidental or randomly produced blot or stain, eg of ink or watercolour.

blotting off *n*
The process of lifting a surface layer of wet paint by pressing a clean piece of paper or fabric over it. This may be done to produce a textured effect in the paint film or to remove excess moisture before continued application of paint.

blow forming *n*
A method of shaping sheet plastic by heating it until soft and subjecting it to a concentrated blast of air which stretches and inflates the material. This is done in a machine specially designed for the purpose: the plastic sheet is clamped in place over the air channel so the pressurized air can be released to act directly on the material once it is pliable.

blueing *n*
The process of heating the surface of metal under a direct flame until it darkens and takes on a blue tinge. This forms a distinctive surface finish and at the same time cleans away surface dirt and impurities.

blunger *n*
A machine for processing dry or plastic clay with water to produce liquid clay (slip). The blunger is fitted with rotary paddles that break down chunks of clay into particles. Mixed with water, these form a suspension that can be drawn off in the form of a smooth liquid. Dried clay can be returned to a plastic state if treated first in a blunger, then passed through a FILTER PRESS.

blunging *n*
The process of liquidizing dry or plastic clay performed by a BLUNGER.

blush *n*
A cloudy or opaque effect in a coating of transparent lacquer, the equivalent of BLOOM in an oil varnish.

board *n*
1 The classification of a range of paper products in stiff or rigid sheet form. A board may be made from paper pulp or made up of compressed or glued layers of paper sheets. Various types are produced for different purposes, as supports for painting and

drawing, as mounting and framing materials etc. See also BRISTOL BOARD, ILLUSTRATION BOARD, MOUNT BOARD, PASTEBOARD.
2 A relatively thin, flat sheet of sawn timber or a composite wood product. See also CHIPBOARD, HARDBOARD.

boaster *n*
1 (*carving*) A heavy chisel with a broad cutting edge, used in the first stage of roughing out a form in a stone block. Also called a boasting chisel.
2 (*modelling*) A simple flat tool made of wood or metal, rounded at one end and squared at the other, used to work soft clay or wax.

boasting *n*
A preliminary stage in stone carving, when the stone block is worked with a large, heavy chisel to break up the surface and give it rough shape.

boasting chisel *n*
See BOASTER.

bocage *n* (*Fr* grove, thicket)
A cluster of modelled porcelain flowers, leaves or tree branches designed as a background for modelled porcelain figures.

body *n*
1 A mixture of natural clays and mineral additives used in making ceramic forms. The ingredients are chosen to give the body particular properties for working and firing, eg a high or low degree of plasticity, specific maturing temperature, degree of shrinkage etc.
2 An object made from a clay body.
3 The substantial quality of a heavy or dense material.

body art *n*
A term loosely including various forms of art in which the human body, that of the artist or of someone directed by the artist, is the primary means of expression. This may come under the heading of PERFORMANCE ART, or be a matter of using parts of the body itself to create an object, eg as the instrument of applying paint, as the model for cast sculpture etc.

body colour *n*
1 Paint which is applied as a relatively heavy, opaque layer, as compared to that which is applied in transparent washes or glazes. The opacity is due to white pigment or filler in the paint. This does not necessarily affect the intensity of the colour and the

further admixture of white paint or pigment is required to lighten the tone.
2 See GOUACHE.

bole *n*
1 A fine, red, natural clay deriving its colour from high iron content, used as a ground for laying gold leaf. The bole may be mixed with SIZE to encourage adhesion of the leaf. Traditionally, red bole has been used as the ground for gilding in panel painting and three-dimensional work because the rich red gives depth to the metallic overlay. Also traditional is the use of the more specific term Armenian bole, although there are various sources of supply. China clay is sometimes used as a ground for gilding and in this context is called white bole.
2 A natural red earth, a form of iron oxide, used as a colouring agent, eg in ceramic glazes.

bolus ground *n*
A ground of red BOLE used in painting or gilding.

bone ash *n*
A form of calcium phosphate produced by roasting ground animal bones, usually ox bone. It is a primary ingredient of bone china and is used as a flux in opaque ceramic glazes.

bone china *n*
A type of ceramic ware first developed in England in imitation of Chinese porcelain. It is white and translucent, made with a mixture of bone ash, china clay and china stone. It is fired at a high temperature and glazed at a lower temperature.

bone glue *n*
Any type of glue manufactured from animal bones.

book of hours *n*
A medieval book of prayers, hand-written and usually richly illuminated, giving appropriate prayers for different hours and days in the Christian calendar. Such books were used for private devotions rather than official services.

boss *n*
1 A projecting section in a block of material used for sculpture or architectural construction. It may be shaped or decoratively carved.
2 An ornament or decorative device projecting from the main body of a three-dimensional form.

boucharde *n*
A hammer used in stone carving. The head is made of metal and the striking faces are cut into rows of sharp, pyramidal teeth. The

pounding of a boucharde loosens the stone surface, giving purchase for the chisels subsequently used to shape the block. Also called bushhammer.

bow drill *n*
A drill traditionally used in stone carving, to bore holes in a stone block which either provide rough shaping of the form or open up the stone so it can be easily split. The drill itself has a tipped metal shaft set in a cylindrical handle: it is operated by moving the string of a bow, shaped like an archery bow, rapidly back and forth across the handle, causing a corresponding movement of the tool which penetrates the stone.

boxwood *n*
The tough, close-grained, yellow wood of the box tree. It has a fine texture and is capable of taking intricate carved detail. Apart from use as a carving material, it is commonly the material of end-grain blocks used in WOOD ENGRAVING.

bozzetto *n* (from *It bozzo* = rough stone)
1 (*sculpture*) A small work in wax or clay, made as preparation for a large, detailed version which may be carried out in a more durable material usually stone. See also MAQUETTE.
2 (*painting*) Less accurately, the term is sometimes used to refer to a small or quickly executed study made as part of the preparation for a large painting.

brayer *n*
An inking roller, used in various forms of printmaking, made of a plastic or rubber composition and set in a metal frame attached to a wooden handle. The frame is designed to hold the roller rigidly suspended, so the tool can be turned upside down and the back of the frame rested on a worktop without the roller itself or its coating of ink making contact with the surface. It can be used for inking a wood or lino block, lithographic stone or metal printing plate.

braze *vb*
To join pieces of metal by BRAZING. **brazed** *adj*.

brazing *n*
A method of joining two pieces of metal using brass or a similar copper-zinc alloy as an adhesive in the joint. The process is similar to soldering, but the alloy has a higher melting point than other types of solder and forms a stronger joint. The colour of the alloy may also be an important consideration and brass is sometimes preferred as a visual element in metal sculptures in which the joints remain visible.

breakfast piece *n*
A traditional form of still life composition in which items of food and drink are depicted piled on a table in an apparently disordered fashion, though the arrangement of the items may in fact have symbolic value.

bright *n*
A brush with short hairs or bristles of equal lengths arranged in a flat, rectangular shape and forming a straight line across the tip.

bristle *n*
A stiff, relatively coarse hair used in making certain types of brushes, eg for oil painting, either a natural material such as hog's hair or synthetic fibre.

bristol board *n*
A smooth, lightweight paper board used as a support for artwork, illustration, ink drawing, printing etc.

broken colour *n*
1 A colour obtained by mixing two or more pure hues. See also COLOURED GREY, TERTIARY COLOUR.
2 The effect obtained when paint is applied in textured strokes which leave fragments of previously applied colours showing through the upper layer. See also DRAGGING, DRYBRUSH, SCUMBLING.
3 The effect of covering a support with small dabs of colour, to create the impression of a greater variety of hues by OPTICAL MIXING.

bronze[1] *n*
1 An alloy of copper and tin, sometimes containing a small proportion of other metals, zinc and lead among others. There is no single formula for bronze and its colour depends upon the relative proportions of the different metals in its content, though copper is always the major element. Bronze is the traditional material for cast metal sculpture because it is durable and has great tensile strength, but is also highly responsive and capable of reproducing fine details of surface form and texture.
2 An object made of bronze, typically a sculpture produced by a casting process.

bronze[2] *vb*
To apply a process or substance to the surface of a metal or other material to give it the appearance of bronze. **bronzed** *adj.*

bronzing *n*
A term covering various techniques of giving a metal or non-metallic material the appearance of bronze. These include

creating an artificial patina to simulate weathered bronze, or applying bronze leaf or powder over an adhesive size or paste to create a metallic surface effect.

bruising *n*
The effect of a faulty stroke in stone carving, when the surface layers of a stone block are stunned but not cut by a chisel or point applied at the wrong angle. Bruising forms a mark particularly noticeable in stones with a slightly translucent quality, eg alabaster or marble, showing as a white, opaque patch which may be quite a deep flaw.

brush[1] *n*
A tool consisting of a collection of hairs or bristles, of natural or synthetic fibres, assembled in a particular shape and attached to a rigid handle. See BLENDER, BRIGHT, FILBERT, FLAT, ROUND, STENCIL BRUSH.

brush[2] *vb*
1 To apply a brush to a medium or surface.
2 To apply a fluid material using a brush. **brushed** *adj*.

brush drawing *n*
1 A drawing entirely executed with a brush, or one in which a brush is the principal tool giving the drawing its character.
2 The technique of executing such a drawing. Brush drawing is particularly associated with oriental traditions in which the fluid motions of brush-written calligraphy are extended into the creation of pictorial images.

brushing out *n*
A general term for the practice of obliterating part of an image by application of a layer of opaque paint.

brushwork *n*
The manner in which an artist uses a brush to apply paint to a support, as visible in the marks in the paint surface which demonstrate the movement of the brush.

bullnose chisel *n*
A stone carving chisel with a curved cutting edge.

bung *n*
1 A vertical stack of SAGGARS containing ceramic ware for firing.
2 A vertical stack of ware placed directly on a kiln shelf.

buon fresco *n* (*It* true fresco)
See FRESCO.

burin *n*
An engraving tool used for cutting into the surface of metal or wood. It consists of a steel rod, square in section, obliquely angled at one end to form a cutting edge. The other end is set in a wooden handle rounded to fit the palm of the hand. For line engraving on metal, the cutting edge is honed at an angle of 45° to the shaft; for use on a wood block, the angle is 30°. A burin sharpened at 60° may be used for stippling and linear textures. Also called graver.

burlap *n*
A coarse woven cloth, usually made of jute, which has various uses as a covering material and is sometimes used as an inexpensive painting support, though far inferior to linen or cotton fabrics marketed as artists' canvas.

burning in *n*
The final stage in the process of encaustic painting, when the wax colours applied to the support are heated to fuse the paint layers and render the surface permanent. The heat is sufficient to make the surface cohesive, but not so great as to destroy the surface textures by melting down the wax.

burnish *vb*
To carry out a process of BURNISHING. **burnished** *adj*.

burnisher *n*
1 (*intaglio printing*) A metal hand tool used to smooth and polish the surface of a metal plate. It is a rod of polished steel, typically set in a wooden handle, which is slightly flattened and tapered at one end and may be straight or slightly curved at the tip. It is used to eradicate flaws or errors in the plate surface, or as a drawing instrument for working on the roughened plate surface in the AQUATINT or MEZZOTINT processes.
2 (*metal sculpture*) A similar tool used for smoothing and polishing processes in any form of work in metal. There are various types for use with different metals and working processes.
3 (*gilding*) A hand-tool made of semi-precious stone, usually agate, used to rub down and polish gold leaf. The stone tip, set in a handle, may be a narrow point or hook, or a blunt wedge-shape or cylinder, depending upon the stage of the process in which it is used and the fineness of the work.

burnishing *n*
1 (*intaglio printing*) The process of smoothing and polishing areas of a metal plate to eradicate any unwanted mark or texture which would hold ink and therefore be visible in the printed image.
2 (*metal sculpture*) The process of rubbing a metal surface with a

special tool or compound to make it more lustrous and reflective.
3 (*gilding*) The process of rubbing gold leaf when it has adhered to a ground, to compact the surface and bring up the shine.
4 (*relief printing*) The method of printing a relief block by hand, by placing a sheet of paper over the inked block and systematically rubbing it down over the image area. This can be done with a BAREN, specially designed for the purpose, or with any smooth, rounded implement, eg a spoon or polished stone.
5 (*ceramics*) The process of rubbing the surface of a clay form, usually at the leather-hard stage, to consolidate the material and create a surface sheen.

burr *n*
In DRYPOINT, ENGRAVING and MEZZOTINT, the roughened edges of the mark made by the cutting tool on the surface of the metal plate. In engraving, the burr is removed to leave a clean, sharp-edged cut, while in drypoint and mezzotint it contributes to the printed effect.

bush chisel *n*
A hand tool used in stone carving. Unlike other chisels, it has a square striking face flattened at right angles to the shaft and this is covered with pointed teeth. Like other chisels, it is driven vertically against the stone but has the effect of stunning the surface, in the same way as a BOUCHARDE, rather than cutting it.

bushhammer *n*
See BOUCHARDE.

bust *n*
A form of figure sculpture representing the head and shoulders only. See also PORTRAIT BUST, PORTRAIT HEAD.

bust peg *n*
A wooden support used as the basis of an armature for modelling of a head or bust. The bust peg is typically a thick wooden dowel set vertically in a baseboard. Other materials such as wire or metal rod are attached to the peg, to build the armature to a suitable shape.
Also called head peg.

butterfly *n*
A small cross made of two pieces of wood bound together. It is suspended horizontally within an armature to provide extra support for heavy masses of modelling material.

butt joint *n*
Any form of joint between two sections of a material in which they are brought together edge to edge rather than overlapped or

interlocked. The method of sealing the joint corresponds to the type of material used, eg welding for metal.

C

cabinet picture *n*
A small painting, suitable for hanging in a room of moderate dimensions and intended to be seen from close range.

cadmium colours *n pl*
Synthetic organic pigments in the colour range red, orange and yellow, primarily derived from the mineral compound cadmium sulphide. They are vivid, opaque and permanent colours.

calligram *n*
An image or design formed entirely from calligraphy, ie one in which pen- or brush-written letterforms are arranged in lines and masses to create a picture or motif. Depending on the form, the text within the image may or may not be legible.

calligrapher *n*
A person skilled in the techniques and practice of CALLIGRAPHY. See also SCRIBE.

calligraphic *adj*
A descriptive term which can be applied to work in two or three dimensions, implying qualities typical of written forms, such as linearity, fluidity and rhythmic patterning.

calligraphy *n*
The art of fine writing, or handwriting as an art. The term refers to lettering written directly with a pen or brush and which depends upon the shape of the tool for its characteristic form. It differs from ordinary handwriting in that the aesthetic qualities have equal importance with the meaning of the text and there are established conventions of style and technique. It is also distinguished from the broader field of graphic lettering in that it has a fluidity derived from the letters being written, not drawn or mechanically constructed. Broadly speaking, penmanship is a tradition of western calligraphy while the brush is the tool of oriental and Islamic traditions.

calliper *n*
A sculptor's instrument for measuring three-dimensional forms.

It consists of two metal arms hinged together at one end: at the other end, each arm is pointed and curved inwards, so the points come together when the instrument is closed. To take a measurement, the arms are opened out and fitted on either side of a form or projection, the points touching the surface of the sculpture.

camaieu *n* (*Fr* cameo-like)
1 (*painting*) The technique of painting in monochrome, using only two or three tones of the same colour. See also CIRAGE, GRISAILLE.
2 (*enamelling*) A tonal effect obtained by laying white enamel over a dark ground and working a design in outline, cutting through the white to expose the dark layer.

came *n*
A narrow strip of lead grooved on either side, traditionally the material forming the framework for the sections of coloured glass in stained glass decoration.

cameo *n*
A small sculpture or decorative object made in a natural stone which consists of two or more different coloured layers, so a relief design cut in one layer stands out from a background of a different colour.

camera lucida *n* (*Lat* light chamber)
A device operating on the same principle as a CAMERA OBSCURA, but employing a specially shaped glass prism to concentrate the transmitted image at a required size.

camera obscura *n* (*Lat* dark chamber)
A device arranged either in a box or in a small room, for projecting the image of an object or scene outside the chamber onto a sheet of paper or glass screen inside, from which it can be traced in outline. The chamber is dark, and light enters through a small hole cut in one wall, projecting an inverted image of its outside source on the opposite wall, or on a surface placed to intercept it. A lens and mirror may be used to focus the image and turn it right way up.

cancelled plate *n*
A printing plate from which no more impressions are to be taken, commonly scored through or otherwise marked so further prints would be imperfect. It is cancelled to ensure the value of a limited edition, or to indicate that wear and tear on the plate surface have caused deterioration of the image.

canvas *n*
1 A closely-woven fabric used as a support for painting,

particularly for work in oils or acrylics. Linen is regarded as the best fibre for painter's canvas, as it is evenly woven and durable, but cheaper cotton substitutes are now commonly used.
Canvases are available in different weights and textures, in the natural buff colours associated with linen and the creamy white tones of cotton. The best qualities of canvas for a particular work are a matter of personal choice for the painter.
2 By extension, a painting executed on a fabric support. See also STRAINER, STRETCHER.

canvas board *n*
A prepared support for oil or acrylic painting consisting of canvas pasted to stiff card. The boards are usually ready-primed and available in a range of sizes.

canvas pin *n*
A metal pin pointed at both ends and fitted with a section of cork around the centre. Pins are used to separate two canvases which must be stacked or carried together while still wet, eg when brought in from painting outdoors. The pins are driven into the corners of the canvases and the corks act as a cushion between the two.

canvas pliers *n*
A hand tool consisting of two hinged metal arms, each with a wide flattened head, between which the edges of a piece of canvas can be firmly gripped in order to pull it taut over a STRAINER or STRETCHER when preparing a canvas for painting. This is especially necessary with canvas that is primed before stretching, as it is more resistant than an unprimed fabric.

capital *n*
The head or crowning section of a COLUMN, broader than the width of the shaft and usually decoratively shaped or carved. The capital directly bears the weight of the superstructure supported by the column.

capriccio *n* (*It* caprice)
1 A painting, print or drawing showing an imaginary scene, but one composed of real architectural features or landscape rendered in faithful detail, eg buildings from several different places put together as if seen from a single viewpoint.
Also called veduta ideata.
2 A fanciful or fantastic picture of any kind.

carborundum *n*
A silicon-carbide compound used as an abrasive. It is available in the form of a powder, a coating on cloth or a solid block.

cardboard *n*
A stiff, lightweight sheet material made from pulped vegetable fibres. The term is a classification of papers having a certain range of thickness and density. Cardboard is sometimes used as a support for painting and drawing, but is mainly produced as a packaging material. See also BOARD.

caricature *n*
A portrait, whether a drawing, painting, print or sculpture, in which the subject's physical characteristics are exaggerated and distorted for comic effect, frequently as a means of passing satirical comment.

carmine *n*
A fugitive red lake pigment made from a dye extracted from the cochineal insect, now generally superseded by more reliable synthetic substitutes.

carpet page *n*
In a handwritten and illuminated book, a full page consisting entirely of abstract patterns and ornaments decorated with gold and colours.

cartellino *n* (*It* small paper)
A realistically painted scroll or small piece of paper in the background or foreground of a composition, used as a device for displaying a motto or inscription, often the place where the artist's signature is written.

cartoon *n*
1 A full-scale drawing used as the model for a large easel painting, fresco or mural, or as a design to be executed in mosaic, stained glass or tapestry. The drawing may be in line or colour and is copied on or transferred to the main support. See also POUNCING, SPOLVERO.
2 A comic drawing, or series of drawings forming a narrative.

cartouche *n* (from *Lat carta* = paper)
A decorative framing device, designed to look like a scroll of paper, surrounding a text or inscription. The word is used for any such ornament, whether it is carved, engraved, painted, drawn or printed.

cartridge paper *n*
A strong, hard, relatively lightweight and inexpensive drawing paper made from wood or vegetable pulp, available in white, off-white and a range of colours. It takes its name from its original use as a wrapping for gun cartridges.

carve *vb*
To shape a mass of material by CARVING. **carved** *adj.*

carving *n*
1 The process of shaping a mass of solid material by breaking down the surface and using pointed, tipped or sharp-edged tools to cut away sections of the material. The term also broadly includes the use of abrasive tools and substances for shaping and finishing. Stone and wood are the traditional, most commonly used materials for carving but a range of other substances, eg soap, plaster, plastics, can be employed for various purposes.
2 An object produced by a process of cutting and abrading a solid material.

caryatid *n* (*Gr* woman of Caryae)
A statue of a clothed female figure which acts as a structural support to a section of a building, eg in place of a column. Commonly several figures are grouped within the framework or arranged at intervals in a straight row. The caryatid was a feature of classical Greek architecture but the form has been borrowed in later periods.

case *n*
1 An outer shell formed around a piece mould in which the sections of the mould can be reassembled and held firmly together while a cast is made. The case is usually of plaster and is cast around the mould so that when set, the inner surface of the case corresponds exactly to the outer form of the mould. It is made in two or more pieces, simpler in construction than the mould inside and seamed along different lines to provide proper support for the mould pieces. Also called jacket.
2 An outer mould of plaster made to fit around a flexible rubber or gelatin mould, to support it in the correct form while it is filled with a casting material.

casein *n*
Milk protein used as an adhesive or as a binder for paint. It is a powder made from the curd of soured skimmed milk, which is separated, washed and dried. In commercial manufacture, hydrochloric acid is added to the milk to improve the quality of the casein. The powder does not dissolve in water alone and ammonia is added to produce a casein solution. The natural product dries to a matt and brittle surface: for use as a paint binder it may be mixed with oil or gum to give flexibility, but casein preparations available commercially are formulated to have the appropriate qualities for painting.

cast[1] *n*
A three-dimensional form produced in a mould. It is usually a reproduction of an originally modelled, carved or constructed form, although the term can include items made from an original negative mould.

cast² *vb*
To produce a three-dimensional form by CASTING a raw material in a mould. The term may also apply to certain ways of making the mould itself, eg if it is of a material applied in liquid or paste form around the original master. **cast** *adj.*

casting *n*
The process of making a three-dimensional object within a mould, usually to reproduce the form of an original sculpture in a different, more durable material or to produce several identical forms. Typically the raw material is run into the mould as a liquid and allowed to set, so the external shape of the cast follows precisely the interior shape of the mould. Bronze and plaster are materials traditionally used in casting processes: concrete and thermosetting plastic resins are also now widely used. See COLD CAST METAL, HOLLOW CASTING, LOST WAX PROCESS, SAND CASTING, SLIP CASTING. See also MOULD MAKING.

cast shadow *n*
In pictorial terms, a shadow on a surface or object caused by another object interposed between this and the source of light. Compare CONTAINED SHADOW.

cast stone *n*
A general term for refined cement or concrete mixtures intended to resemble stone when cured. See also PORTLAND CEMENT.

catalogue raisonné *n* (*Fr*)
A complete listing of all known works by a particular artist, giving the provenance, current location and condition of each work, and biographical details as appropriate. It also includes a record of works attributed to the artist or after major works by the artist.

catalyst *n*
1 Generally, a substance which induces a chemical change in another substance.
2 Specifically, the term is used to refer to the additive which starts the hardening process in synthetic resins, which must be an ingredient of resins used for casting or laminating.

cavo rilievo *n* (*It*)
SUNKEN RELIEF.

celadon *n*
Ceramic ware glazed in a green or grey-green tone, originally a feature of oriental stoneware. The range of colours comes from a small proportion (1 – 3%) of iron oxide in the glaze which turns green when fired in an atmosphere deprived of oxygen. See also REDUCTION FIRING.

cellulose acetate *n*
1 A compound made by the action of acetic acid on cellulose, a raw material originating from plant cells. It is the basis of a number of different materials, including paper, textiles and plastics.
2 Specifically, a clear plastic film available in different weights and thicknesses, used for various purposes including artwork overlays and protection of drawings, prints and illustrations.

cement¹ *n*
1 A fine grey powder made by grinding, roasting and regrinding a mixture of limestone and clay. When mixed with water it gradually sets hard into a solid material resembling stone. It can be used in its own right for casting and modelling and also has an important sculptural use as the main ingredient of CONCRETE.
2 More generally, any material in paste form used as a binder or adhesive for sculpture materials.

cement² *vb*
To bind or join materials using a cement. **cemented** *adj.*

centring *n*
The process of manipulating and pressuring a lump of clay on a rotating potter's wheel, to establish it centrally so that the clay spins on the same axis as the wheel itself. This is a preliminary to THROWING and if the clay is not properly centred, the form made from it will not be symmetrical. Centring is achieved by pulling and pressing the clay into a roughly central position, then checking and perfecting its rotation by a method known as CONING.

cera colla *n* (*It* wax glue)
An emulsion of wax and size formerly used as a vehicle for pigments, no longer current.

ceramics *n*
1 The techniques and processes involved in making clay forms that are brought to a finished state by firing. See COILING, HOLLOW BUILDING, MODELLING, PINCHING, SLABBING, SLIP CASTING, THROWING. See also GLAZE.
2 The finished products made by such techniques.

ceramic ware *n*
The collective term for objects made of clay and brought to a finished state by firing. In context, the term is often abbreviated to WARE. See also EARTHENWARE, FLATWARE, GREEN WARE, HOLLOW WARE, STONEWARE.

cerography *n*
1 Any process of painting in which wax is used as the binder for pigments. See ENCAUSTIC.
2 Any technique of engraving or inscribing on wax.

chalcography *n*
The process of engraving on copper or brass.

chalk¹ *n*
1 A soft, fine-grained white limestone, consisting mainly of calcium carbonate, which can be used in its natural form as a drawing material or, when ground to powder, as an inert pigment or filler. Traditionally the term also includes black and red mineral substances also used in their natural state as drawing materials.
2 A drawing material in stick form, consisting of pigment bound in gum, used as a substitute for natural chalks. In this connection, chalk is also a synonym for PASTEL.
3 An artificially prepared calcium carbonate in the form of a fine white powder, used in making pastels and as an ingredient of grounds for painting in oil or tempera.

chalk² *vb*
To draw on or otherwise mark a surface with chalk.

chamfer¹ *n*
A bevelled edge on a solid section of material.

chamfer² *vb*
To cut a chamfer. **chamfered** *adj*.

champlevé enamelling *n* (*Fr* raised field)
An enamelling technique in which the surface of a metal form or object is partly cut away to leave a raised design. The recesses are filled with coloured enamels and the whole piece is fired. Compare CLOISONNÉ ENAMELLING.

charcoal *n*
A drawing medium made by charring fine sticks of wood, usually willow or vine twigs, under intense heat in an atmosphere starved of oxygen. The dense black material is available in different thicknesses and grades of hardness; all are liable to crumble. Charcoal is best used on a support with a surface tooth, eg paper with a coarse grain, and is commonly used to sketch a composition in outline on canvas before paint is applied. When used solely as a drawing medium the image is easily smudged and finished work is usually sealed with a FIXATIVE.

charcoal pencil *n*
A length of thin charcoal encased in wood, a form which is

cleaner to handle than raw charcoal and can be more easily sharpened to a point. Charcoal pencils are available in hard, medium and soft grades.

charge *vb*
1 (*sculpture*) To fill a mould with a casting material.
2 (*painting*) To load a brush with paint. **charged** *adj*.

chase[1] *vb*
To refine or decorate a metal object by CHASING. **chased** *adj*.

chase[2] *n*
A rectangular metal tray or adjustable frame in which RELIEF PRINTING blocks, pieces of TYPE and FURNITURE can be assembled in a particular form for printing.

chasing *n*
1 The process of removing imperfections from a cast metal sculpture or adding detail to the surface using any of a number of tools such as fine chisels, files, matting tools, punches etc.
2 A method of decorating a metal object or surface with relief or intaglio designs, eg by EMBOSSING or ENGRAVING.

chiaroscuro[1] *n* (*It* light-dark)
The distribution of light and shade in an image, particularly in a painting where there is a marked contrast between the lightest and darkest tones or the forms are heavily modelled by means of abrupt tonal gradation.

chiaroscuro[2] *adj*
The description of an image which features a pronounced pattern of light and shade, used of two- and three-dimensional images.

chiaroscuro woodcut *n*
A woodcut in two or more colours or tones, usually based on a key block giving a black outline with other colours printed from separate blocks. It is designed to give the effect of a line and wash drawing in which tonal contrasts are used to model forms within a basic outline.

chill *n*
See BLOOM.

china clay *n*
A white primary clay of low plasticity deposited through the decomposition of granite. It is the purest of natural clays and is an essential ingredient of porcelain and bone china. It has various industrial uses. In the manufacture of art materials it serves as an extender or filler in paints, a binder for drawing materials and as

an ingredient of surface coatings on certain types of paper. Also called kaolin.

china stone *n*
A natural rock formed from partly decomposed granite with a high content of felspar. It is an essential ingredient of porcelain and bone china and is commonly used in the preparation of earthenware bodies and ceramic glazes. Also called Cornish stone, pegmatite or petuntse.

Chinese ink *n*
See INDIA INK.

Chinese white *n*
See ZINC WHITE.

chinoiserie *n*
A term used of artefacts, motifs or images appearing in western art which are borrowed from or intended to imitate traditional Chinese forms.

chipboard *n*
A rigid sheet material made of wood chips compressed and bound in a synthetic resin.

chipping out *n*
The process of releasing a cast from a waste mould, when a plaster mould is chiselled or hammered to break it away from the cast form.

chisel[1] *n*
A cutting tool made of metal, used primarily for carving wood or stone, but also for cutting other rigid materials such as metal or set plaster. It is usually made of steel: one end of the shaft is flattened and honed to a cutting edge while the other end is blunted or fitted in a wooden handle to receive the impact of a hammer or mallet used to drive the tool into the material. There are many different types and sizes of chisel, designed for use with particular materials and different techniques of carving and cutting. See also BULLNOSE CHISEL, CLAW CHISEL, COLD CHISEL, FLAT CHISEL, SKEW CHISEL.

chisel[2] *vb*
To cut and shape a material using a chisel. **chiselled** *adj.*

chisel draft *n*
A shallow band or indentation cut in the surface of a stone block, making a guideline for ROUGHING OUT a form.

chopped strand mat *n*
A thin fabric made of randomly distributed short lengths of glass fibre held in a binder which is soluble in synthetic resins, used as reinforcement for resins in casting or laminating processes. It can also be used as reinforcement for concrete.

chroma *n*
The quality of a colour residing in the combination of its hue and saturation.

chromatic colours *n*
All colours except black, white and grey, ie the pure hues of the colour spectrum.

chromolithography *n*
The technique of producing a colour lithograph by printing each colour in the image from a separate plate or stone. The term is not now commonly used.

chryselephantine *adj*
The description of sculpture made of or decorated with ivory and gold, a tradition originating in ancient Greece where ceremonial statues were made with ivory to represent the flesh and draperies of beaten gold.

ciment fondu *n* (*Fr*)
A fine, dense cement, available in black or white, relatively quick-drying and capable of reproducing delicate surface detail when used as a casting material. When cured it is extremely hard and resistant.

cinnabar *n*
A natural red crystalline form of mercuric sulphide, originally the source of VERMILION, now obsolete as an artists' pigment.

cirage *n* (*Fr*)
A monochrome painting in tones of yellow. See also CAMAIEU.

circular saw *n*
A mechanical power-driven saw consisting of a circular toothed metal blade that rotates at high speed to cut through a material. The blade may be set in the flat top of a workbench or fixed to a moveable arm mounted over a base frame.

cire perdu *n* (*Fr* lost wax)
See LOST WAX PROCESS.

ciselure *n* (*Fr*)
The final CHASING of a cast metal sculpture.

cissing *n*
A defect occurring in paint applied to a smooth or non-absorbent surface, when the paint layer retracts leaving bare, ragged-edged streaks and patches.

clad *vb*
To construct a form by CLADDING.

cladding *n*
A technique used in construction of shaping a solid form by covering an open framework with a flexible sheet material, eg hardboard over a timber frame. The form is relatively lightweight in relation to its scale but appears solid when the covering is complete.

classical *adj*
1 A description of art forms deliberately composed after the style of early Greek and Roman art.
2 Less specifically, art forms based on rational principles of scale and proportion, typically featuring balanced or symmetrical composition with careful refinement of shape and structure.

claude glass *n*
A small, convex black glass that reflects a scene in miniature and reduces colour, so the artist sees a broadly simplified tonal image. This device was at one time commonly used by landscape artists and was named after the seventeenth-century French painter Claude Lorraine.

claw chisel *n*
A chisel used in stone carving for shaping the form after the initial process of roughing out. The characteristic of the claw chisel, as distinct from other types, is the toothed cutting edge. This leaves striations in the stone which are removed by further cutting with a flat chisel, or by abrasion. Claw chisels are made in various sizes and numbers of teeth to suit different weights of material and stages in the carving process.

claw hammer *n*
A hammer with the head flattened at one end to form a striking face, the other end consisting of two strong metal prongs which can be used for grasping and levering.

clay *n*
A term broadly covering various earthy substances primarily composed of hydrated aluminium silicate combined with other minerals. Clay deposits resulting from natural decomposition of rocks are found in a variety of colours and textures and are cleaned and refined for use in sculpture and ceramics. The

important property of any clay so used is that it should be malleable but retain a given shape when formed. Different ingredients are combined to make clay bodies for ceramic ware, according to the properties required in working and firing the clay. Pottery clays are generally required to be less plastic and more fine-grained than those used for modelled sculptures which are not finished by firing. See also BALL CLAY, CHINA CLAY, PRIMARY CLAY, SECONDARY CLAY.

clay wash, clay water *n*
A thin solution of clay mixed with water, of about the same consistency as milk, used as a PARTING AGENT in plaster moulds.

clear casting *n*
A method of making cast sculpture with a specially formulated synthetic resin which is poured into a mould without any reinforcing material and when cured produces a transparent, solid cast.

cleavage *n*
A defect in an oil painting consisting of the separation of layers of varnish, paint and ground, causing the paint to crack and flake off. This may be the result of improper priming or the use of materials which are not sufficiently adherent.

cliché-verre *n* (*Fr* glass negative)
1 A method of printing a hand-drawn image photographically. A glass plate is coated with an opaque ground and a design drawn in the ground with a needle. It is then placed over a sheet of photographic paper and exposed to light, so the image is imprinted on the paper and is developed as black line on a white background.
2 An image obtained by this method.

cloison *n* (*Fr* partition)
A single section of a design in CLOISONNÉ ENAMELLING, ie an individual area bounded by wire or metal strip and filled with coloured enamel.

cloisonné enamelling *n* (*Fr* partitioned)
An enamelling technique in which a design is created in raised outline by soldering thin wire or metal strip to a metal base. The recesses between the wires are filled with coloured enamels and the whole piece is fired.
Compare PLIQUE À JOUR.

closed composition *n*
A composition in which the forms and apparent directional movements are designed to be contained within the picture area,

rather than to suggest a continuing space beyond the immediate image.

closed form *n*
A sculpture shaped within the limits of a solid mass of material without noticeable projection into the surrounding space, particularly a carving which corresponds closely to the original form of the block.
Compare OPEN FORM.

coated paper *n*
A general term for types of paper given a smooth, matt or glossy surface with a fine coating of china clay or a mineral compound of similar qualities. It is used particularly for printing when a perfectly smooth, even surface is necessary to obtain a sharp image. A paper sheet may be coated on one side only or on both sides. Papers are available in a range of colours, some with a different colour on either side of the sheet. The coating reduces the flexibility of the paper as it can crack.

cobalt colours *n pl*
Synthetic inorganic pigments in the colour range blue, green, violet, and also yellow, prepared from compounds based on the metallic element cobalt and other metal oxides. The colours are generally lightfast and relatively transparent.

coelanaglyphic relief *n*
See SUNKEN RELIEF.

coiling *n*
A technique of building a hollow form from long, narrow rolls of clay which are laid one on another and built up gradually to form clay 'walls'. When the form is roughly shaped in this way the coils are gently stroked to merge the layers together into a continuous surface. This is basically a pottery technique but can also be used to make hollow sculptures.

coil pot *n*
A ceramic vessel formed by the technique of COILING.

cold cast metal *n*
A term applied to cast polyester resin in which the gel-coat has been mixed with a metallic powder filler to create a bronzed or other metallic surface effect.

cold chisel *n*
A specially toughened steel chisel designed to cut cold metal, also used in stone carving.

cold cure rubber compound *n*
A synthetic material used in making flexible moulds for casting processes. It is applied cold in a fluid or paste form and can be used to take a mould from a wax model or other material that would be damaged by exposure to heat. See also LATEX, SILICONE RUBBER.

cold-pressed oil *n*
A drying oil produced by crushing a raw material in a press without heat action and filtering the extracted oil. Linseed and poppy oils are produced by this process. The method of extraction has an effect on the properties of the oil, eg cold-pressed linseed oil is lighter in colour and clearer than raw hot-pressed linseed oil, which has to be further refined to be useful as a vehicle or medium in artists' paints.

cold-pressed paper *n*
A category of papers which have a relatively coarse or open texture, the term cold-pressed referring to the method of finishing.

collage *n* (from *Fr coller* = to stick)
1 The technique of creating an image or design by sticking paper, card, fabric, printed matter, string and other materials to a flat support. It is often combined with painting and drawing techniques.
2 An object or image created in this way. Its surface may be flat or in shallow relief, depending on the materials used. See also ASSEMBLAGE, MONTAGE, PHOTOMONTAGE.

collar *vb*
To shape a clay form by COLLARING. **collared** *adj*.

collaring *n*
A technique used in throwing a pot on a wheel, to control the form if it begins to flare out too widely as it is shaped. The top of the pot is enclosed between both hands, preventing outward expansion. Collaring is also used constructively to narrow and shape the neck of a pot.

collograph *n*
1 The process of assembling and printing from a block on which an image is built up as a collage of different materials, producing a raised and textured surface that will accept ink. Depending on the form, the block can be printed as relief or intaglio, or both.
2 A print obtained by this process.

colloid *n*
A substance composed of extremely small particles which will

not dissolve in a liquid but forms a fine suspension in which the liquid and particles do not readily separate, ie the solid matter does not settle in a mass if left to stand as do coarser particles in a suspension. A variety of fluid media used as art materials have this property.

colophony *n*
See ROSIN.

colour *n*
1 A visual sensation obtained from an object, substance or surface in respect of the wavelength of light which it reflects or transmits. See also HUE, SATURATION, VALUE.
2 The term is also used in referring to a paint or pigment, the colour sensation it emits being a major property of its usefulness.

colour circle, colour wheel *n*
A diagram arranged to show the relationships of PRIMARY COLOURS and SECONDARY COLOURS and the chromatic colours formed by mixtures of these hues. The simplest device shows the colours in six sections of a circle, running in the sequence red, orange, yellow, green, blue, violet, and it becomes progressively more complex by the insertion of red-orange, orange-yellow, yellow-green, green-blue, blue-violet and red-violet. This shows the simple progression through related hues and contrasts are demonstrated by the pairings of colours lying opposite each other in the circle. See also COMPLEMENTARY COLOUR.

coloured grey *n*
A grey produced by mixing complementary colours (red and green, blue and orange, yellow and violet) as distinct from a neutral grey made by mixing black and white. In fact, such a colour is not a grey by conventional standards; because of the behaviour of relatively impure pigments when mixed, coloured greys tend to be in a range of subtle, muddied browns, grey-greens and mauves.

coloured ground *n*
1 A painting ground treated with a thin glaze of colour. See IMPRIMATURA.
2 A painting ground which is coloured by the addition of a pigment in the preparation stage. Often the base layers on the support are white and only the final layer of the ground is coloured in this way.

coloured pencil *n*
A drawing tool consisting of a fine stick of pigment bound in china clay encased in wood. See also PENCIL.

coloured print *n*
A print in which the basic image has been printed in one colour only and subsequently hand-coloured with watercolour washes or any other appropriate technique. Compare COLOUR PRINT.

colouring agent *n*
A pigment or dye which forms the element of colour in any type of artists' material, whatever the other ingredients.

colourist *n*
The term applied to an artist who has particular skill in applying colour and manipulating colour effects.

colourman *n*
The traditional term for a manufacturer and supplier of artists' paints and pigments.

colour perspective *n*
See ATMOSPHERIC PERSPECTIVE.

colour print *n*
A print in two or more colours made by printing a separate block or plate for each different colour in the image, or by inking a single block or plate with more than one colour.
Compare COLOURED PRINT.

column *n*
A vertical pillar, usually circular in section, which is an architectural feature commonly having a load-bearing function but also of aesthetic value in the overall design of a building. It consists of a base, shaft and CAPITAL, any or all of which may be decoratively carved or incised.

combing *n*
1 A method of working patterns in clay slips used as surface decoration of ceramic ware. A toothed tool of wood, leather or plastic is used to draw linear patterns in the coating of wet slip.
2 A similar technique applied to creating texture in a layer of wet paint.

commercial graphics *n*
See GRAPHIC DESIGN.

complementary colour *n*
One of a pair of colours which may be described as opposite and mutually enhancing. Each of the primary colours -- red, blue, yellow -- is paired with the secondary colour formed by mixing the other two primaries. Thus the complementary pairs are red and green (blue and yellow); blue and orange (red and yellow); yellow and violet (blue and red). These are the most intense

pairings since no trace of the primary colour is contained in its complementary colour, but the effect is also present in the juxtaposition of mixed hues paired on the same principle, eg red-violet and yellow-green.

composite form *n*
A ceramic object assembled from two or more components which may be formed by different techniques, ie as distinct from a pot made in a single operation by THROWING a mass of clay.

composition *n*
1 The organization of different elements within the overall structure of a work of art, eg in painting, composition refers to the relationship of different elements such as line, mass, tone and colour, and also to the arrangement of the subject matter within a picture area. It is a general term that also relates to graphic design and three-dimensional forms. Although attempts have been made at various times to establish rules of 'correct' composition, the term describes a concept of form which in individual works is governed purely by the decisions of the artist, made before and during execution of the work, and these may arise from theory or practice.
2 More generally, the ingredients or components of a physical substance or material, and their combination within the mass.

composition board *n*
A sheet material made from compressed wood chips, blocks or layers of wood, rather than cut from a solid section of timber.

composition clay *n*
A term used of various substances marketed as modelling materials, which are artificial compounds with an oil or wax ingredient to keep them indefinitely malleable and non-drying.

compressor *n*
An electrically-powered machine designed to supply a constant flow of pressurized air to an AIRBRUSH. There are two basic types: one which passes air directly through the machinery and a more complex version which stores air at constant pressure and replenishes the supply automatically if the pressure begins to drop. Both feed air into the airbrush via a narrow connecting hose.

conceptual art *n*
A term used broadly of work by artists in which a physical object is not a necessary end-product, the idea of a work and examination of its theoretical value being the primary motivation, with the written word as an important vehicle of presentation. In fact, there is commonly some actual evidence of

the work, eg a statement by the artist or photograph of a particular situation chosen or set up by the artist, but the term has been applied to a variety of processes and activities and is not precisely defined.

conceptual colour *n*
A colour used in figurative painting which is symbolic or expressive, rather than realistic.

concrete[1] *n*
An extremely heavy, durable sculpture material with a stone-like appearance, made from a mixture of cement, water and aggregate. It is usually used as a casting material, to form a complete sculpture or a component of a construction, but can also be crudely modelled, or set as a coating over a solid form.

concrete[2] *vb*
To fill or cover a form with concrete.

concrete[3] *adj*
The description of a thing which is actual and physical rather than abstract and notional.

coning *n*
A technique which forms part of the process of CENTRING a mass of clay on a potter's wheel. When the clay is roughly positioned at the centre of the rotating wheel the potter holds it between both hands and exerts pressure to draw the clay up into a cone. It is then cupped with one hand and pressed firmly down from the top with the other hand. If the clay is off-centre, this can be seen by the irregular shape and motion of the cone. The process is repeated a number of times until the clay mass is perfectly centred.

conservation *n*
The term which broadly refers to all techniques and processes involved in preserving works of art in prime condition, restoring works in which the original materials have deteriorated, and repairing works which are actually damaged, ie broken or torn. Conservation includes investigation of proper conditions of temperature, humidity and lighting under which works may be safely stored and displayed. See also RESTORING.

conservator *n*
A person skilled in any of the techniques of conservation of works of art.

construction *n*
1 The process of building up or assembling a sculpture from component materials, as distinct from carving or modelling a

mass of a single material. The component parts are often preformed and joined together, though cutting and shaping processes may be applied as the pieces are assembled. Wood, metal and plastic are materials commonly used in construction but the range includes all sorts of raw materials and manufactured items, including found objects.
2 A sculpture made by this process.

contained shadow *n*
In pictorial terms, a shadow on a form which describes its shape in relation to the light falling upon it. Compare CAST SHADOW.

Conté crayon *n*
A proprietary brand of square-sectioned drawing chalks in black, white, sanguine and sepia.

content *n*
The subject matter of a work of art, as distinct from its material form or style of imagery. The term is used both of an overall theme or concept and of the figures, objects or motifs by which it is represented.

contour *n*
The boundary of a solid form or mass, often expressed as an outline but descriptive of more than the simple shape of an object. The term is used of two- and three-dimensional forms. The contour can show not only the shape of a form but also some indication of its volume, emphasis and texture.

contrapposto *n* (*It* placed in opposition)
The pose of a sculpted figure in which the apparent movement of the upper part of the body opposes that of the lower part; eg on a central axis through the body, if the torso is turned to the right, the hips and legs are turned towards the left.

conversation piece *n*
A painting, usually small-scale, showing a group of people acting informally in a domestic or everyday setting. Typically the figures constitute a group portrait of members of a family and are shown full-length rather than in close view.

cool colour *n*
Any colour in the range of blue, blue-green and blue-violet hues, which can be said to have an apparent coolness.

copal varnish *n*
A varnish used in oil painting made by melting copal, a fossilized natural resin, in hot linseed oil. It forms an extremely hard, glossy film but the natural resin has a tendency to crack or discolour with age.

coping *n*
A method of splitting off a section of a stone block to remove a relatively large amount in the first stage of carving. A number of holes are made across the surface of the block with a POINT or chisel. Several sharp points are inserted in the holes and are struck with a hammer in sequence until the stone cracks and the outer section splits away.

coping saw *n*
A hand-held saw consisting of a fine metal blade, toothed on one side, set in a three-sided metal frame attached to a wooden handle. It is used for fine cutting around curves and angles in sheet metal or wood.

copolymer *n*
1 A synthetic compound consisting of large molecules formed by chemical combination of two different, smaller molecular units in a repeated pattern.
2 A binder or emulsion used in paint manufacture which is a compound of this type. See also POLYMER.

copy^1 *n*
1 Strictly, a drawing, painting or sculpture made in exact imitation of an original work of art, by someone other than the original artist, but not intended as a FAKE.
2 A work made by an art student in imitation of an original by a well-known or established artist, in order to study the composition and technique.
3 See REPLICA.
4 See REPRODUCTION. Compare FACSIMILE, VARIANT.

copy^2 *vb*
To make a copy.

core *n*
A filling of refractory material inside a hollow wax sculpture used as the model for a bronze cast. The core is pinned in place in relation to the INVESTMENT around the model and when the wax is melted out the space left between core and investment determines the thickness of the metal cast. The core may be a base over which the wax is modelled or the core material can be packed into a hollow-cast wax form.

Cornish stone *n*
See CHINA STONE.

coroplastics *n*
A collective term for sculpture and decorative relief work in TERRACOTTA.

costruzione legittima *n* (*It*)
A system of LINEAR PERSPECTIVE in which the elements in a composition are arranged between a base line and vanishing point dictated by the assumed height of a figure standing in the foreground plane. A diagrammatic scheme establishes regular measurements between these points in which the degree of recession towards the vanishing point is fixed on successive vertical planes.

cottling *n*
1 The process of constructing a temporary container for liquid plaster in forming a one-piece mould around a clay object. It consists of simple walls of any solid and relatively non-porous material built around the clay form: any gaps or joints in the construction must be sealed and made watertight. The liquid plaster is poured in to cover the model and when it has hardened sufficiently to be self-supporting, the container can be dismantled.
2 A construction made for this purpose.

cotton duck *n*
A heavy, closely woven, light-coloured cotton fabric used as a support for painting. It is less expensive than linen fabrics sold as artists' canvas and is relatively firm and durable.

coulisse *n* (*Fr* wings, in a theatre)
A style of composition in painting in which pictorial elements, typically of landscape or architecture, are placed at each side of the picture in a manner that directs focus towards the centre.

counterproof *n*
A proof taken not directly from a plate or block but from a print on which the ink is still wet. The original impression is covered with a sheet of clean paper and run through the press. The counterproof shows a reversed image from that of the print and this corresponds to the image on the plate or block. It is less distinct than a direct impression but useful as reference for making corrections or planning further stages of the work.

covering power *n*
The ability of a liquid paint to cover a support, technically expressed as a measurement of area in relation to a measured volume of paint. The term is often wrongly applied to the HIDING POWER of a paint.

crackle *n*
A network of hairline cracks in a ceramic glaze. This may be the result of different rates of shrinkage between body and glaze or due to rapid cooling after firing. Crackle is the term used when

these conditions are deliberately set up to produce a decorative effect or to simulate ageing of a glaze. When a glaze cracks accidentally it is usually known as CRAZING.

cradle *vb*
To reinforce a wood panel by CRADLING. **cradled** *adj.*

cradling *n*
A method of strengthening a wood panel used as a painting support, the purpose being to control warping and movement of the wood which might cause the panel to split. The traditional method, used in conservation of old paintings, is to glue down slotted wooden strips running parallel at intervals across the back of the panel, then to insert a second row of wood strips crosswise, running through the slots but not glued down so they are free to move if the panel expands or contracts. The term is also more generally used to describe any method of strengthening a panel with a network of wood battens.

craft[1] *n*
1 A particular skill or technique used in making an image or object from physical materials.
2 A process or activity involving the use of such a skill.

craft[2] *vb*
To make an object or image, or part of one, by skilful manipulation of materials.

Crank mixture *n*
A coarse clay body consisting of fireclay mixed with grog, used for modelling and for the shaping of heavy, irregular forms which would be liable to crack in firing if made from a finer body. The mixture was originally developed as a refractory material for making kiln shelves and SAGGARS.

craquelure *n* (*Fr* cracking)
1 The fine network of cracks that may appear in the surface layers of an oil painting, due to ground, paint and varnish hardening or contracting at different rates as they age. The pattern of cracking varies with the type of ground and medium used, and this may help to establish the age and authenticity of a work.
2 The term is sometimes used to describe cracking in ceramic glazes. See CRACKLE, CRAZING.

crawling *n*
1 The shrinking of a ceramic glaze, leaving cracks or raw areas on the surface of a form. This may be caused by grease or dust on the surface before the glaze is applied, or be a fault in the composition of the glaze.

2 Unwanted marks on the surface of a cast metal sculpture, caused by the molten metal cooling too quickly on coming into contact with the interior of the mould.

crayon[1] *n*
A drawing material in stick form, made of pigment bound in gum, oil or wax.

crayon[2] *vb*
To apply colour to a support using a crayon.

crayon engraving *n*
See STIPPLE ENGRAVING.

crazing *n*
The cracking of a ceramic glaze as it cools after firing, due to different rates of contraction in the clay body and glaze. This often occurs if the fired ware is removed too quickly from the kiln. It is a particularly damaging fault if the glaze is intended to seal porous earthenware. Crazing which is deliberately induced is known as CRACKLE.

creeping bite *n*
The process of graduating the depth of etched lines or aquatint texture by partially submerging an etching plate in acid and gradually increasing the area exposed, eg by tilting the acid bath or pushing the plate further into the acid solution.

crevé *n* (*Fr* punctured)
A fault in the surface of an etching plate caused by the breakdown of the ground between exposed lines, when the acid bites through to create a small area of OPEN BITE. It is usually due to the acid solution being too strong or the plate being left in it too long.

criblé *n* (*Fr* sieved)
See DOTTED MANNER.

crosscut saw *n*
A hand-held saw with fine, closely spaced teeth, used to cut across the grain of a solid material eg wood or soft stone.

cross hatch *vb*
To create an area of tone by CROSS HATCHING. **cross-hatched** *adj*.

cross hatch and slurry *n*
A method of joining sections of damp or leather-hard clay by scoring the faces of the joint with a criss-cross pattern and using thick liquid clay as an adhesive between the sections.

cross hatching *n*
1 An extension of the technique of HATCHING, used to create areas of tone in a drawing. It involves working two sets of closely-spaced parallel lines crossing each other at right angles. It is used in the same way as hatching but necessarily creates a more dense textured effect which at a distance is seen as an unbroken tone.
2 An area of tone created by this technique.

crucible *n*
A deep pot made of refractory material, the container for metal which is being made molten in a furnace, eg bronze for casting.

cure *vb*
1 To undergo the process of CURING.
2 To cause or promote curing in a material. **cured** *adj.*

curing *n*
The hardening process of a material worked in moist or liquid form, eg concrete, plaster, resin. This is not a simple process of drying out by evaporation of the moisture content, as the material undergoes physical changes in which it acquires the durable characteristics of its solid form.

curvilinear *adj*
The descriptive term for a design or image which is primarily composed of or characterized by curving lines.

cutting *n*
The process of adding bulk to a quantity of dry pigment by addition of an inert pigment or filler.

cylinder press *n*
A mechanical printing press for RELIEF PRINTING from wood or linoleum blocks. It consists of a flat metal bed on which the inked block is placed, across which travels a heavy cylinder coated with a thick rubber blanket. Paper is attached to the cylinder and as this moves over the block the paper is pressed down on the inked surface and picks up an impression of the image.

d

dabber *n*
1 A pad used for laying the ground on an etching plate. Commonly it consists of a mass of soft fibre, such as wool or cotton, covered with leather, felt or a similarly tough fabric. This is formed into a smooth pad on one side: on the other side the edges are drawn together and either twisted into a finger grip or set in a handle. The same tool can also be used to lay ink on a printing block or plate.
2 See DOLLY.

damar, dammar *n*
A name given to any of a number of natural resins obtained from certain species of forest trees native to south-east Asia. Damar is used as an ingredient of oil painting mediums and varnishes and is available in the form of small glassy chunks, colourless or pale yellow in colour.

damar varnish *n*
A varnish made by dissolving damar resin in turpentine, one of the most commonly used varnishes for oil painting.

damascening *n*
The technique of decorating a base metal with fine inlays of precious metal, gold or silver. The form of the decoration is commonly a pattern of wavy lines or arabesques.

dead clay *n*
Clay that has lost its plasticity and resilience due to age or poor conditions of storage.

dead colour *n*
The colour used to lay in a monochrome UNDERPAINTING, typically a dull brown, green or grey.

dead plaster *n*
Plaster that has lost its useful setting property through exposure to damp.
Compare KILLED PLASTER.

dead stone *n*
A stone block that has been weathered too long, in which the texture is dulled and unresponsive to carving processes.
Compare LIVE STONE.

de-airing *n*
A treatment applied to clay to consolidate the mass, eliminating air pockets and creating an even texture throughout. This is done by passing the clay through a de-airing PUGMILL, in which it is mechanically shredded and compressed.

decal *n*
1 A transfer motif printed in a slightly adhesive oil colour or lacquer on a paper backing sheet. The motif is pressed on a suitable surface and the paper backing is soaked with water and peeled away. Decals can be used to lay motifs on materials such as ceramics, glass or painted wood.
2 The process of transferring a decal to the surface of an object. Also called decalcomania.

decalcomania *n*
1 See DECAL.
2 A method of creating a painted image by dabbing paint on a sheet of paper and pressing a clean sheet over the surface to spread and lift the wet colours. This partly random process may be used as a starting point for development of the image.

deckle edge *n*
The irregular edge on a sheet of handmade paper, occurring naturally in the settling of the pulp fibres. The name comes from the frame (deckle) in which the pulp is spread and drained to make a paper sheet. The rough edges are artificially simulated in some types of machine-made papers.

décollage *n* (from *Fr decoller* = to unstick)
A reversal of the technique of COLLAGE: materials applied in layers one on top of the other are partially torn away to create an image by a subtractive process which breaks up the original surface. This is associated with large-scale areas consisting of posters and printed materials, but the principle is applicable on any scale.

découpage *n* (*Fr* cutting out)
The technique of decorating a surface with shapes and designs cut from paper, a form of COLLAGE typically applied to ornamental and utilitarian objects. The surface may be varnished to seal and strengthen the paper layers.

deep etch *n*
The technique of etching heavily recessed areas in a metal plate by long immersion in acid. This usually applies to broad, open shapes rather than line work, achieved by scratching away wide areas of ground or by painting a design on a clean plate surface with stopping out varnish. The deeply etched areas print as a grey

tone surrounded by a heavy black line where the edges of the bite hold more ink. Alternatively, the plate can be printed in relief by rolling ink over the surface of the raised areas. This can also be combined with inking the intaglio to produce a two-colour print. See also RELIEF ETCHING.

deflocculant *n*
A substance, or combination of substances, which disrupts the natural bonding of clay particles. It is used in the preparation of SLIP since its action on the clay greatly reduces the amount of water needed to render the clay into liquid form. A casting slip made in this way undergoes less shrinkage in firing. Sodium silicate and sodium carbonate are commonly used as deflocculants.

deflocculate *vb*
To treat clay with a DEFLOCCULANT. **deflocculated** *adj*, **deflocculation** *n*.

degraded colour *n*
A colour that is reduced in clarity and intensity by the admixture of another colour or a neutral grey.

del *abb* **delineavit** *vb* (*Lat* has drawn it)
Lettering which appears on a print accompanying the name of the artist who created the original image from which the print was made. It is seen on old engravings.

Delft ware *n*
See MAJOLICA.

dental plaster *n*
A superfine, brilliantly white form of PLASTER OF PARIS, used as a casting material or binder.

deposition *n*
A traditional image in Christian art; the lowering of Christ's body from the cross.

design[1] *n*
1 The composition of an image, ie the overall organization of elements in a drawing, painting, print or sculpture.
2 The basic plan for the assembly of different elements or components in an artefact or functional object, including the construction of individual forms and their interrelationships and taking account of the method of production and intended use of the item.
3 The process of conceiving and executing a composition or plan.

design² *vb*
To plan the organization of component elements into a unified form.

designer *n*
1 A person skilled in any technique or process of DESIGN, especially one who designs particular items as a professional line of work.
2 The person responsible for the design of an individual image or object, sometimes also responsible for actually making the finished item.

designers' colours *n pl*
Fine quality GOUACHE paints, intended for use in ARTWORK and ILLUSTRATION. They provide a flat, opaque film of colour with a matt surface or slight sheen. Since they are commonly used for work intended for reproduction, the colours are not all completely permanent.

devalued *adj*
A term describing the condition of a paint or pigment in which the original hue is significantly altered by the admixture of another colour or addition of an impure adulterant or filler.

device *n*
1 A tool or instrument designed and constructed for a particular purpose.
2 An individual form or motif in a composition which has a symbolic or explanatory role in terms of overall content.
3 A motif or design in which a number of elements are combined as a single unit.
4 A motif or symbol which represents an artist's signature or printer's trademark.

devitrification *n*
The crystallization of a ceramic glaze, caused by slow cooling or by a substance in the glaze mixture that tends to promote this reaction. The effect is sometimes exploited in the firing of a MATT GLAZE.

diaglyph *n*
An image carved in SUNKEN RELIEF.

diamond point tool *n*
1 A drypoint needle in which the cutting tip is made of diamond. It is regarded as a more sensitive drawing tool than the softer steel needle and is more hardwearing.
2 A similar tool used to incise lines on metal, plastic or glass.

dichroism *n*
The property of a substance which gives different colour effects according to whether it is mainly reflecting or transmitting light. This can occur with the pigment in a paint, which has a certain colour when spread as an opaque film and shows a different hue when applied as a transparent glaze. See also MASS TONE, UNDERTONE.

die *n*
1 An INTAGLIO image cast or incised in a solid material which can be used to stamp or emboss a soft material, eg paper, leather, molten wax, plaster, with a reversed impression of the image.
2 A hollow cylinder of metal with a THREAD spiralled around the inside and split vertically to form a cutting edge, used to cut a corresponding thread on the outer surface of a basically cylindrical component.

diluent *n*
1 A liquid which can be used to thin or dilute a particular substance, but which does not dissolve it.
2 Specifically, a liquid used to alter the fluidity and covering power of a paint, commonly the same liquid which forms the VEHICLE in the paint.

diorama *n*
1 A scenic painting housed within a given location, which is made of a combination of transparent and opaque materials and displayed under special lighting effects to give an impression of three-dimensional reality and live atmosphere.
2 Depending upon scale, the box, case, room or building in which such a painting is housed.

dipper *n*
A small metal pot designed to clip on to the edge of a flat palette, for holding a diluent or medium conveniently close to the paint. Also called palette cup.

dipping *n*
The process of coating a clay object with an even layer of glaze or slip by simply immersing it in the liquid.

diptych *n*
A painting or relief sculpture worked on two separate panels which form a single unit in terms of composition or are conceived as companion pieces to be viewed together. The panels may be hinged together or mounted in a single frame. See also POLYPTYCH, TRIPTYCH.

direct carving *n*
A method of carving in which the form is directly shaped in a

block of material, not copied from a model or sketch. This takes into account the particular features of the block, eg the grain of stone or wood, any knots, veins or blemishes, so the work is defined by the nature of the material as well as the form imposed by the sculptor. Also known as *taille directe* (*Fr*).

direct painting *n*
See ALLA PRIMA.

direct sculpture *n*
A general term for sculpture techniques in which a form is shaped or constructed directly in the materials of which it is finally composed, as distinct from copying a model on a larger scale or casting processes in which a transitional material used to shape the form is ultimately replaced by the casting material. See also DIRECT CARVING.

direct stencil *n*
An image created directly on the fabric mesh of a screen used in the SCREENPRINTING process. The methods of direct work include painting the mesh with a solution of gum or glue which blocks holes in the mesh as it dries; drawing on the mesh with a wax crayon; or applying a photographic image by passing light through an intermediary image onto a screen coated with light-sensitive emulsion.

disegno *n* (*It* design)
A term which can mean both drawing and design, therefore referring to the overall composition of a painting and possibly also alluding to the artist's preliminary concept of the work.

disposable palettes *n pl*
Sheets of non-absorbent paper packed together in pad form. Colours are laid out and mixed on the pad, as on any form of palette, and the used sheet is then torn off to leave a fresh surface. The pad is usually rectangular with a hole cut in one end to form a thumb grip.

distemper *n*
An impermanent paint consisting of pigment and a powdered filler, eg chalk, in a binder of glue size, sometimes used as ground or colours for a mural, for interior decoration, or painting of temporary structures such as theatre sets, but not of a quality suitable for works intended to have lasting value.

distilled water *n*
Water which has been vaporized and condensed to remove all impurities, often used as a diluent for watercolours in preference

to ordinary tap water as its purity ensures no interference with the quality of the pigments.

dolly *n*
1 A tight roll of paper, scrim or other suitable fabric, used for applying ink to an INTAGLIO PRINTING plate. The flat end of the roughly cylindrical form is used to pick up ink and rub it into the intaglio. Also called dabber. See also À LA POUPÉE.
2 A platform mounted on wheels on which a large sculpture or mass of heavy material can be moved around a studio.

donkey *n*
A piece of studio equipment which combines an easel and a stool. It is a narrow bench, one end of which can be raised to form an adjustable support for a drawing board or small canvas: the artist sits astride the remaining flat portion of the bench.

dotted manner *n*
A technique for producing an image printed from an engraved metal plate on which the design is developed with masses of small dots indented in the plate by means of metal punches driven with a hammer. The process is often combined with line engraving and may be printed as intaglio (black dots on white ground) or relief (white dots on black ground). The technique is also called *manière criblée* (*Fr*): the abbreviated form *criblé* is also used.

dotted print *n*
An image produced by the DOTTED MANNER method of print-making.

double run *n*
A method of obtaining a heavily defined impression from an inked intaglio plate by running it through the press twice before lifting the paper.

dowel *n*
A small, narrow cylinder of wood which can be used to peg a joint between two sections of wood, eg in a construction or a wood carving made from more than one block. A hole is drilled in each face of the joint and the dowel is inserted in one hole and fitted to the other: it is usually coated with an adhesive to secure it in place.

dragging *n*
1 The technique of dragging thick, undiluted paint over a surface to produce an effect of ragged streaks and rough-textured patches of colour. The charged brush is dragged lightly across a textured support or over a previously applied paint layer which is still tacky.
2 See RETROUSSAGE.

dragon's blood *n*
A natural blood-red resin, at one time used as a colouring agent in painting and manuscript illumination. Being impermanent, it has long since been discarded in this role, but the material is also sometimes used as a varnish ingredient.

draughtsman, draughtswoman *n*
1 An artist skilled in techniques and processes of drawing.
2 The term is often used specifically to refer to an artist employed professionally to make technical drawings, plans and projections, eg related to architecture or engineering.

draughtsmanship *n*
1 An artist's skill in drawing.
2 The quality of drawing skill apparent in a particular work or works. This does not apply only to drawings, but also to painting, printmaking etc when referring to organization of a composition and realization of forms within the image.

draw *vb*
1 To pursue a process of drawing or to make a drawing, by whatever method.
2 To remove fired ceramic ware from a kiln. **drawn** *adj*.

drawing *n*
1 A process of creating a two-dimensional image by manipulation of any of various tools and materials. Commonly, drawing is understood as differentiated from painting by reliance on linear and tonal characteristics rather than use of mass and colour, but broadly the term covers many different forms of representation and the processes of drawing and painting are essentially interlinked.
2 An image created by such a process.
3 (*ceramics*) The process or activity of unpacking fired ceramic ware from a kiln.

drawing board *n*
A thick, flat, rectangular sheet of wood to which paper or board can be clipped, pinned or taped to form a rigid support for drawing or painting. The type of wood used for this purpose varies: it may be timber, plywood or a laminated or composition board. It should be strong, inflexible and resistant to warping: some boards are reinforced with metal strips at top and bottom.

drawknife *n*
A cutting tool used in wood carving and construction processes, consisting of a strong metal blade with a handle at either end. It is used for stripping bark and shaving the outer surface of wood.

draw trial *n*
A method of checking the progress of ceramic ware while it is being fired, by placing test pieces in the kiln which can be withdrawn at different stages of firing to examine changes in the materials. The process is less commonly used with modern electric kilns and has largely been replaced by the use of the PYROMETRIC CONE.

drier *n*
A substance added to oil paint to speed drying, typically metallic salts combined with oil or resin. The salts chiefly derive from lead, manganese or cobalt and the oil or resin content is low, being necessary principally to facilitate mixing of the drier with the paint.
Also called siccative.

drill[1] *n*
A tool consisting of a metal shaft with an edged or pointed tip which is rotated rapidly to bore a hole into a solid material. Hand-operated and power-driven drills are used in various sculpture processes, eg stone and wood carving, construction. See also AUGER, BOW DRILL, TAP DRILL.

drill[2] *vb*
To bore a hole in a solid material using a drill.

drybrush *n*
A painting technique which produces an effect of ragged, mottled colour. The brush is either barely charged with paint or heavily charged with colour and then blotted almost dry. It is pulled across the support, held at a shallow angle to the surface so the flat of the brush makes contact, rather than just the tip. The textural qualities are most fully exploited if the support has a noticeably coarse grain or tooth.

dry colour *n*
Dry powdered pigments of high quality, as available for artists' use in mixing paints in the studio, eg for tempera painting where egg is used as the binder and the process involves frequent mixing of relatively small quantities of fresh paint.

drying oil *n*
The general term for any one of a number of vegetable oils used as a vehicle or medium for oil paint. Commonly used drying oils are linseed, poppy, walnut and safflower oils. They dry by chemical change when exposed to oxygen, not by evaporation, and form a durable film which binds the pigment and adheres firmly to the support.

drying rate *n*
The relative speed of drying of a pigment dispersed in oil. Every pigment has a natural drying rate and these can vary widely. Adjustments may be made to the composition of oil paints in manufacture to compensate for fast or slow drying rates, bringing the colours within a smaller range of variation.

dry mounting *n*
A method of bonding paper to board by placing a thin sheet of adhesive film between them and pressing them under a metal hotplate in a specially designed press. The heat melts the adhesive film and this forms a permanent, firm bond between the two materials.

drypoint *n*
1 An INTAGLIO PRINTING process in which an image is worked on a metal plate by scratching into the surface with a pointed tool. It is thus distinct from etching, in which acid corrodes marks in the metal, and engraving, in which lines are cleanly incised. In drypoint, the rough burr thrown up along the scratched marks is an essential feature. It retains ink and imparts a soft, velvety quality to the printed image but wears down relatively quickly, limiting the number of impressions that can be taken from the plate. The process is sometimes combined with etching.
2 A printed image resulting from this process.

drypoint needle *n*
A rigid steel point set in a wood or metal holder. The needle is used to inscribe lines and textures on a metal plate and must be tough and extremely sharp. See also DIAMOND POINT TOOL, ETCHING NEEDLE.

dummy *n*
A small, heavy mallet with a cylindrical striking head made of metal, usually iron, used to drive a stone carving chisel.

dunting *n*
The cracking of a ceramic form during firing, due to the tension of a glaze contracting over the clay body or a too rapid rise or fall in temperature within the kiln.

dust box *n*
A box fitted with a mechanical device for laying aquatint resin on an etching plate. The box contains a thick layer of powdery resin which is agitated by means of a bellows attachment or revolving paddles within the box. When the resin dust has formed a dense cloud inside the box the metal plate is inserted on a wire tray and left until an even layer of dust has settled on the surface. When

the plate is removed it is heated to liquefy the resin particles, which set in place as they cool.

Dutch mordant *n*
An acid solution used in etching, called 'Dutch' because it corresponds to a formula used in seventeenth-century Holland. It is a solution of hydrochloric acid and potassium chlorate and is particularly accurate in etching fine lines on copper.

dye[1] *n*
A colouring agent which is soluble in a liquid vehicle and imparts colour to a surface or material by being absorbed. A dye may be fixed on an insoluble substance to create a PIGMENT. See also LAKE PIGMENT.

dye[2] *vb*
To colour a substance or material with a dye. **dyed** *adj*.

e

earth colours *n pl*
A general term for pigments derived from metal oxides occuring naturally in clay, rock or soil. These include a variety of red, yellow, brown and green colours, including ochres, umbers and terre verte. They are typically stable and permanent in any medium and are among the least expensive of artists' pigments.

earthenware *n*
Ceramic ware fired at a relatively low temperature, generally below 1100°C (2012°F), in which the clay body is opaque and remains porous after firing. It can be sealed with a glaze, which is also low-fired. See also STONEWARE.

earthworks *n pl*
The term used for forms of LAND ART in which the artist works directly with the natural geography of a particular location using the native substances in situ, eg earth, stone, water etc.

easel *n*
A framework of wood or metal designed to hold a painting at a convenient height and angle while work is in progress. See RADIAL EASEL, SKETCHING EASEL, STUDIO EASEL, TABLE EASEL.

easel painting *n*
A term used to refer to particular types of painting, generally

implying that the work is moveable and relatively small-scale, studio-executed and demonstrating conventional painting techniques, ie a painting that can be worked at an easel. This differentiates from a mural or fresco attached to a wall and from images and designs executed by unconventional methods.

ébauche *n* (*Fr* rough outline)
1 The initial stage of UNDERPAINTING, in which a composition is sketched out roughly on the support.
2 Any rough sketch, outline or plan of a composition.

ebony *n*
A dense, close-grained, heavy hardwood obtained from various tropical trees native to Africa, Asia and South America. It is pure black in colour and sufficiently compact and resistant to take finely detailed carving and a highly polished surface finish.

échoppe *n* (*Fr*)
An etching needle with a bevelled oval tip. When used to draw lines in an etching ground it creates a fluid, swelling line.

eclectic¹ *adj*
1 The description of a method of work which consists in borrowing forms and concepts from established sources and combining them to produce works which supposedly benefit from the synthesis of elements considered to have particular excellence in their own contexts.
2 The description of an artist, or work by that artist, who practises this principle.

eclectic² *n*
A person whose method of work is eclectic.

écorché *n* (*Fr* flayed, skinned)
A drawing, painting or sculpture showing the musculature of a human figure or animal, ie the figure is represented as if the skin had been removed. Such items were once commonly used as aids in teaching anatomy to artists.

edition¹ *n*
1 (*printmaking*) A number of identical impressions taken as a complete set from a plate, block or stone in its final state. The prints are numbered consecutively, showing both the individual number in the sequence and the overall number of prints in the edition, eg 10/50. Each one is signed by the artist. See also LIMITED EDITION.
2 (*sculpture*) A set of cast sculptures taken from the same mould or master. The edition usually consists of no more than six casts and each one is signed and numbered. Though each cast in an edition

might have a lower value than a unique piece, it may be a more effective way of offsetting the costs of an expensive process such as bronze casting.

edition[2] *vb*
To produce a number of works that form an edition.

editioning *n*
The process of pulling a required number of identical prints to form an EDITION.

egg-oil emulsion *n*
A paint medium made by mixing egg yolk with a drying oil, sometimes used in tempera painting when the paint is required to have more body than can be obtained using egg yolk alone as the binder. There are several recipes for studio preparation of egg-oil emulsions.

egg tempera *n*
The true method of tempera painting in which pure egg yolk is used as the binder for pigments and water as the vehicle.

electrolyte *n*
A chemical substance or solution that is a conductor of electricity. Deflocculants used in turning plastic clay to slip are electrolytes: it is not fully understood how their electrical capacity acts on the clay to make it fluid, but the effect is reliable in practice.

electroplating *n*
The process of laying a metal coating on another metal or non-metallic object by immersing the material in a metallic salt solution and passing an electric current through the solution, which causes it to deposit an amount of its metal content on the surface of the immersed object.

emboss *vb*
To create a design by EMBOSSING. **embossed** *adj.*

embossing *n*
1 Any method of creating a raised design or image on a sheet material, eg paper, leather, metal, by hammering, pressing, stamping or moulding it from front or back. See also REPOUSSÉ.
2 More broadly, any method of creating a design or image in low relief on metal, eg carving, chasing, moulding.

emery *n*
1 An extremely hard ABRASIVE in the form of granules or powder, made by pulverizing a crystalline mineral compound mainly composed of alumina.
2 A synthetically produced substance with similar qualities.

emulsifier *n*
A substance capable of combining two immiscible liquids as an EMULSION, eg casein, egg or wax, which are agents used in production of oil and water emulsions.

emulsify *vb*
To convert immiscible liquids into an EMULSION. **emulsified** *adj.*

emulsion *n*
1 A fluid composed of a mixture of two liquids which do not normally mix, one being suspended throughout the other in the form of tiny droplets. An emulsion may be a natural substance, eg egg yolk, or artificially produced through the agency of an emulsifier.
2 A fluid of this type used as a vehicle or medium in painting.
3 The term is also used of a number of hardwearing paints specially formulated for interior and exterior use and marketed under various brand-names. These may have appropriate uses as art materials, eg for mural painting or as surface finish for outdoor sculpture.

enamel¹ *n*
1 A vitreous material which is a compound of silica and mineral ingredients, used for surface decoration of metal. The compound is ground to a powder and can be applied in dry form to a flat or hollowed surface or to an adhesive ground of gum, or it can be mixed with water to form a malleable paste. When heated the material melts into a smooth, glassy coating. Depending upon the ingredients, an enamel may be transparent or opaque, colourless or coloured. See also FLUX.
2 A ceramic glaze fired at a low temperature, typically a powdered colouring agent in an oil medium which can be painted over an existing glaze.
3 A liquid paint consisting of pigment ground in a varnish medium, which dries to a tough, glossy film of opaque colour. It is generally used for surface decoration or finishing of three-dimensional objects and solid materials, less commonly as a medium for painting pictures.

enamel² *vb*
To apply or decorate an object with an enamel. **enamelled** *adj.*

enamelling *n*
1 The process of decorating a metal surface or object by applying vitreous enamel powders or pastes and firing them at a relatively low temperature to melt the enamel into a smooth, glossy surface coating.

2 The process of colouring or decorating a ceramic object with a low-fired enamel. See ON-GLAZE DECORATION.
3 The process of painting the surface of an object with enamel paints.

encaustic *n*
1 The technique of painting with pigments bound in molten wax. Refined beeswax is used as the binder, often with the addition of DAMAR resin. The wax colours are applied with a brush, spatula or painting knife and are kept warm during application so they can be easily manipulated. The paint can be applied as thin glazes of colour or thick IMPASTO layers, translucent or opaque. When the painting is complete an overall heat treatment is applied, to bond the surface without changing its qualities, and the final surface is polished with a soft cloth to produce a characteristic sheen. The technique was first used in ancient Greece, using charcoal burners to heat the colours. The modern equivalent involves use of electrically heated palette and tools, plus a mounted bulb or heating element to warm the support and burn in the finished surface. Burning in, the final heat treatment, is considered the true sign of encaustic technique, as compared to other types of painting with wax in which resins and oils are added to keep the paint fluid.
2 Paint consisting of pigment bound in wax.

end-grain block *n*
A block used for wood engraving taken from a hardwood, eg boxwood, and sawn across the grain rather than in line with the fibres. The block surface is compact and when given a smooth finish is suitable for the engraving of fine lines and complex detail.
Compare PLANK-GRAIN BLOCK.

engobe *n*
A clay slip used as a thin coating on a clay body, as surface decoration or to form a ground for coloured glaze. It may be applied before the body is completely dry or after biscuit firing. The term identifies a slip used only in this way, as distinct from one used to create a form, as in SLIP CASTING.

engrave *vb*
To create an image or design by a process of ENGRAVING.
engraved *adj.*

engraver *n*
1 A person skilled in the technique of engraving.
2 A person responsible for engraving and printing of a particular image.

engraver's cushion *n*
See SANDBAG.

engraving *n*
1 Broadly, any process of creating a linear design or image on the surface of a hard and durable substance, eg metal, wood, glass, with fine cutting tools.
2 A design or image made by such a process.
3 Specifically, an INTAGLIO PRINTING process in which an image is incised directly in the surface of a metal plate, usually copper, with a fine cutting tool known as a BURIN. In the basic process of line engraving, the tool is held at a low angle and pushed evenly through the surface of the metal, creating a narrow incised line with a ragged burr along the edges. The burr is removed with a scraper to leave the line clean and sharp. The deeper the line, the more ink it will retain. Curved lines are cut by turning the plate under the tool rather than pushing the burin round the curve. Tonal areas are created by HATCHING, CROSS HATCHING and STIPPLING with the tool. See also STIPPLE ENGRAVING, WOOD ENGRAVING.
4 A printed image produced by this process.

en plein air *adv* (*Fr* in the open air)
The term applied to the practice of painting out of doors to capture directly the effects of light and atmosphere, eg in landscape painting. The term originally differentiated this practice from the long-established tradition of making sketches and notes out of doors and using these as reference for a painting executed in the studio.

environmental art *n*
The term applied to forms of art in which the art object is a large-scale construction or assembly of materials, of either a permanent or temporary nature, which the viewer can enter or pass through.

epoxy resin *n*
A synthetic thermosetting plastic resin used as a sculpture material. It is obtained in liquid form and is mixed with equal parts of a specially formulated hardener, or curing agent. It has similar properties to those of POLYESTER RESIN, but is less commonly used: it hardens more slowly though the original liquid form has less tendency to deteriorate if stored over a period of time.

erase *vb*
To rub away or obliterate marks on a support. **erased** *adj*.

eraser *n*
Any material that will lift or rub away the marks of a drawing or painting medium from a support. Erasers vary from soft gum, plastic or rubber compounds to gritty abrasives: in many cases they act effectively by rubbing away a fine surface layer from the support itself, though the softer types can lift a drawing medium by adhesion. See also AIR ERASER, KNEADED ERASER.

erasure *n*
The area on a support where an eraser has been used to lift the marks of a drawing or painting medium. Generally, an erasure can be identified by faint traces of the original marks or a change in surface texture where the support material has been abraded.

esquisse *n* (*Fr*)
SKETCH.

etch[1] *vb*
To create a design or image on metal by exposing parts of the surface to the corrosive action of acid. **etched** *adj*.

etch[2] *n*
An acidic gum solution spread over a lithographic plate or stone after the design has been drawn. The solution desensitizes the surface and fixes the greasy drawing in place. The term can seem misleading in this context as the solution does not actually corrode the surface or alter the level of the exposed areas.

etcher *n*
1 A person skilled in the technique of etching.
2 A person responsible for etching and printing a particular image.

etching *n*
1 An INTAGLIO PRINTING process in which a design or image is made on a metal plate, usually copper or zinc, by corroding parts of the surface with acid. The plate is coated with a thin layer of waxy ground and the image is drawn in the ground with a pointed metal tool, which does not actually scratch the surface of the metal. The back and edges of the plate are coated with acid-resistant varnish and the plate is immersed in acid solution which bites into the lines exposed through the ground. To produce both light and heavy black lines in the print, parts of the plate are coated with varnish and it is returned to the acid so the lines still exposed are more deeply bitten. Tonal areas can be added with OPEN BITE or AQUATINT. When the ground and varnish are cleaned off the image is seen cleanly bitten into the plate surface and the corroded lines can be filled with ink and printed. The whole process can be repeated more than once on

the same plate to develop the image in detail. See also RELIEF ETCHING, STOPPING OUT.
2 A printed image produced by this process.
3 A similar process used to create a RELIEF SCULPTURE in a solid piece of metal. This also involves protecting certain areas of the metal with acid-resistant varnish and corroding the exposed parts with acid solution to shape them as required.

etching ground *n*
A waxy substance applied to the surface of an etching plate to form a thin, acid-resistant coating. It is melted onto a warmed plate and spread evenly with a DABBER or roller, then allowed to cool. An etching needle is used to draw into the ground, exposing lines and areas of the plate surface. These can be cleanly etched in acid while the remaining ground protects the unexposed areas from corrosive action. See also HARD GROUND, SOFT GROUND.

etching needle *n*
A steel point set in a wood or metal holder, used for drawing into the waxy ground covering an etching plate. Compared to a drypoint needle it is lightweight and relatively blunt as it is not required to cut into the metal surface.

etching press *n*
A mechanical printing press designed for printing from flat metal plates, as used in DRYPOINT, ENGRAVING, ETCHING and MEZZOTINT. The basic construction is a heavy vertical frame bearing two large metal rollers, between which passes a flat metal bed on which printing plate and paper are carried. The rollers are turned by means of a large geared wheel and as the bed travels between them the top roller applies even pressure across the plate, forcing the paper down into the inked intaglio. The plate and paper are usually covered with two or three layers of felt blankets which help to distribute the pressure evenly and cushion the impact between plate and roller.

eutectic *adj*
The property of a mixture of substances which in combination melt and fuse at a temperature lower than the melting point of any single constituent. The phenomenon so described is made use of in the addition of fluxes to ceramic glaze mixtures.

exc *abb* **excudit** *vb* (*Lat* has published it)
Lettering which appears on a print accompanying the name of the person who printed or published it, as distinct from the artist responsible for the original image.

exothermic *adj*
The term describing a material that spontaneously generates heat

in changing from one state to another, eg polyester resin, which gives off heat as it cures.

expanded polystyrene *n*
A lightweight foamed plastic material, white with a dense, granular texture, formed by extruding molten polystyrene in the presence of heat and a specific chemical agent which expands the material up to 40 times its original mass. Expanded polystyrene is easily cut and shaped: it is used as a base over which heavier materials are modelled, as a lightweight construction material and to form original sculptures which may be reproduced in metal by the process of LOST PATTERN CASTING.

extender *n*
An inert substance added to paint to give it extra body or to alter the texture. If the substance has no particular colour or opacity of its own it may improve the texture or covering power of the paint, but some extenders degrade the colour and tactile quality and are used primarily to increase bulk in inexpensive paint ranges.

extrude *vb*
To shape a plastic material by EXTRUSION. **extruded** *adj*.

extrusion *n*
The process of forcing a plastic material through a shaped aperture to produce a length of the material with a particular shape in cross section, eg round or polygonal. Clay emerges from a PUGMILL in this way after it has been processed into a uniform mass. Extrusion is applied to various materials in industrial manufacturing processes, eg to make rods or tubes, via machines designed for the particular purpose in hand.

eye level *n*
In a painting or other two-dimensional composition, an actual or imagined line running through the picture horizontally which represents the artist's line of vision in relation to the subject and indicates the position from which the overall viewpoint is taken. See also HORIZON LINE.

f

facing *n*
1 A process in conservation of paintings in which the image area of a work is stabilized by the application of layers of tissue stuck on with a water-soluble adhesive, to maintain the surface while the painting is transferred to a fresh support or repairs are carried out on the basic fabric of the original, eg a canvas or panel.
2 The layers of tissue applied in this process.
3 The first layer of an INVESTMENT, ie the coating of material which forms the inner face of a mould and directly shapes the surface of the cast.

facsimile *n*
1 An exact copy of a work of art, made as far as possible using the same materials and techniques as applied to the original work.
2 A reproduction of a work of art which is not immediately distinguishable from the original. Particularly associated with prints and calligraphy.

facture *n* (*Fr*)
HANDLING.

Faience *n*
See MAJOLICA.

fake[1] *n*
A COPY or VARIANT of an existing work of art, or a work made in imitation of a well-known artist's style, produced with the specific intent of passing it off as an authentic work by the original artist.

fake[2] *vb*
To make or produce a fake.

fan blender *n*
A brush with the bristles set in a splayed, flat fan shape. The fan may be of hog bristle, sable or synthetic hairs. It is used to blend and diffuse different colours and tones in paint which is already applied to the support. The shape and light weight of the brush make it unsuitable for use in the initial application of paint.

fat *adj*
1 A term used to describe the quality of oil paint which is viscous

and mixed with a generous proportion of oil. Compare LEAN.
2 See LONG CLAY.

fat over lean *n*
A technique of oil painting in which thick layers of paint rich in oil (fat paint) are laid over thin layers of paint containing little oil or thinned with a solvent (lean paint). The lean paint dries more quickly and contracts less than the fat, so it is necessary to work fat over lean to ensure that the paint layers remain stable as they dry. Also called lean to fat painting.

fattura *n* (*It*)
HANDLING.

feathering *n*
1 (*etching*) The method of clearing gas bubbles that develop on exposed areas of an etching plate while it is immersed in an acid bath, simply by using a feather to disperse the bubbles. If left, they interfere with the action of the acid and cause an uneven, textured bite.
2 (*painting*) Light brushwork used to blend and diffuse colours applied to the support. The brush is moved over the surface with quick, lifting strokes.
3 (*ceramics*) A method of creating a decorative pattern in coloured slips applied as surface decoration for a clay body. A thick slip is applied in trails over a finer coating of a different colour and a feather is used to draw the wet trails into fine lines and criss-cross patterns.

fec *abb* **fecit** *vb* (*Lat* has made it)
Lettering which appears on a print accompanying the name of the printer, as distinct from the artist responsible for the original image.

felspar, feldspar *n*
An insoluble mineral found in igneous rocks, appearing in different forms all basically composed of alumina and silica with the addition of other elements such as sodium and calcium. It is a component of granite and when decomposed forms natural clays. It is extensively used as an ingredient of clay bodies and ceramic glazes.

ferroconcrete *n*
Concrete reinforced at the casting stage by the insertion of steel bars or mesh.

ferrule *n*
The hollow section of a brush, usually made of metal, in which the hairs or bristles are set and held in the required shape. It forms

the junction between the hair tip and the wooden handle of the brush.

festoon *n*
A carved, modelled or painted ornament in the form of a garland of foliage, fruit and flowers suspended in a loop between two points, sometimes further embellished with ribbons, tassels etc. This is commonly a form of architectural decoration but the motif may also be used in a painting. Also called swag.

fête champêtre *n* (*Fr* rural festival)
A painting showing courtly and well-dressed figures enjoying a feast or entertainment in a setting of parkland or open countryside.

fête galante *n* (*Fr* festival of courtship)
A variation of the FÊTE CHAMPÊTRE, with particular emphasis on the romantic nature of the festivities.

fettle *vb*
To carry out a process of FETTLING. **fettled** *adj*.

fettling *n*
1 The process of cleaning and finishing a metal sculpture, eg trimming seams or joints, smoothing areas of rough texture etc.
2 The process of trimming and smoothing a ceramic object prior to firing, to refine the form when the clay is in a leather-hard or almost dry condition.

fettling knife *n*
A flexible, tapering metal blade set in a handle, used for trimming and scraping damp or leather-hard clay.

fibreglass *n*
See GLASS FIBRE.

figurative *adj*
The description of an image which depicts recognizable forms, eg figures, objects, landscape, though these may be broadly interpreted and not necessarily shown as a realistic or accurate representation.

figure *n*
1 A representation of a human figure, eg in painting or sculpture.
2 An individual motif in a composition.
3 A surface pattern on wood, other than the grain pattern, eg growth rings, knots and natural variations of colour.

figure-ground relationship *n*
In a two-dimensional composition, the relationship between a particular motif or form and the area surrounding it. When

something is drawn or painted on a flat surface, the viewer tends to see it as standing out from a background. This sense of relative position may be exploited to create apparent depth within a picture or a composition may be deliberately organized to stress the flatness of the picture area and the equal balance of figure and ground.

figure painting *n*
1 The category of paintings in which the human figure is the principal subject.
2 A painting of a human figure.

figurine *n*
A small model, carving or cast representing a human figure.

filbert *n*
A brush with hog-hair or synthetic bristles arranged in a crimped FERRULE to form a flattened head with a curving or arch-shaped tip.

file *n*
A metal tool used to smooth and shape rigid materials by abrasive action. It has a rough surface of projecting ridges or sharp teeth: there are many different types, ranging from fine to coarse and suitable for a variety of materials such as wood, stone, resin and metal. See also RASP, RIFFLER.

filler *n*
1 An inert material in powdered or granulated form added to a sculpture material to give it extra physical bulk.
2 A specially formulated additive mixed with a synthetic resin used for casting or lamination processes, which adds colour or opacity to the basically transparent material.
3 An inert white pigment added to paint to increase the bulk, alter the texture or act as reinforcement of the paint film as it dries. The filler generally has no colouring property of its own and does not necessarily affect the opacity of the paint, though in some cases it is used to improve handling qualities, giving the paint smoother texture and greater covering power.
4 See FILLING COMPOUND.

fillet *n*
A WINDOW MOUNT of thin paper or board, cut with a slightly smaller opening than the full picture mount and inserted between mount and picture to create a narrow inner surround for the image, commonly in gold or a different colour from that of the main surround.

filling compound *n*
Any of various substances, consisting of natural or synthetic

ingredients, used to fill a crack, indentation or other flaw in a surface, eg in plaster, stone or wood. Generally such a substance is applied in paste form and gradually hardens, when it can be abraded or cut to lie flush with the surrounding surface.
Also called filler.

film *n*
1 A continuous layer of paint, varnish or other medium applied to a surface. The term is used particularly of a dried coating.
2 A thin, flexible sheet material, eg plastic, paper, especially one which is transparent.

filter press *n*
A machine designed to restore clay slip to a plastic state by squeezing out the excess moisture. The slip is poured into canvas bags which are compressed mechanically, allowing the water to drain through the fabric.

fine art *n*
A term used broadly to encompass processes and products in art which are judged primarily in terms of their aesthetic value and theoretical significance, as opposed to those which have a specific practical function, as in APPLIED ARTS. Traditionally, architecture has been included with painting, sculpture and related arts under the heading of fine art and the term originally included music and poetry.

finish^{1} *n*
1 The actual surface of a completed object or image, eg the outer appearance and texture of a painting or sculpture.
2 A surface coating or treatment applied to an object or material.
3 The quality of detail in an image, ie the completeness of a complex rendering.

finish^{2} *vb*
1 To apply a process or substance to the surface of an object or material which alters, protects or enhances its particular qualities.
2 To render an image in considerable detail. **finished** *adj*.

fireclay *n*
A coarse, highly refractory natural clay formed in or near coal seams. In a raw state it is hard and black: after processing it may retain its dark colouring but this is usually lost in firing as bituminous matter within the clay is burnt off.

firing *n*
1 The application of intense heat to ceramic materials under controlled conditions. This has different effects according to the materials and the stages of processing. It fuses the components of

individual substances, renders clay hard and durable and fuses a glaze to a clay body. Each material has a maturing temperature at which the required changes take place, but efficient firing is a combination of time and temperature, involving gradual heating and cooling: abrupt changes, unless carefully calculated, are generally damaging and the process must be highly controlled to achieve predictable effects.
2 The application of heat to enamelling materials, to melt enamel powders or pastes into continuous films of colour and fuse them to a metal framework or base. This is generally a more rapid and less complex process than firing of ceramic ware.

fit *n*
The relationship between a clay body and a ceramic glaze, in terms of their rates of expansion and contraction during firing and cooling.

fitch *n*
1 A brush with a squared, slightly splayed head, the tips of the bristles being trimmed to create a chamfered edge.
2 The hair of a polecat, one of the types of SABLE hair used in making brushes.

fixative *n*
A thin, colourless varnish used to bind and seal the surface of a drawing in pencil, pastel, charcoal or similar unstable medium. It fixes loose particles of the medium on the support and prevents accidental smudging of the image. Fixatives are now commonly sold in aerosol cans for even and convenient application.

fl *abb* **floruit** *vb* (*Lat* flourished)
An identification used in art historical references and cataloguing to signify that the accompanying dates show the period when a particular artist was known to be actively at work, given when birth and death dates are unknown.

flag *n*
The minutely branched, natural split in the tip of a hog bristle. The flags in a hog bristle brush make it particularly effective in holding and spreading a quantity of viscous paint.

flake white *n*
A white lead pigment at one time widely used in oil painting, because of its opacity and covering power when ground in oil, and the flexibility of the dried paint film. It is one of the oldest known artificial pigments but is poisonous and has more recently been superseded by titanium white, which is not poisonous but has similar functional properties.

flaking *n*
A defect in an oil painting caused by poor adherence of the materials, when the paint film cracks and flakes of paint detach from the support completely. Also called scaling.

flame-cutting *n*
A process of cutting through sheet metal by heating it to melting point along a narrow path and simultaneously directing a jet of oxygen onto the molten metal which effectively parts the material. See OXYACETYLENE TORCH.

flat *n*
A brush with long hairs or bristles arranged in a flat, rectangular shape and forming a straight line across the tip.

flat chisel *n*
A chisel with a squared tip and straight cutting edge, as commonly used in stone and wood carving and various other cutting processes.

flat colour *n*
An area of colour in a painting applied as an even, opaque layer of paint showing no brushmarks nor any change in tone or hue throughout the paint film.

flattened relief *n*
1 A category of carved or modelled sculptures in which forms project very slightly from a background plane, in many cases being apparent as no more than a slight swelling of the surface. Finely incised lines are added to develop detail and emphasize contours. The effect relies equally on drawing and the sculptural aspects of the material and technique.
Also called *rilievo stiacciato* (*It*).
2 An individual sculpture displaying these qualities.

flatware *n*
The collective term for items of pottery such as plates and shallow dishes or bowls, which are broad and open in form. Compare HOLLOW WARE.

floriated *adj*
The description of something which is decorated with motifs shaped like flowers and leaves.

flux[1] *n*
1 (*ceramics*) An ingredient in a clay body or glaze which lowers the melting point of other ingredients so they will fuse more readily in controlled firing. A number of substances can be used in this way, eg metal oxides and various mineral compounds.
2 (*sculpture*) A chemical substance applied to metals in preparation

for the processes of brazing, soldering or welding, which cleans away impurities and encourages the free flow of molten metal. **3** (*enamelling*) A compound of silica and other substances which forms a clear glass when fired. It is the basic component of enamels, given opacity and colour by the addition of metal oxides. Also called *fondant* (*Fr*).

flux² *vb*
To use or apply a flux. **fluxed** *adj*.

fluxing *n*
1 The process of adding a FLUX to a clay body or ceramic glaze. **2** The process of treating metals with a flux.

focal point *n*
The area of a pictorial composition which tends to command the viewer's attention, whether through subject matter, eg a figure or main group of figures, or formal elements, eg a dominant colour or shape. Other elements in the composition may be contrived to lead the eye back to the focal point of the image.

folk art *n*
The general term for the native arts and crafts of any particular region, arising from traditional cultural forms which are practical rather than theoretical and handed on between individuals without the development of formal systems of training.

fondant *n* (*Fr*)
FLUX.

foreshortening *n*
The technique of representing in two dimensions the spatial depth and position of a figure or object. This can be done artificially by applying principles of perspective. In practice, it requires keen perception of the apparent shape and size of different parts of a form as seen from a particular viewpoint, regardless of actual dimensions and relative proportions. A vertical line or plane is represented as such: anything which lies at an angle to the artist's line of vision must be in some degree foreshortened. A geometric example is the use of ellipses of varying widths to represent a circle turned through different angles away from the picture plane. A common figurative example is a figure with hand and arm outstretched towards the viewer: the hand appears disproportionately large and the length of the arm is severely truncated.

form *n*
1 The style or composition of a work of art, as distinct from the content.

2 (*painting, drawing*) The depiction of a figure or object, or a motif of any kind.
3 (*sculpture*) An individual piece of sculpture, eg a carved or modelled shape, or the interior shape of a mould.
4 In either of these contexts, a particular part or component element of the image which has an identifiable shape or mass.
5 Generally, the type or condition of an object, material or substance.

formal *adj*
1 The description of a stylized or conventional representation of a figure, object or scene.
2 A term used of the qualities of a work derived from the materials and techniques applied in making it, rather than those related to the subject matter or imagery.

formalism *n*
A term applied to forms of art in which the interest in materials and techniques is apparent as central to the character of the work and more important than a concern with content: eg in painting, a work in which the image is arrived at by the process of applying paint, rather than the paint being primarily the means of conveying a specific image.

format *n*
1 The shape, dimensions and proportions of a two-dimensional image.
2 The overall arrangement of elements in a design.

former *n*
1 A constructed MOULD in which a material can be cast into a regular solid form, eg an open wooden box used for casting a block of concrete or plaster.
2 A shape carved, modelled or constructed in relief to serve as the pattern for shaping sheet plastic in VACUUM FORMING.
3 A device for shaping a specific form in plaster, consisting of a metal template fixed to rotate or move back and forth on a particular path across a base board of wood. A mass of damp plaster is built up under the template until it overlaps the shaped edge. The template is then moved continuously to scrape the plaster surface and more plaster is added until the mass has been scraped smoothly into the outer form dictated by the shape of the template.

foul biting *n*
1 The action of acid which breaks through an etching ground and bites into the metal plate in an area not intended to be etched. This may be due to an uneven ground, excessively strong acid solution or too long a period of immersion.

2 The marks or areas of corrosion caused by this action, which retain ink and will appear in proofs taken from the plate.

found object *n*
An object presented as or included in a work of art, though not in itself of particular aesthetic merit or related to conventional artists' materials. In effect, the object is given aesthetic significance or symbolic value by the artist's decision to use it in a work.
Also known as *objet trouvé* (*Fr*).

foxing *n*
A defect in paper, caused by exposure to damp conditions. It appears as small brown spots which are actually fungus growths.

frame[1] *n*
1 A structure designed to enclose or surround a picture, for decorative effect, to protect the image and the materials of which it is made, or to strengthen the basic support. The frame for a painting on canvas, panel or other durable support typically consists of lengths of MOULDING fitted precisely to the edges of the picture, made into a continuous surround by strong and unobtrusive joints between the component pieces. A frame for a work on paper commonly consists of an outer frame of this type, somewhat larger than the image area of the picture, a sheet of glass fitting the frame, a MOUNT surrounding the image and a backing board which seals and strengthens the assembly. A frame is ideally custom-built for a particular work, but a variety of frames can be bought readymade in standard sizes.
2 More generally, the outline of the image area in a two-dimensional work.

frame[2] *vb*
1 To enclose a picture within a frame.
2 To arrange elements of a composition within a given format, ie as if enclosed by a frame. **framed** *adj*.

framing *n*
The techniques and processes of constructing and assembling picture frames.

free-standing *adj*
The description of a sculpture that can be viewed from all sides, as compared to RELIEF SCULPTURE which is permanently attached to a background or fixed support. Free-standing does not necessarily mean self-supporting, as the work can be anchored by concealed fixings in the base which do not interfere with the essential form.

freestone *n*
A limestone or sandstone with a uniform grain, fine-textured and compact, which can be easily carved in any direction.

French chalk *n*
See TALC.

fresco *n* (*It* fresh)
1 A wall-painting technique in which ground pigments suspended in water are painted on wet lime plaster freshly applied to the wall. The surface is prepared by coating the wall with one or two coarse plaster layers and drawing the image in outline. A smooth topcoat of plaster is applied in small sections, corresponding to particular areas of the drawing, and each area is painted while the plaster is wet. No binder is used in the paint as a chemical reaction binds the pigments into the surface of the plaster as it dries. This method is the true fresco technique, also called *buon fresco*. See ARRICCIO, INTONACO, SINOPIA. Compare FRESCO SECCO.
2 A painting made by this technique.

fresco secco *n* (*It* dry fresco)
A wall-painting technique in which pigments bound with glue are applied to a surface of dried plaster. This is a less durable but more convenient technique than true fresco. It has also been used as a method of retouching or adding detail to a fresco originally painted on wet plaster.

fret *n*
An ornamental pattern composed of vertical and horizontal lines joined or interlocked at right angles to form a continuous band of spiralled motifs. This is commonly seen as a form of painted or carved architectural decoration. Also called key pattern or meander.

frieze *n*
1 A broad band of painted decoration or relief sculpture, especially on a wall. The name comes from the element of architectural construction known as a frieze which is commonly decorated with painted or sculpted forms.
2 A band of brickwork or stonework running between sections of moulding set across the top of a line of columns or around the top of an interior wall.

frilling *n*
A surface defect in liquid paint or varnish applied to a support standing vertically, consisting of a horizontally looped effect caused by the medium flowing irregularly down the surface, which is retained in the paint film as it dries.

frit[1] *n*
An ingredient in ceramic glazes, consisting of silica and a soluble FLUX, or more than one, heated together to melting point, cooled and ground down as a single substance, in the form of an insoluble powder.

frit[2] *vb*
1 To combine two or more substances to make a frit.
2 To add a frit to a glaze mixture. **fritted** *adj*.

frontality *n*
A term applied to the characteristic of forms of art in which a figure or object is represented as from a direct, facing viewpoint, without any attempt to convey continuous depth or perspective. When used of sculpture in the round, it implies that views from front, back and sides are each approached in this manner, without full realization of relationships throughout the form, and the primary viewpoint intended is that seen centrally from the front.

frottage *n* (*Fr* rubbing)
1 The technique of taking a direct impression of a surface pattern, texture or relief image by laying a sheet of paper over it and rubbing lightly and evenly with a soft pencil or crayon. The technique is used to reproduce both natural and man-made surfaces. Rubbed textures and patterns are commonly used as components of COLLAGES.
2 An impression made by this technique. Both technique and product are also called rubbing.

frottis *n* (*Fr*)
A thin film of colour, eg a GLAZE or VEIL.

fugitive colour *n*
1 A pigment or other colouring matter that fades over time, under exposure to light or owing to atmospheric conditions such as heat or dampness.
2 The term is also used of a pigment if its colour deteriorates or is seriously devalued when it is mixed with other substances.

furniture *n*
1 Strips and blocks of wood or metal used to surround a RELIEF PRINTING block or pieces of TYPE on the bed of a press, to keep them in place and to provide a continuous level surface on which paper can be laid for printing.
2 See KILN FURNITURE.

g

gaiter *n*
A thin rod of iron or steel used as reinforcement for the interior of a hollow cast sculpture. A number of rods are set in place to follow the interior form as shaped by the thickness of the casting material.

gamboge *n*
A strongly coloured natural yellow gum, originally used as a yellow watercolour paint but unsuitable as a colouring agent for oil paint. It has been superseded by synthetic equivalents.

ganosis *n*
The process of toning the surface of stone sculpture by polishing it with wax, sometimes with pigments added to provide appropriate colouring.

gauffrage *n* (*Fr*)
See BLIND PRINTING.

gel *n*
1 A thick, transparent painting medium added to oil or acrylic paint to give it a heavy consistency for IMPASTO effects in which the colours are relatively transparent.
2 The term referring to a synthetic resin used in sculpture processes at the stage when a catalyst or hardening agent has been applied and the resin takes on a thick, even consistency as the first phase of the curing process.

gelatin, gelatine *n*
An organic protein obtained by boiling animal matter, eg skins, bones, ligaments. It is available in powder, granule or tablet form and prepared in water is used as an adhesive, binder or size. A viscous solution of gelatin will set in a solid but flexible form and can be used to make sculpture moulds.

gelatin mould *n*
A flexible mould made from gelatin, used to cast a wax or plaster form. The gelatin can reproduce fine detail from an original model and is typically used in preparing a wax cast from a master form which is then used as the model for bronze casting by the LOST WAX PROCESS.

gel coat *n*
The first application of resin in gel form to a mould or surface in the processes of CASTING and LAMINATING. The gel is usually painted on and eventually forms a hard, smooth outer layer on the sculpture which is backed up by further applications of resin reinforced with glass fibre.

gemstone *n*
A precious or semi-precious stone used in jewellery or other forms of highly crafted decorative work.

genre *n*
1 The collective term for paintings showing scenes from daily life, the common activities of domestic work, everyday commerce and recreational pursuits, including informal entertainments such as circus, fete and carnival.
2 Any particular category of painting, or other works, defined by subject matter, eg portraiture, landscape, history painting. The word was originally used in this way and may have taken on the more specific meaning by virtue of there being no other term previously used to describe paintings of everyday scenes.

gesso *n*
1 A ground basically consisting of a white powdered material, eg chalk, whiting or slaked plaster, in a water-based, slightly adhesive binder, eg SIZE. An active white pigment may be added to give the mixture extra brilliance. There are a number of different recipes for gesso and it has a number of uses. Primarily, it is the traditional ground for TEMPERA painting on wood panel: it is applied in liquid form, in several successive thin coats, and dries to a smooth, hard, absorbent and brilliantly white surface. It is brittle and therefore not suitable as a ground for a flexible support such as canvas. It is also used as a ground for gilded or painted decoration on carved wood sculpture, picture frames or furniture and can be lightly modelled or incised to elaborate the surface decoration. It is also commonly used as a ground for RAISED GOLD illumination.
2 A white acrylic PRIMER specially formulated for use with acrylic paints. Though marketed under the name gesso, it is not of the same composition as the traditional material.

gesso grosso *n* (*It* coarse gesso)
Gesso made with unslaked plaster, used as the first coarse layers of a gesso ground for tempera painting.

gesso sottile *n* (*It* fine gesso)
Gesso made with slaked plaster, used as the finishing layers of a gesso ground for tempera painting.

gestural *adj*
A description of styles of painting in which the brushmarks and application of colour show the physical movement of the painter's hand and arm holding the brush, particularly evidence of broad or vigorous movements.

gild *vb*
To decorate an object or surface by GILDING. **gilded** *adj*.

gilder *n*
A person skilled in the technique of gilding.

gilder's cushion *n*
A small, firm, rectangular cushion made of a heavy fabric with a surface nap, on which gold leaf is laid to be cut or trimmed.

gilding *n*
The decoration of a surface by the application of gold, in the form of gold leaf laid over a flat or raised adhesive ground, or powder gold in an adhesive binder applied with a quill or brush. Gold leaf is the most brilliant and durable form. The small leaves are laid on the ground and rubbed down lightly. When fully adhered they are burnished more vigorously to compact the surface and create a high shine which is a lasting characteristic. Powder gold painted on a surface can also be burnished when dry, but has less brilliance and tends to dull relatively quickly. Gilding strictly refers to the application of gold, but the term is also more loosely used to refer to metallic decoration, eg in silver or bronze, produced by similar methods.

giornata *n* (*It* day's work)
A single section of the INTONACO layer of a fresco painting. The term originally referred to the amount of plaster that could be painted, literally, within a day's work.

glair *n*
A solution of egg white used as the binder for gesso on which gold leaf is laid in RAISED GOLD illumination, and also as a binder for pigments used in painted decoration of a manuscript. The egg white is beaten until frothy and mixed into water: the solution is left overnight to clarify.

glass fibre *n*
A lightweight but durable material used as reinforcement for synthetic resins in various sculpture processes. The basic material is glass drawn out in very fine filaments, which have a degree of strength and flexibility not typical of glass in solid form. The fibres are made into thin fabrics, narrow strips of tape or loosely

stranded rope. Also called fibreglass. See also CHOPPED STRAND MAT, ROVING.

glaze[1] *n*
1 A thin film of transparent oil paint laid over an UNDERPAINTING, designed to add colour to a form modelled in monochrome, modifying but not concealing the previously applied paint layers. The paint is thinned with a good proportion of oil or oil-varnish medium to achieve the necessary transparency.
2 More generally, any thin film of paint which is transparent and slightly glossy, owing to use of a suitable medium in the paint. The term is typically used of oil or acrylic paint applied in this manner. Compare WASH.
3 A vitreous coating applied to a ceramic object to decorate or seal the surface. A ceramic glaze is a mixture of silica and other ingredients, eg metallic oxides, which give particular qualities of colour and texture. It is applied as a liquid coating by suspension of the ingredients in water and is fired in a kiln, when the heat hardens the glaze and fuses it to the surface of the clay.

glaze[2] *vb*
1 To apply a glaze.
2 To cover a picture with a sheet of glass to protect it from deterioration or damage. See also FRAME. **glazed** *adj*.

glazing *n*
1 The process of applying an oil glaze over a dry or partially dry UNDERPAINTING.
2 The process of coating a ceramic object with a glaze.
3 The process of framing a picture under glass.

glory *n*
In Christian art, the general term for depiction of a radiance surrounding a sacred figure. See AUREOLE, HALO, MANDORLA.

glost *adj*
The descriptive term for objects and processes involving ceramic glazes: hence glost ware is ceramic ware which has been glazed; glost firing is the process of fusing the glaze to the clay body.

glue size *n*
See SIZE.

glyptic[1] *adj*
The descriptive term for an object or image shaped by carving or incising a material, as opposed to modelled forms which are described as plastic.

glyptic[2] *n*
A sculpture or decorative object formed by carving or incising, especially one worked in a precious stone or gemstone.

glyptics *n*
The art of carving and incising gemstones and precious stones.

golden mean *n*
See GOLDEN SECTION.

golden section *n*
A principle of proportion applied to composition in art and apparently corresponding to a commonly occurring natural proportion. Simply stated, it is that a line should be divided at a point where the ratio of the shorter section to the longer is the same as that of the longer section to the whole. It is expressed approximately in numerical terms as a ratio of 5:8.
Also called golden mean.

gold leaf *n*
Gold beaten into the form of a paper-thin sheet. It is flimsy and clinging and for convenience of handling is sold in book form, consisting of a number of small leaves separated by chalk-coated papers. It is used for gilding on flat, raised or moulded surfaces and is laid on an adhesive ground of gesso, bole or size. See also GILDING, ILLUMINATION.

goldpoint *n*
See METALPOINT.

gold size *n*
1 A paste consisting of red bole, glue and water mixed with a solution of gelatin or other SIZE, which is brushed on a surface to form an adhesive ground for gold leaf.
2 A synthetic, fast-drying varnish preparation used for the same purpose.

goo *n*
A thick, fluid mixture of cement and water applied to the interior of a mould in making a hollow-cast concrete sculpture. It bonds with the concrete subsequently applied but is smoother in consistency and as the first layer in the mould forms an even outer skin on the cast.

gone off *adv*
A term used to indicate the condition of a material that has begun to harden after being worked in a liquid or plastic form.

gouache *n*
1 A type of paint broadly defined as opaque watercolour,

consisting of pure pigment in a gum binder with a white pigment or filler added to give the paint opacity. Unlike watercolour, it completely obscures the support and dries to a flat, semi-matt finish: the colours tend to lighten as they dry. It is used as an independent painting medium and for adding emphasis to details in otherwise transparent watercolour paintings. It is available as a viscous fluid packaged in tubes or as solid, slightly moist cakes set in pans. The term BODY COLOUR is sometimes used as a synonym for gouache.

2 A painting executed in this medium.

gouge *n*

A hand tool for cutting wood, similar to a chisel but with a curved or V-sectioned blade. Small versions are used for cutting a block in WOODCUT printmaking or for detailed carving: larger curved gouges are used to shape wood or soft stone.

gradation *n*

A gradual transition between tones or colours, eg from black to grey to white, without abrupt change or defined boundaries.

graffito *n* (*It*)

See SGRAFFITO.

grain *n*

1 The texture and internal structure of a solid material as formed by the arrangement of its constituent fibres or particles, resulting from a natural process of growth or formation.

2 The surface pattern or texture of a material corresponding to this basic structure.

3 A surface texture artificially simulating a natural grain.

granite *n*

A hard rock, igneous in origin, used as material for stone carving. It is found in colours ranging from white through pink and grey to black. Among its component elements are quartz and felspar, which may be present in the form of large crystals that impart a piebald appearance to the cut stone and give it a sparkling surface quality. These elements are also harder than steel and granite is worked with special cutting tools, heavier and tougher than those used for marble and other stones.

granulation *n*

1 A tendency sometimes occurring in water-based paints for a wash of paint to dry with a grainy texture as the vehicle is absorbed into the support and the pigment particles are deposited on the surface.

2 A method of decorating a surface with tiny granules of gold, usually applied to a flat ground of gold.

graphic art *n*
1 A term commonly used to refer to artists' works on paper, eg drawings and original prints.
2 The term is also used of forms of art, particularly paintings, drawings and prints, in which the principal characteristics are linear drawing and stylized forms of representation.
3 See GRAPHIC DESIGN.

graphic design *n*
A term broadly covering art and design processes associated with reproduction in a commercial context, eg design for publishing, advertising, packaging and display, film and television. It involves the use of letterforms, symbols and images designed to convey specific information in calculated ways and includes various disciplines such as illustration, layout, technical illustration and typography. Methods of reproduction are usually based on photographic techniques, now often controlled by computerized systems.
Also called commercial graphics.

graphics *n pl*
1 *abb* GRAPHIC ART.
2 *abb* GRAPHIC DESIGN.
3 Images, diagrams or symbols inset in printed text.
4 Typography, lettering or graphic symbols connected with filmed images.

graphite *n*
A natural form of carbon; a black, crystalline and slightly greasy substance. It is used in stick form as a drawing medium, in a pure state or mixed with a china clay binder, and is the basic ingredient of lead pencils. When applied to a support, it lays down heavy blacks and greys with a slight surface sheen.

graver *n*
See BURIN.

green *adj*
A term used to describe wood that is moist and unseasoned or raw clay that has not been fired.

green glaze *n*
A glaze applied to ceramic ware before biscuit firing. Also called once-fired glaze or raw glaze.

green ware *n*
Ceramic ware that has not been fired.

grisaille *n*
1 A painting executed entirely in tones of grey, often intended to

simulate the appearance of a RELIEF SCULPTURE.
2 An UNDERPAINTING executed in grey tones to establish the modelling of forms which are subsequently coloured by the application of transparent paint glazes. This is typically an oil painting technique.

grog *n*
Fired clay ground into powder or granules. It has various uses in ceramic work: mainly it is mixed into a clay body to coarsen the texture, speed drying and reduce shrinkage. It may also be used as a base layer on which clay is modelled or fired, the loose surface allowing the clay body to contract freely as it dries.

grotesque *n*
A fanciful motif or decorative image contrived from a combination of human and animal forms, commonly embellished with decorative flowers, foliage and ornamental patterns.

ground *n*
1 (*painting*) A coating laid over the surface of a support to which the paint is applied. It may be white or tinted and the material used depends upon the medium to be applied. The function of the ground is to provide a firm surface texture for adhesion of the paint layers, to reduce the absorbency of the support, to protect it if necessary from chemical reaction in the paint that could cause deterioration of the fabric, and to improve or modify the intensity of colours subsequently applied. See also GESSO, PRIMER, SIZING.
2 (*etching*) A dark waxy substance applied to an etching plate to form a thin acid-resistant coating. See also ETCHING GROUND, HARD GROUND, SOFT GROUND.
3 (*ceramics*) The surface of a clay object which is in a condition to accept decorative glazes.
4 In painting, drawing and relief sculpture, the picture area in which images and symbols are arranged. In this sense the term is used in a similar way to BACKGROUND, but it does not necessarily imply an illusion of spatial depth.

ground laying *n*
A technique for applying enamel decoration to glazed ceramic ware. A base layer of oil is painted over the glaze and is buffed with a silk pad as it dries. Enamel powder is then dusted over the oil to form an even coating and is fired when completely dry.

ground line *n*
A device used in simple pictorial images, whether drawing, painting or low relief. It is simply a line which indicates the ground level or base on which figures and objects stand. Stylized

pictorial forms may employ several ground lines establishing tiers within which a sequence of images is arranged.

ground plane *n*
In pictorial terms, a plane apparently receding horizontally from the vertical picture plane, which forms the ground level for figures and objects in the picture.

guild *n*
In the medieval period, an association of artists, craftsmen and traders which formed part of the system regulating the training of artists and standards of workmanship in the arts and crafts. After a period of apprenticeship and general practice, an artist might apply to become a master and only when recognized as such by the guild was allowed to practise independently and run a workshop in which apprentices and assistants were employed. Guilds were largely superseded in this role by academies of art.

gum *n*
A hard sap exuding naturally or extracted from various species of trees and shrubs, which is soluble in water or swells and softens when exposed to water. This differentiates gums from natural resins, which are not water-soluble. Gums are variously used, eg as adhesives, binders and ingredients of preparations used in painting.

gum arabic *n*
A natural gum obtained from various species of acacia native to North America and northern Africa. It may vary in colour from pale yellow to red-brown and is soluble in hot water. It is traditionally the binder used in making watercolour paints.

gum-etch *n*
A solution of gum containing a proportion of ETCH, used as the first treatment for the surface of a lithographic plate on which an image has been drawn. See LITHOGRAPHY.

gumming up *n*
The process of coating a lithographic plate or stone with a gum solution to protect the image and the surrounding surface at any stage in the process of LITHOGRAPHY, eg after the image has been drawn or when the plate or stone is stored between printings.

gum tempera *n*
A water-based paint consisting of pigment mixed with a gum binder. See TEMPERA.

gum tragacanth *n*
A natural gum obtained from various species of thorny shrubs native to the eastern Mediterranean and Asia Minor. It is not

directly soluble in water but will swell to a jelly-like mass that can be used in this form as an adhesive or squeezed and filtered to produce a liquid gum. It is traditionally the binder used in making pastels.

gypsum *n*
A natural crystalline form of calcium sulphate occurring in sedimentary rocks and clays. It is colourless, white or in a range of tints from green to brown. The purest varieties are the raw material for PLASTER OF PARIS.

h

hachure *n* (*Fr*)
HATCHING.

hacksaw *n*
A hand-held saw consisting of a strong, narrow, toothed blade set in a three-sided metal frame attached to a handle, used for cutting wood, metal or rigid plastics.

half life-size *adj*
The description of a painted or sculpted figure made on a scale corresponding to half its actual dimensions and proportions.

halo *n*
In Christian art, the depiction of a circle of light around the head of a sacred figure. Also called nimbus.

hammer *n*
A hand tool consisting of a solid, heavy head, usually of iron or steel, set crosswise on a straight handle of wood or metal, used for driving, striking and beating actions. See BALLPEEN HAMMER, CLAW HAMMER, LUMP HAMMER. See also BOUCHARDE, MALLET.

hand-coloured *adj*
The description of a print in which the basic image is printed, usually in black, and is then developed with painted colours, traditionally watercolours but any suitable medium can be used, depending upon the effect required.

handling *n*
1 The particular uses of tools and materials characteristic of the

work of an individual artist. Also known as *facture* (*Fr*) and *fattura* (*It*).
2 More generally, the characteristics of any individual art object which show the technical skill and method applied by the artist.

handmade paper *n*
A category of papers made from rag pulp, each sheet being made individually in a wire mesh frame of a size that can be conveniently handled by one or two people. The main characteristics of handmade papers are the uneven DECKLE EDGE and the slight variations of dimensions, surface texture and thickness in a batch of sheets owing to the individual processing. Handmade papers have traditionally been favoured supports for watercolour painting, fine drawing and printmaking, but they are no longer widely or readily available. MACHINE-MADE PAPERS are produced which correspond in many ways to the qualities previously appreciated in handmade papers.

Hansa yellow *n*
The original trade name of a synthetic organic yellow pigment, extremely stable and permanent, the basis of a small range of yellow pigments variously marketed under manufacturers' trade names.

hardboard *n*
A relatively thin, stiff but flexible sheet material made from shredded wood and sawdust compressed under heat in a resin binder.

hard-edge painting *n*
A style of abstract painting characterized by the use of flat colour in shapes with clearly delineated edges.

hardening *n*
1 The process whereby a liquid material becomes solid, including simple drying by evaporation and the more complex process of CURING.
2 The process of heating and rapidly quenching a metal, to alter its physical characteristics and make it more durable.
3 A surface treatment applied to concrete, involving application of a chemical solution.

hardening on *n*
The process of low-firing ceramic ware decorated with colouring matter bound in an oil medium. The firing burns off the oil before a final glaze is applied.

hard glaze *n*
A ceramic glaze fired at a high temperature.

hard ground *n*
An acid-resistant coating applied to the surface of an etching plate. It is a mixture of beeswax, bitumen and rosin and is sold commercially in the form of a small shiny cake or ball, dark brown in colour. Hard ground is resistant and durable in acid but is easily lifted by an etching needle, so lines drawn in it are clean and sharp. See also ETCHING GROUND, SMOKING, SOFT GROUND.

hard paste *n*
The name given to the mixture of substances used in making true porcelain, of the form originated in China. It is a compound of china stone, china clay and flint which is fired and glazed at 1300° C (2375° F) or over. Also called *pâte dure* (*Fr*).

hard soldering *n*
See SOLDERING. See also BRAZING.

hardwood *n*
A general classification of the woods obtained from deciduous, broad-leaved trees. These are typically close-grained, tough and durable, but the term does not refer to actual physical hardness which varies considerably across the range. Mahogany and oak are among the hardwoods traditionally used for wood carving.

hatch *vb*
To create an area of tone by HATCHING. **hatched** *adj*.

hatching *n*
1 The technique of creating an area of tone with linear marks. Closely-spaced parallel lines are drawn to define the area. The tone can be varied by making the lines fine or heavy and altering the spaces between them. The technique is particularly associated with drawing, and with engraving and etching, but the principle is applicable to any medium in which linear qualities are appropriate to the work and can be employed with the tools involved, eg a brush or incising tool. Also called *hachure* (*Fr*).
2 An area of tone created by this technique. See also CROSS HATCHING.

head peg *n*
See BUST PEG.

heat work *n*
The relationship between the maximum temperature required in a kiln and the time allowed for that temperature to be achieved for successful firing of ceramic ware. Both elements vary according to the condition of the ware and the intended effect of firing.

heightening *n*
The addition of white or very pale colours in a painting or drawing, to raise the KEY of the work or emphasize contrasts of light and shade.

heroic *adj*
1 In a technical sense, the description of a statue which is considerably larger than life-size.
2 In a more general sense, the term is used of subject matter which is evocative of grand physical scale or noble sentiments.

hiding power *n*
The opacity of a paint or pigment, ie its ability to cover and conceal colours previously applied to a support.
Compare COVERING POWER.

hieratic *adj* (from *Gr hieros* = sacred)
The description of forms and styles in art which adhere to particular conventional systems of representation, generally because they are used for religious or ritualistic images.

high-fired *adj*
The descriptive term for ceramic ware fired at a high temperature.

highlight *n*
The lightest tone in a drawn or painted image, particularly a small dash or patch of white representing the point of maximum light reflection on a surface.

high relief *n*
1 A category of various types of sculpture in which forms project from a background plane by more than half their natural proportional depth. In some cases, the forms may be heavily undercut or almost fully rounded, but still attached to a background and therefore best seen from a fixed range of basically frontal viewpoints. Also called *alto-rilievo* (*It*).
2 An individual sculpture conforming to this principle of composition. See also LOW RELIEF, MEDIUM RELIEF.

history painting *n*
1 A category of paintings covering works in which historical scenes, literary or legendary events are realistically depicted, usually in a formal and grandiose style.
2 An individual work of this type.

hollow building *n*
A technique of constructing a composite ceramic form by shaping components out of slabs, tubes and rolls of clay and joining them when they have dried to a leather-hard condition.

hollow casting *n*
1 A method of casting a three-dimensional form by painting the interior of a mould with a liquid or paste material to build up a required thickness, rather than by filling the mould completely with the material. This technique is used particularly for making resin or wax casts.
2 In the LOST WAX PROCESS, the method of casting from a hollow wax model filled with a CORE of refractory material.

hollowing out *n*
1 The process of shaping the interior form of a clay object in THROWING.
2 The process of cutting out clay from the interior of a terracotta sculpture at the leather-hard stage, to reduce the weight of the material for firing.

hollow ware *n*
The collective term for items of pottery, eg cups, jugs, vases and similar containers, which are relatively deeply hollowed. Compare FLATWARE.

horizon line *n*
In linear perspective, a line drawn horizontally through a pictorial composition representing the artist's eye level and the furthest point of sight on the ground plane, at which lines receding horizontally from the picture plane converge on a vanishing point. See PERSPECTIVE.

hot air blower *n*
A hand-held electrical tool, similar to a hairdryer, designed to emit a powerful jet of hot air which can soften plastic rod or sheet to a point where the material is pliable and can be modelled or moulded into a required shape.

hot-pressed oil *n*
A drying oil produced by steam-heating and crushing the raw material. This is a more economical way of extracting oil than cold-pressing, but the quality of the oil tends to be inferior and oils so produced, eg from linseed or poppyseed, are refined and bleached for use in oil paints.

hot-pressed paper *n*
A category of papers which in manufacture are rolled or pressed between hot metal plates to produce a compact, relatively smooth, sometimes slightly glazed surface finish.

hot wire cutter *n*
A tool used to cut sheets or blocks of EXPANDED POLYSTYRENE, consisting of a fine wire held taut between two terminals attached

to a frame. The wire is electrically heated and cuts by melting the materials along a fine seam. There are hand-held and bench-mounted versions of the tool.

hue *n*
The basic quality of a true colour, eg red, orange, orange-red, not referring to the possible range of tones of an individual colour, eg light red, dark red.

humectant *n*
A HYGROSCOPIC substance added to a material to keep it moist, eg glycerin added to watercolours to maintain moisture content and encourage solubility.

hygroscopic *adj*
The description of a material or substance that absorbs and retains moisture from the surrounding atmosphere.

i

icon, ikon *n*
1 A portrait of a sacred figure in the form of a painting, mosaic or low relief, usually small-scale. This is a traditional form of Christian art, particularly in eastern Europe.
2 More generally, a formal or symbolic pictorial image.

iconography *n*
A field of art historical study dealing with the identification of symbolic images, themes and motifs in figurative art.

iconology *n*
A field of art historical study dealing broadly with the interpretation of meaning in symbolic images, motifs and themes in art in the context of particular cultures and historical periods.

igneous rock *n*
Rock formed by the cooling and solidifying of molten masses from within the earth which have risen closer to the surface. All types of igneous rock are hard, compact and durable. The category includes granite and basalt.

illuminate *vb*
To decorate a manuscript with ILLUMINATION. **illuminated** *adj*.

illumination *n*
1 The art of decorating a hand-written manuscript with ornamental devices, colours and gilding. The term is used broadly for any type of decoration, but strictly should refer to the use of gold or silver that can be burnished to a highly reflective finish.
2 An image or design, particularly one that is gilded, used to decorate an individual letterform, block of text or margin in a hand-written manuscript.

illusionism *n*
The general term for styles and techniques of figurative painting that attempt to deceive the eye into accepting a two-dimensional image as three-dimensional or real. Pictorial devices employed to create this effect include FORESHORTENING and PERSPECTIVE and the use of tonal contrasts and shading to accentuate modelling of forms.

illusionistic *adj*
The description of a quality in painting where forms and images are depicted in a realistic manner giving an impression of actual space or solidity on a two-dimensional surface. This applies to individual motifs and to detailed compositions, eg a painting on a wall which creates the illusion of a view through a window or into an adjoining room.

illustrate *vb*
To make an ILLUSTRATION.

illustration *n*
1 An image designed to accompany a written text, especially one intended to be printed with the text by a commercial reproduction process, eg in a book or magazine.
2 Any technique or process used to create such an image, eg painting, drawing, montage.

illustration board *n*
A prepared support for drawing and painting, made by mounting a good-quality paper on a stiff board made from paper pulp. Illustration boards are made in a range of sizes, thicknesses and grades of surface finish.

illustrator *n*
1 An artist whose professional line of work is illustration.
2 The person responsible for the image, or images, accompanying a particular text.

image *n*
1 The actual form or total appearance of a work of art, ie the

composition of the various elements and the way in which they are expressed or depicted.
2 A motif or figure represented on a background plane.

imagery *n*
The motifs, figures, objects or scenes in a work of art, ie the individual components of a composition and the ways in which they are assembled or related.

Imari *n*
A type of decorated oriental porcelain typified by a blue underglaze embellished with red and gold enamelling.

imp *abb* **impressit** *vb* (*Lat* has printed it)
Lettering which appears on a print accompanying the name of the printer, as distinct from the artist responsible for the original image.

impasto *n*
1 Thickly applied paint that forms a low relief effect on the support and in which the marks of brush, palette knife or similar tool are usually visible. This effect can be achieved in oil, acrylic, encaustic or gouache painting, since the paint has sufficient substance to retain the weight and texture, whereas watercolour and tempera are generally too fluid to achieve the richness of texture.
2 The technique of applying paint in this manner.

impression *n*
1 A final proof or print from a block, plate or stone prepared for relief or intaglio printing, ie the paper bearing the inked image which has been impressed upon it.
2 The effect of contact between the inked surface of a block, plate or stone and the material which receives the image: thus a light or blurred image is referred to as a poor impression.
3 An image obtained by pressing a plastic material against a rigid relief or intaglio surface.

imprimatura *n*
A thin glaze of colour laid over a white ground applied to canvas or other painting support. The purpose of applying the colour tint is to establish a middle tone, whether warm (red, brown) or cool (blue, green) against which a full range of dark and light tones can be developed. A fine glaze of oil or acrylic paint applied for this purpose also renders the ground less absorbent. Also called coloured ground.

inc *abb* **incidit** *vb* (*Lat* has cut, incised it)
Lettering which appears on an engraving accompanying the name

of the engraver, as distinct from the artist responsible for the original image.

incise *vb*
To cut or carve a hard or resistant surface with a sharp tool. **incised** *adj*.

incising *n*
The technique or process of cutting into a hard surface with a sharp tool, especially used of making fine or detailed work such as lettering and linear designs.

incrustation *n*
Any form of decorative INLAY, applied to an object or architectural feature, which consists of an arrangement of varied and contrasting materials.

India ink, Indian ink *n*
A pure black, permanent drawing ink, available in liquid or stick form. Its traditional composition is lamp black pigment in an aqueous gum binder, but there are various forms containing different ingredients, eg a waterproof type in which shellac is the binder. Also called Chinese ink or sumi ink.

indigo *n*
1 A deep violet-blue pigment or dye, originally obtained from plants of the *Indigofera* genus, subsequently produced synthetically from coal-tar.
2 The violet-blue colour associated with this pigment.

indirect carving *n*
A method of carving in which a small-scale model is copied proportionately on an enlarged scale by means of a mechanical technique. Typically, this applies to stone carving when a clay, wax or plaster model is reproduced by POINTING.
Compare DIRECT CARVING.

indirect stencil *n*
An image applied to the fabric mesh of a screen used in the SCREENPRINTING process which is fully prepared before application, eg a cutout paper stencil or a transparent, self-adhesive plastic film, either of which physically cover parts of the mesh; or a photographic image prepared on a soft film of light-sensitive emulsion and transferred to the screen by pressing the emulsion into the screen mesh.

inert pigment *n*
A substance in powder form which has no capacity to colour a paint but may be used as an ADULTERANT, EXTENDER or FILLER, or as an ingredient of a GROUND for painting. A white pigment

of this kind will become colourless when mixed in oil and contributes little or no opacity to the paint. In a water-based medium, it may have a degree of opacity but should not devalue the pigment used as the colouring agent. Mixed with an aqueous binder, it may be sufficiently white and opaque to form an effective ground.

inflatable *n*
A sculpture or architectural construction made from flexible plastic sheeting, which achieves its proper form when filled with air.

in-glaze decoration *n*
Decoration applied to ceramic ware over an unfired glaze, eg by painting with metal oxides, which merges into the glaze when the piece is fired.

Ingres paper *n*
A range of medium-weight coloured papers with a rough surface tooth, particularly suitable for chalk or pastel drawings. The colours are typically subtle tints, plain or finely mottled with dark fibres, but there is an extensive range of choice among the various proprietary brands of this type of paper.

ink[1] *n*
1 A liquid medium for drawing and painting, consisting of a pigment or dye suspended or dissolved in an aqueous vehicle. Coloured drawing inks are not always fully permanent but are used particularly for illustration work and other purposes where permanence is not a primary requirement, because the colours are vibrant and transparent. See also INDIA INK.
2 A viscous liquid or paste medium, commonly consisting of pigment finely ground in an oil or varnish vehicle, used for printing an impression by an INTAGLIO, PLANOGRAPHIC or RELIEF PRINTING process. For intaglio processes, the ink may be prepared as needed by grinding a pigment in oil: for all processes prepared inks are generally available from manufacturers and suppliers of printing materials.

ink[2] *vb*
To apply INK to a material or surface. **inked** *adj.*

ink and wash *n*
See LINE AND WASH.

inking *n*
1 The process of completing or colouring a drawing using a liquid ink, eg applied with a pen or brush.

2 The process of coating the image on a printing plate, block or stone with ink prior to taking an impression.

inlaid *adj*
1 The description of an object decorated with an INLAY.
2 The description of the materials applied to form an inlay.

inlay *n*
1 Any form of decoration in which small pieces of various materials, or similar materials in different colours, eg ceramics, wood, metal, are sunk into the surface of a large object or mass of a single material. The decoration is usually finished flush with the original surface.
2 Any individual process of creating such decoration on a surface or object. See also INTARSIA, MARQUETRY.

inorganic pigments *n pl*
The classification of the range of pigments derived from mineral sources, eg natural coloured earths or stones, including synthetic mineral pigments which are chemically manufactured.

inpainting *n*
A process in conservation of paintings in which a blemish or blank patch in an image is repainted in colour without covering or interfering with the existing, original paint layers.

intaglio *n*
An image which is cut back from the flat surface of a solid material, so that whether it lies in one or several levels of the material, no part of the image projects from the original surface. See also INTAGLIO PRINTING.

intaglio printing *n*
The process of taking an inked impression from a design or image which is engraved, etched or scratched in the surface of a hard material, typically a metal plate. The plate is covered with ink which is pressed into the recessed lines and areas: the surface of the plate is then wiped clean, leaving ink only in the intaglio. This process can be carried out on a cold plate, but it is common practice to warm the plate to encourage spreading and lifting of the oily ink. The plate is laid on the bed of a heavy press and covered with a sheet of dampened paper. When passed through the press, the paper is forced down the inked intaglio and picks up the ink. The impression on the paper is a reversed image, slightly raised and textured, according to the depth and character of the original intaglio. See AQUATINT, DRYPOINT, ENGRAVING, ETCHING, MEZZOTINT. See also ETCHING PRESS, WIPING.

intaglio relief *n*
See SUNKEN RELIEF.

intarsia *n*
A method of decoration applied to furniture and architectural forms, consisting of small sections of materials such as bone, ivory, mother of pearl and coloured woods inlaid in a solid background.

intermediate varnish *n*
A thin layer of varnish laid over an UNDERPAINTING to provide a moist surface that ensures adhesion of subsequent paint layers and allows painting to continue on the principle of WET INTO WET. This is particular to oil painting.

intonaco *n*
A smooth topcoat of plaster on which the colours are applied in FRESCO painting. The colours must be applied to wet plaster so the intonaco is laid in sections. See also GIORNATA.

inv *abb* **invenit** *vb* (*Lat* has devised it)
Lettering which appears on a print accompanying the name of the artist who created the original image from which the print was made.

investment *n*
A heavy coating of refractory material which forms the mould around a wax model in the LOST WAX PROCESS of casting. It is built up directly around the original model and also encases the wax rods applied to form RUNNERS and RISERS. Typically the investment consists of a fine coating painted directly over the model and a thick, course outer layer which completely encases the form. There are various mixtures which can be used to make an investment: materials such as ciment fondu, plaster, sand and grog are common ingredients.

isocephaly *n*
A form of figure composition used especially in relief sculpture, in which figures are shown all at the same height, regardless of posture, eg whether standing or sitting.

ivory *n*
Strictly, the material of elephant tusks, though in the context of sculpture materials, the tusks and teeth of several other mammals are also included under the term. It is a dense, slightly translucent substance, clear white or yellow-tinged, which can be carved into intricate forms and takes a high polish. It is typically used for small-scale carvings and is also a traditional support material for miniature paintings.

j

jacket *n*
See CASE.

japan *n*
1 A varnish composed mainly of a resin and solvent, used as a medium mixed with oil paints to speed drying and contribute a glossy surface quality.
2 A type of inexpensive enamel paint, sometimes used as a decorative or protective coating for sculpture materials, particularly sheet metal. The composition may vary: some types dry in air while others require heat treatment, but most contain bitumen and are black or very dark in colour.

japanning *n*
Any of various methods of decorating an object or surface with lacquers, in imitation of the effects of oriental lacquer work.

japonaiserie *n*
A term used of artefacts, motifs or images appearing in western art which are borrowed from or intended to imitate traditional Japanese forms.

jig *n*
A device made to hold metal components in correct position or relation while work such as cutting, shaping or soldering is carried out. A jig is custom-built for a particular purpose and is especially necessary when the same process is applied repeatedly to sections of a material to produce a number of identical components.

jigger *n*
1 A machine for forming FLATWARE, consisting of a revolving convex mould over which clay is laid and an adjustable arm carrying a template which trims and shapes the clay as the mould rotates.
2 A wooden box, open at one end, on which an intaglio printing plate is placed while it cools after a ground has been applied or is kept warm during the inking process. The jigger stands next to the hotplate used to heat the plate and the interior is commonly used for storing grounds, dabbers, rollers etc.

jiggering and jolleying *n*
The technique of forming ceramic ware mechanically using a JIGGER and JOLLEY. This is mainly a commercial manufacturing process, not commonly applied in studio potteries.

jigging *n*
The preparation of metal components for sculpture of decorative metalwork, involving use of a JIG.

jigsaw *n*
A mechanical power-driven saw consisting of a short, narrow metal blade set vertically in heavy machinery, operating with a rapid up-and-down motion to cut through sheet materials such as wood, metal or plastic.

jolley *n*
A machine for forming HOLLOW WARE, consisting of a revolving concave mould into which clay is pressed and an adjustable arm carrying a template which cuts into the clay and shapes the interior form of the ware as the mould rotates.

junk art *n*
Any type of art in which discarded objects and materials, eg anything from packaging materials to broken industrial machinery, are used as the components for forming art objects.

jute *n*
A plant fibre used to make coarse string, rope or woven fabric. See also BURLAP, SCRIM.

k

kaolin *n*
The anglicized form of the Chinese name for CHINA CLAY.

key *n*
1 (*painting*) The overall impression of colour and tonal values in a painting. A painting in which bright colours and light tones predominate is said to be high key: one in which dark colours and tones predominate is said to be low key.
2 (*painting*) See WEDGE.
3 (*casting*) A device set in the seam of a mould made in two or more pieces, which ensures that the mould can be dismantled and then reassembled exactly as it was originally made. Typically, in

a plaster mould the key is made by cutting a small V-shaped or rounded inset in the dried seam edge of one piece, which is filled when wet plaster is cast against it to create the second piece, and so on. Thus the first piece has a depression in the seam, the second a projection which fits it exactly, and these must be fitted together precisely when the mould is reassembled.
Also called natch.

key block *n*
The block used as the master design in a colour print. It usually holds the outline or dominant form of the image which serves as the guide from which other blocks can be made to print the different colours in register. The principle applies also to a printing plate or lithographic stone used in this way, called key plate or key stone.

key pattern *n*
See FRET.

kick wheel *n*
A potter's wheel operated on a mechanical system powered by a bar or treadle at the base which is pushed with the foot.

kidney *n*
A flat, kidney-shaped piece of metal, rubber or plastic used to scrape and smooth the surface of clay, eg in finishing the form of a thrown pot or firming a sheet of clay laid into a press mould.

killed plaster *n*
Plaster used for repairing a damaged plaster cast, to fill flaws in the surface etc. It is deliberately swamped with water, either by allowing a plaster mix to harden slightly and then mixing in more water, or by leaving plaster in powder form to stand in water before stirring it to an even consistency. The texture and colour then correspond more closely to those of the cured plaster of which the cast is composed.
Compare DEAD PLASTER.

kiln *n*
An oven which can be heated to high temperatures under controlled conditions for the firing of ceramic ware, glazes and slips or enamelling materials. Kilns are available in different sizes and types for domestic, studio and industrial use, and may be fired by electricity, gas, oil or solid fuel. Electricity is now commonly used in studio work as it is convenient, clean and reliable.

kiln-dried *adj*
A description of wood that is artificially seasoned, its moisture

driven off when the wood is baked in a kiln at high temperatures. This is an industrial technique used for large amounts of timber, since it is uneconomic to store it for the period of several months required for natural seasoning.

kiln furniture *n pl*
The collective term for a variety of objects used to support ceramic ware being fired in a kiln. These supports, which have descriptive names such as castle, pillar, prop, ring, stilt and thimble, are made of refractory material which is unaffected by high temperatures in the kiln.

kinetic sculpture *n*
1 The term used for various forms of sculpture which are designed to move or have moving parts. Motion may depend upon mechanical or motorized functions built into the sculpture, or may occur simply in response to air currents or movements made by the artist or viewer.
2 An individual sculpture of this type.

kitsch *n* (*Ge* trash)
A term used for artefacts with a crude, sentimental or vulgar quality, whether mass-produced or individual art objects.

kneaded eraser *n*
A soft, pliable eraser in the form of a small block of a slightly adhesive rubber compound that can be twisted into any shape and which does not wear away in use. It picks up the powdery colour put down by a soft drawing medium such as chalk, charcoal or pastel and the marks of a soft graphite stick or pencil. Also called putty rubber.

kolinsky *n*
The best quality of hair used in the manufacture of red sable brushes, taken from the small animal called kolinsky or Siberian mink. The hairs are particularly finely shaped, resilient and durable.

kore *n* **korai** *pl* (*Gr* maiden)
A stylized statue of a young woman, a typical form of early Greek sculpture. The posture is basically similar to that of the KOUROS, but the female figure is draped.

kouros *n* **kouroi** *pl* (*Gr* youth)
A stylized statue of a young man, a typical form of early Greek sculpture. The nude figure is basically symmetrical and stands with one leg slightly forward in a formal pose designed for a frontal viewpoint.

kraft paper *n*
A strong, lightweight brown paper made from wood pulp, produced as a packaging material but also used in picture framing as a protective, dust-excluding backing for frames.

l

lacquer *n*
Any of a number of natural or synthetic resin materials dissolved in a volatile solvent, to form a vehicle for a paint or varnish medium which may be applied as a liquid coating and hardens to a tough, resistant and glossy finish.

lacuna *n* **lacunae** *pl* (*Lat* gap, hole)
A damaged area in a painting or manuscript where a section of the image or text is completely missing.

laid paper *n*
Paper which, held to the light, shows a ribbed pattern in its internal structure crossed by widely spaced parallel lines. This was originally a feature of handmade papers made in a wire mesh frame reinforced with straight parallel wires. The pattern shows in the paper because the wires cause variations in the thickness of the material. The laid pattern may otherwise be artificially pressed into machine-made paper made on a close-weave mesh. See also WOVE PAPER.

lake pigment *n*
A pigment manufactured from a liquid dye which is fixed on an inert pigment base to make a substance that can be ground and mixed with paint vehicles. This is necessary to produce a colouring agent that contributes body, and sometimes opacity, to the paint where a liquid would merely dissolve into the vehicle. The process can also reduce the concentration of particularly strong colours so they do not flood or contaminate other colours in use. Lakes have been produced for centuries from certain natural dyes, but those produced since the invention of synthetic dyes have greatly expanded the range of artists' colours.

laminate[1] *vb*
1 To construct a material by bonding two or more layers of a substance.

2 To cover or surface a structure with a layer of material.
laminated *adj.*

laminate² *n*
1 A material made of bonded layers.
2 An individual layer or collection of layers in a laminated material.

laminating *n*
1 Generally, the process or activity of making a laminate.
2 Specifically, a technique of constructing a sculpted form with an outer shell of synthetic resin, by applying layers of resin and glass fibre reinforcement to a basic framework, eg of wood. As with other methods of making a hollow form in resin, the outer layer consists of a gel-coat without reinforcement which is allowed to harden slightly before further reinforced layers are applied. This produces a smooth, refined finish on a tough, resistant thickness of cured resin.

lamination *n*
1 A process of laminating.
2 An individual layer or collection of layers in a laminate.

land art *n*
Forms of art dealing directly with natural landscape, objects and elements which the artist manipulates, rearranges or records. A work may produce a major change in the actual geography of a particular location or may be concentrated in an activity by the artist which is documented or represented by materials taken from the location, but makes little permanent impression on the landscape itself.

landscape *n*
1 A painting, or other representation, of a view of natural forms, eg open countryside, parkland or forest, often covering a considerable range of distance. Figures may be included to give a sense of scale, but they are entirely subordinate to the view as a whole.
2 The broad category, or genre, of works of this type.
3 The basic format of any picture in which the dimension of width exceeds height. The term derives from the fact that paintings of landscape are commonly arranged in a horizontal format. See also PORTRAIT.

lapis lazuli *n*
A rich blue, natural mineral, originally the source of the blue pigment known as ultramarine, which is now made artificially. It is a semi-precious stone used for ornamentation.

latex *n*
An emulsion of synthetic rubber suspended in water, used as the basis of certain adhesives and as a cold cure rubber compound for making small, finely detailed moulds. It is applied to an original model in fluid form, brushed or sprayed on in successive coats, and solidifies into a highly flexible skin. Reinforcement of cotton SCRIM can be added in outer layers and a latex mould requires a plaster case to be made which will hold it in shape for a subsequent casting.

lath *n*
A thin strip of wood, capable of providing rigid but relatively lightweight reinforcement for a malleable material.

lathe *n*
A machine with a horizontally rotating part to which a section of rigid material, eg wood, plastic, metal, can be attached and is then shaped as it rotates by a cutting tool brought into contact with the surface. The tool makes a continuous cut around the outer layer of the material and in this way a perfectly symmetrical form can be shaped.

lawn *n*
A fine mesh made of bronze wires, used for sieving a slip or ceramic glaze. Different gauges are made, giving a range of fine and coarse meshes.

lay figure *n*
A jointed, wooden doll-like figure constructed in correct human proportions. It can be arranged in a variety of poses, clothed or draped, as an aid to drawing or painting a figure study or composition. Originally, lay figures were life-size models: modern versions are generally small and proportionately scale down, consisting of simple cylindrical and ovoid forms with moveable joints.

laying in *n*
The process of applying the first layers of colour to a support to establish the basis of a composition in painting. This can refer to a relatively detailed UNDERPAINTING, or any broad manner of defining an overall plan at the beginning of a work which may subsequently be modified or completely obliterated.

laying up *n*
The process of rolling out clay into thick sheets and laying them out on bats, in preparation for HOLLOW BUILDING, PRESS MOULDING, or SLABBING.

layout *n*

1 In graphic design, the basic plan of the arrangement of different elements in a design as they will appear together in printed form, eg for a book or magazine page. The layout shows the positioning of text, illustrations and other features and may be marked directly with instructions to the printer on size, colour, tone etc of the individual items.
2 The process or activity of preparing such a plan.
3 More broadly, the basic form of a composition, especially in painting and graphic arts.

layout paper *n*

Lightweight but strong white paper with a hard, smooth surface, used for making rough designs, layouts and sketches.

lean *adj*

1 A term used to refer to the quality of oil paint that contains little oil and is well-diluted with turpentine. See also FAT, FAT OVER LEAN.
2 See SHORT CLAY.

lean to fat painting *n*

See FAT OVER LEAN.

leather-hard *adj*

The condition of clay that has partially dried but still contains enough moisture to retain a degree of flexibility and surface sheen. A leather-hard body can be moistened and reworked: it is more resistant than fresh clay but not hard enough to break cleanly.

lettering *n*

1 Letterforms and words included in a design or composition which are hand-drawn or painted, rather than written or printed.
2 Any technique of drawing or painting such letterforms.
3 An abbreviated word, or full word, appearing on a print giving information about the artist or printer, particularly associated with old engravings. See DEL, EXC, FEC, IMP, INC, INV, P, SC.

life drawing *n*

1 The activity or process of drawing a human figure by direct observation of a live model.
2 A drawing made by such a process.

life-size *adj*

The description of a figure painted or sculpted in the same scale as its actual dimensions and proportions.

lift ground *n*

A method of painting an image directly on an etching plate and subsequently processing it to print as a positive, tonal image of the original painting. The image is painted in a mixture of sugar and INDIA INK on the clean surface of the plate. The whole plate is then coated in STOPPING OUT VARNISH and, when this is dry, immersed in warm water. The sugar gradually dissolves, lifting the varnish covering the image and exposing the metal in these areas only. The exposed areas can then be etched directly as OPEN BITE or given a flat or gradated tone by the AQUATINT process. Alternatively, the whole process can be carried out on a plate already covered with aquatint resin. Also called sugar lift.

lifting *n*
A method of creating an area of texture in a painting by pressing a piece of absorbent cloth or paper over a layer of wet paint to pick up colour from the surface.

lightfast *adj*
The description of a substance which does not lose its colour on long or continuous exposure to natural light. When used of artists' pigments, it is a guarantee of permanence.

light sculpture *n*
A collective term for forms of art in which light and the effects of light are principal elements of the composition, through use of actual light sources, eg fluorescent and neon tubes, or reflective materials, eg glass, mirror, polished metal. It includes constructions which incorporate a special lighting effect or beams of light directed in particular ways to illuminate space and form.

lignum vitae *n*
An extremely hard, dense, heavy and close-grained wood, native to central America. It varies in colour from grey-green to dark brown. Because of its density it is not easily carved, but may be chosen as a carving material for its durability and stone-like tactile qualities. It is also used for making strong and resilient mallets used in wood and stone carving.

limestone *n*
Stone consisting primarily of calcium carbonate, sedimentary in origin, a traditional and widely used material for stone carving. Limestones are durable but relatively easy to carve, varying from close-grained to coarse-grained and found in a range of colours from cream to black, though grey and buff-coloured stones are generally preferred. The compactness dictates the type of finish the stone can take, but a lustrous polish is only applicable to the most dense and close-grained limestones; otherwise the matt, grainy texture is exploited to emphasize the sculptural effect.

limited edition *n*
A run of prints deliberately limited in number to sustain the value of each individual work. It is essentially the same as an EDITION, but if the value as limited is to be guaranteed, the blocks, plates or stones from which the prints are made should be destroyed or defaced. See also CANCELLED PLATE.

limner *n*
1 A painter of MINIATURES.
2 A now obsolete term simply meaning a painter, but often used expressly of portrait painters.

limning *n*
The art or process of painting MINIATURES.

line and wash *n*
A method of drawing using pen and ink to create a linear image which is then elaborated with colour or tone by the application of dilute washes of watercolour or ink. The technique may be reversed, ie line drawing applied over dried washes, and is adaptable to other linear drawing media, eg pencil or charcoal. Also called ink and wash, pen and wash.

linear *adj*
The description of a work in which forms are described primarily by the use of line and contour, rather than by mass. See also PAINTERLY.

linear perspective *n*
The basic system of PERSPECTIVE employing a linear framework constructed on the principle that receding parallel lines appear to converge.

line drawing *n*
1 The technique of drawing with any medium using only line to create the image, ie no solid areas of tone or colour are applied, though tonal effects may be achieved by HATCHING and CROSS HATCHING.
2 A drawing produced by such a technique.

line engraving *n*
See ENGRAVING.

lining *n*
1 A process used in conservation of paintings to strengthen a fragile or damaged canvas by taking it from the original stretcher, mounting it on a fresh piece of fabric and restretching the double layer. A suitable adhesive is used to bond the old canvas to the new fabric base.
2 The practice of painting a fine line or band of colour close to the

inner edges of a WINDOW MOUNT, for decorative effect and to draw attention to the image area.

lining tool *n*
See MULTIPLE LINE GRAVER.

linocut *n*
1 A RELIEF PRINTING process in which an image or design is cut into the surface of a block of linoleum (lino). The lino is relatively soft and flexible, easily cut with knives or small gouges, but because of this softness the image cannot contain much fine detail, as small ridges of lino tend to break down under pressure from cutting tools or in the printing process. The process is similar to WOODCUT and the lino can be mounted on a wood block to give it extra firmness and height for printing on a flat-bed or cylinder press. It is usual to cut a separate block for each colour when printing in two or more colours, but it is also possible to create quite complex effects by overprinting different colours successively from one block, cutting away different parts of the image between printings. The informal term linocut is more commonly used than the technical description linoleum block printing.
2 A printed image obtained from this process.

linoleum block printing *n*
See LINOCUT.

linseed oil *n*
A natural vegetable oil obtained from the seed of the flax plant. It is the most commonly used drying oil forming the vehicle for oil paints and is also used as a medium for painting. It dries by oxidation and forms a tough film, flexible at first but hardening with age, that cannot be reprocessed into its original state. It is usually available in the light-coloured cold-pressed or refined hot-pressed forms and a darker, less pure, raw hot-pressed form. See also STAND OIL.

lithograph *n*
A printed image produced by LITHOGRAPHY.

lithographer *n*
1 A person skilled in the techniques and processes of lithography.
2 The person responsible for preparing and printing a particular image by the process of lithography.

lithographic crayon *n*
A black crayon with a greasy texture used for drawing on a lithographic plate or stone. The crayons, usually square-sectioned, are available in hard, medium and soft grades.

The composition can vary but the basic ingredients are wax, soap and lamp black pigment: other materials such as shellac or tallow may be added to harden or soften the texture.

lithographic ink *n*
A black drawing ink with a dense, greasy consistency, used for drawing and painting on a lithographic stone or plate. It is available in liquid or stick form and the basic ingredients are the same as those of the lithographic crayon. It can be thinned with water to make washes of varying tones. Also called tusche.

lithographic stone *n*
A heavy block of limestone with the upper face ground to a perfectly flat, even surface on which a drawing can be made in lithographic crayon or ink and subsequently treated for printing. When a final run of prints has been taken from a stone, the face can be reground for preparation of a fresh image.

lithography *n*
A method of printing from an image drawn on the flat surface of a block of limestone or a metal plate. The technique depends upon the natural reactions of grease and water in that they are immiscible and mutually repellent. The image is drawn with a greasy crayon or ink: it is dusted with French chalk and coated with a solution of gum containing a small proportion of nitric acid (for stone) or chemical etch (for a metal plate). After a period of several hours the original image is cleaned off with a solvent leaving greasy, colourless marks on the surface and a bituminous solution is rubbed into the marks to boost the grease content. When this is removed the image is rolled up with black printing ink, again dusted with chalk or powdered resin and treated with etch to desensitize the surface surrounding the image. To take a print, the layer of black ink is cleaned off and the plate or stone is thoroughly wetted. The greasy image repels the water and when fresh ink is applied it adheres to the image but not to the wet surface surrounding it. The moisture is then dried off and a print is taken from the inked image. See also OFFSET LITHOGRAPHY.

livering *n*
1 A condition sometimes affecting oil paints of inferior quality or those stored over a very long period. The paint hardens in the tube or can, forming a dense, rubbery mass that is useless for painting and cannot be reconstituted by use of a diluent or solvent.
2 A condition occurring in clay slip that has been treated with a contaminated DEFLOCCULANT; eg soda ash exposed to moisture in the air becomes sodium hydroxide which causes the clay particles to mass together and settle as a thick residue.

live stone *n*
A freshly quarried or well-preserved stone block which has a rich, compact texture suitable for carving, fractures cleanly and makes a vibrant sound when struck with a metal tool.

living sculpture *n*
A form of PERFORMANCE ART in which an activity or pose by the artist in person constitutes the art object, often subsequently represented by photographs, film or videotape of the actual event.

loaded brush *n*
The technique of painting with a brush heavily charged with thick paint to produce an IMPASTO effect.

local colour *n*
The actual colour of an object or surface, ie the colour it reflects naturally under white light, unaffected by shadows or reflections from surrounding objects.

long clay *n*
The term for a clay body which is highly plastic, ie has a soft, workable texture. Also called fat clay.

lost pattern casting *n*
A method of casting in metal from an original sculpture made in EXPANDED POLYSTYRENE. The model is packed in damp sand and channels are made through the sand to allow molten metal to be poured in and gases to escape separately as this occurs. When the hot metal is poured the polystyrene model burns away completely and the space it originally occupied is filled by the metal. The sand packing is removed and the cast is cleaned and chased.

lost wax process *n*
A method of casting a sculpture in metal, primarily used for bronze casting, from a wax model or cast. For small sculptures a solid wax model can be used as the original. For most works the cast is made hollow, for economy in use of bronze, and this can be done directly from a model consisting of a layer of wax shaped over a refractory CORE. Alternatively, a hollow wax cast can be made from a piece-mould of a clay or plaster original, and this also must be filled with a core of refractory material. Metal pins are pushed through the wax into the core, leaving the blunt tips projecting from the model. Wax rods are attached to the model to form RUNNERS and RISERS. The runners are brought together in a cup of wax and these elements form a POURING GATE and channels in the mould through which the molten metal flows and gases escape. The rodded model is completely encased in an outer

jacket of refractory material which traps the outer heads of the pins. This is known as the INVESTMENT: it is baked in a furnace to harden the mould and melt out the wax, when the pins maintain the space between investment and core. The empty mould is sunk in a bed of sand and molten metal is poured through the gate, passes down the empty runner channels and fills the mould. When the cast has cooled the investment is broken away: rods of metal solidified in the runner and riser channels are cut off and the outer surface of the cast is chased and cleaned.

low-fired *adj*
The descriptive term for ceramic ware fired at a low temperature.

low relief *n*
1 A category of various types of sculpture in which forms project from a background plane by less than half their natural proportional depth. Also called *basso rilievo* (*It*) or *bas relief* (*Fr*). **2** An individual sculpture conforming to this principle of composition. See also FLATTENED RELIEF, HIGH RELIEF, MEDIUM RELIEF.

lump hammer *n*
A hammer used in stone carving to strike the cutting tools. The head is rectangular in section and usually made of iron, though a steel head is usable for work on relatively soft stones.

lunette *n*
A semi-circular painting, usually decoration for a wall area of this shape above a window or door.

luting *n*
The method of joining two leather-hard pieces of clay, eg to fit a handle to a cup. The surfaces to be joined are scored with a knife and wetted with slip, then pressed together.

m

machine-made paper *n*
A category of papers now including almost all types commercially available, produced from wood and rag pulps and made by mechanical processes that ensure consistent quality in surface finish, texture, thickness and weight. Typically the paper is produced in a continuous sheet or roll and then trimmed to standard sizes. See also HANDMADE PAPER.

maculature *n*
A weak impression from an intaglio plate, made by pulling a second print without re-inking the plate. This may be done to extract ink left in the etched or engraved lines, or to obtain a spare proof for reference.

madder *n*
Originally, a red or crimson dye obtained from the root of the madder plant (*Rubia tinctorium*) and used in the manufacture of LAKE PIGMENTS. The range of colours obtained from this source have been superseded by synthetic ALIZARIN dyes.

maestà *n* (*It* majesty)
A traditional image of Christian art; the Virgin Mary and infant Jesus enthroned and surrounded by angels.

magilp *n*
Alternative spelling of MEGILP.

mahlstick *n*
A rigid cane or wooden rod with a rounded pad at one end. It is used to steady the hand holding the brush during painting of fine details or over a long period of work. It is held in the free hand with the padded tip resting on the canvas or other support. Also called maulstick.

Majolica, Maiolica *n*
The Italian term for tin-glazed earthenware products. The characteristic is the opacity of the glazed surface, which can be painted with metal oxides to produce a design in rich, bright colours when fired. The name derives from Majorca, once thought to be the original home of such wares. In France, the same type of ware was given the name Faience, after Faenza in Italy which was a centre of manufacture. In England it was

known as Delft ware, because first introduced to England from Holland. All these terms are sometimes used to describe any type of glazed earthenware or, less broadly, earthenware with any type of opaque glaze.

malachite *n*
A natural mineral substance, a form of hydrated copper carbonate, used as a green pigment varying in tone from light to dark according to the medium. It was one of the earliest known pigments but has been entirely superseded by artificial equivalents. It is a semi-precious stone used for ornamentation.

malerisch *adj* (*Ge*)
PAINTERLY.

mallet *n*
A wooden hammer used to drive a wood carving chisel. The striking head is a cylindrical block of wood, usually beech or LIGNUM VITAE, and the curved face is used to strike the chisel. It is also used in carving soft stone. See also DUMMY.

mandorla *n* (*It* almond)
In Christian art, the depiction of an oval or almond-shaped radiance surrounding a sacred figure.

manière criblée *n* (*Fr* sieved style)
See DOTTED MANNER.

manikin *n*
A small LAY FIGURE.

maquette *n* (*Fr* model)
A small sculpture made as a preparatory study for a larger work. Traditionally the form is modelled roughly in wax or clay, but if the full-scale sculpture is to be carved the maquette may also be carved, usually in a less expensive and less durable material than that to be used for the final version.

marble[1] *n*
A crystalline stone, metamorphic in origin, which has traditionally been a favoured material for stone carving. This is because it is hard and durable, though not brittle, and responsive to carving tools and techniques. It occurs naturally in a wide range of colours, from white through pink, red, green and grey to black, attractively streaked and veined. Its crystalline composition gives it a natural sparkle and it can be polished to an extremely smooth and glossy finish.

marble[2] *vb*
To decorate a surface by MARBLING.

marbled ware *n*
Ceramic ware decorated with coloured slips in a surface pattern resembling the veining of marble. See also MARBLING. Compare AGATE WARE.

marbling *n*
1 A method of decorating ceramic ware with coloured slips which are trailed and dotted on a ground of wet slip. The ware is shaken so the colours streak and run together in an effect similar to the patterns of veining in marble.
2 A method of two-dimensional patterning involving use of different types of paint that do not mix, eg oil-based and water-based paints. The liquid colours are run together in a tray or dish, oil floating on water to form a pattern of streaks and whorls. The pattern can be transferred to a piece of paper or fabric laid flat on the surface of the liquid and quickly lifted.

marine painting *n*
1 A category of painting covering works depicting the sea and objects or activities related to the sea, eg naval battles, trading ships, harbour scenes etc.
2 An individual work of this type.

marouflage *n* (from *Fr maroufle* = paint residue)
The process of sticking canvas or a painting on canvas to a flat wall or rigid panel. The term *maroufle* refers to the tacky mixture of paint and oil left in an artist's mixing pot and traditionally the adhesive used for marouflage is a mixture of white lead pigment and linseed oil in a stiff, paste-like consistency, but other substances, eg casein or gum, can be used as suitable. Both the wall and the back of the canvas are coated with the adhesive paste and the fabric is flattened or rolled out over the rigid surface and smoothed into place.

marquetry *n*
A technique of decoration in wood carried out by assembling thin sections of wood or wood veneer in various colours and textures to create an image or pattern inlaid in a solid mass of wood. The inlay may include other decorative materials such as ivory, metal or tortoiseshell and is used to create pictures or to elaborate the design of ornamental and functional items, eg furniture.

Mars colours *n pl*
A range of synthetic inorganic pigments derived from artificially prepared iron oxides, in the colour range brown, red, violet and including Mars black and Mars yellow. The colours are vivid and permanent.

mask[1] *n*
A substance or material used to cover part of a support or a dried area in a painted image while further paint is applied, which protects the specific area from receiving the fresh application of colour. An important quality of the mask is that it should lift from the support without damage to the underlying surface once the process is complete. The simplest form of mask is a piece of paper laid over the support, but there are various materials specially designed for the purpose and in a practical sense any solid material or object can be used.

mask[2] *vb*
To use or apply a mask. **masked** *adj.*

masking *n*
The process or activity of applying a mask.

masking film *n*
A flexible, transparent plastic film with a low-tack adhesive coating on one side, which is laid over a support to act as a mask. Where paint is to be applied, a section of the masking film is cut out and lifted: the remaining film forms a precise and protective surround and colour can then be applied only in the exposed area. This material is primarily used in connection with AIRBRUSH painting, to confine the spray of paint from the tool to specific areas of the support and to build up successive layers of colour. The film can be lifted easily without damage to the underlying surface.

masking fluid *n*
A rubber compound solution which is applied to a support as a liquid and dries to form a thin film of rubber which acts as a mask. It resists application of paint and can later be peeled away. It is used to mask fine details, eg in a watercolour painting or illustration, because it can be applied quite delicately with a fine paintbrush.

masking tape *n*
A strong, opaque, adhesive paper tape which can be used directly as a mask in order to obtain a straight edge around an area of paint, or can be used to anchor loose masking materials, eg paper masks.

mass *n*
1 A fundamental shape or cohesive group of elements in a composition, eg in painting, the basic masses may consist of a central group of figures and the surrounding elements such as landscape or architectural forms, or the general distribution of

light and shade as related to other features of the composition.
2 Specifically in relation to sculpture, mass may refer to the actual substance and weight of the sculpture material.

mass tone *n*
The colour effect of a pigment when spread as a thick, opaque layer at full strength and viewed with light reflecting from the surface.
Compare UNDERTONE.

master *n*
1 A basic form from which a mould or pattern is made.
2 The mould or pattern used for reproducing a particular form.
3 In medieval times, a practising artist who was a member of a guild and in charge of a studio or workshop in which trainees and assistants were employed to help carry out the artist's commissions.

masterpiece *n*
1 A work of art judged by common consent to be of outstanding quality.
2 Originally, the work presented as a demonstration of skill by an artist applying for membership of a medieval guild. Literally, it was a test piece by which the artist could become known as a master of a particular art or craft.

mastic *n*
A natural resin obtained from *Pistachia lentiscus*, a small tree native to countries of the Mediterranean coastline. It is a brittle yellow substance, marketed as roughly spherical or teardrop-shaped granules. It is soluble in alcohol or turpentine and is used as an ingredient in mediums and varnishes for oil painting.

mastic varnish *n*
A picture varnish used on oil paintings, made by dissolving mastic in turpentine.

mat *n*
1 A thin fabric made of glass fibres, used as reinforcement in resin or concrete sculptures. See CHOPPED STRAND MAT.
2 See MOUNT.

matière *n* (*Fr* material, substance)
1 A term used to refer to the actual physical material of which an art object is made, eg paint and canvas, clay, stone, paper and ink.
2 More specifically, the term is used to refer to the PAINT QUALITY in a finished painting.

matrix *n*
1 A mould or basic pattern from which a form is cast or shaped.
2 The binding element of a sculpture material which holds the other ingredients together.

matt *adj*
The quality of a surface which is dull, non-reflective or evenly textured, ie has no lustre or surface sheen.

matt glaze *n*
1 A ceramic glaze which has a dull surface after firing, deliberately induced by allowing an imbalance of one ingredient in the glaze or by introducing a substance known to cause this effect.
2 A liquid medium used as a diluent for acrylic paint or applied as a surface coating to an acrylic painting.

matting tool *n*
A metal hand tool with a specially shaped or textured tip, used to mark the surface of a metal object as part of a CHASING process.

maturing temperature *n*
The temperature at which a clay body or ceramic glaze being fired achieves the qualities required of it in terms of appearance and internal structure.

maul *n*
A wood carver's mallet, shaped from a single piece of wood.

maulstick *n*
See MAHLSTICK.

meander *n*
See FRET.

medium *n* **media** or **mediums** *pl*
1 The fluid constituent of a paint in which the pigment particles are suspended, which gives the paint its particular properties, eg oil, gum or emulsions of various types. See also BINDER, VEHICLE.
2 A fluid substance added to paint during the painting process to modify its handling properties. This may be the same as the medium used in making the paint or a different substance which contributes a particular property.
3 The technical method employed by an artist, eg etching, modelling, painting, carving.
4 The tools and materials necessary to a particular technical method.

medium relief *n*
1 A category of various types of sculpture in which forms project from a background plane by about half their natural proportional depth. Also called *mezzo rilievo* (*It*).
2 An individual sculpture conforming to this principle of composition. See also HIGH RELIEF, LOW RELIEF.

megilp, meguilp *n*
An oil painting medium consisting of mastic varnish mixed with linseed oil. This forms a thick, jelly-like compound which gives the paint a highly workable buttery consistency, but although at one time the medium was extremely popular it has been largely abandoned as it has proved to age badly, becoming brittle and discoloured with time.

melting point *n*
The temperature at which a solid material becomes liquid.

mesh *n*
The term used for any fine, woven fabric which is stretched across a rectangular framework to form a screen used in SCREENPRINTING. Originally the fabric was made of fine silk filaments but synthetic fibres are now commonly used and a variety of fabrics can be suitable, depending on the effect required.

mesh count *n*
The number of threads within a given area of a mesh. The relative fineness or coarseness of a mesh has a definite effect on the surface qualities of a print produced by the SCREENPRINTING process.

metal cut *n*
1 A method of engraving on metal, comparable to wood engraving, to produce an image which is printed from the relief areas of the metal plate; ie the engraved lines and textures show white in the finished print, whereas they would form a black image if printed from the intaglio.
2 A printed image produced by this method.

metalpoint *n*
1 A drawing instrument with a fine metal point, used to make line drawings on specially prepared paper. Gold, silver, lead or copper can be used to draw on paper coated with a slightly abrasive ground of white pigment. The metal deposits tiny particles on the ground and the image drawn with metalpoint is characteristically linear, subtly coloured and delicate.
2 The technique of drawing with this medium.

metamorphic rock *n*
Rock formed by changes in igneous and sedimentary rocks, caused by heat and chemical reactions arising from movement within the earth's crust. The category includes several substances traditionally favoured as stone carving materials, eg alabaster, marble, soapstone.

métier *n* (*Fr* trade, profession)
1 The particular discipline in which an artist specializes, eg carving, oil painting, drawing.
2 The particular subject area in which an artist specializes, eg landscape, portraiture, still life.

mezzo fresco *n*
A variation on the technique of FRESCO painting in which the top layer of plaster is allowed to dry out partially before colours are applied.

mezzo rilievo *n* (*It*)
MEDIUM RELIEF.

mezzotint *n*
1 An INTAGLIO PRINTING process which produces a tonal image. A metal plate is given a uniformly rough texture, worked over the whole plate surface by means of a ROCKER, a curved and serrated tool rocked back and forth systematically to make narrow indentations which throw up a rough burr. When the plate is prepared in this way it would hold ink across the whole surface and print as an even, velvety black. The image is created by smoothing out the texture in various degrees, using a scraper or burnisher, so that parts of the plate surface hold less ink and print as a range of greys: white areas occur where the metal is burnished completely smooth. The grainy texture gradually wears down in printing, limiting the number of perfect impressions that can be taken from a mezzotint plate.
2 A printed image produced by this process.

mineral painting *n*
See WATER-GLASS PAINTING.

miniature *n*
1 A highly detailed painting executed on a very small scale, commonly a portrait. The picture may be worked in tempera, watercolour, gouache or oils, traditionally on ivory, vellum or board.
2 A small, detailed painting forming part of the decorative illumination in a hand-written manuscript, often designed to fill the space inside a large capital letter.

mitre[1] *n*
A corner joint between two pieces of material made by cutting an angled plane at the end of each piece and bringing the planes face to face to form a right-angled section.

mitre[2] *vb*
To make a mitre. **mitred** *adj.*

mitre box, mitre clamp *n*
A device for cutting through sections of wood at an angle to form two components of a mitre joint. There are different versions of such devices, basically consisting of a framework which holds the material in a fixed position and a vertical guide which directs the cut of a saw at a required angle across the wood.

mixed media *n*
A broad categorization of works in which different types of materials are used, eg drawing media or collage combined with paint.

mixed technique *n*
The use in a single work of two or more painting media which require different techniques of application, eg oil glazes over TEMPERA underpainting.

mixing varnish *n*
A varnish used as an ingredient of an oil painting medium, eg when the paint is to be applied as a glaze of transparent colour.

mobile *n*
A sculpture which is supported at a fixed point, hanging or mounted, but is otherwise free to move in response to an air current or light touch. Typically, a mobile consists of flat shapes or lightweight solids suspended on wires or fixed to flexible rods. The elements are carefully planned to maintain a balanced construction while remaining mobile.

model[1] *n*
1 A sculpture made by a process of modelling.
2 A sculpture or other three-dimensional object used as the positive form from which a MOULD is made.
3 A person who poses for an artist as the subject of a particular work, eg a portrait, figure painting or sculpture.

model[2] *vb*
1 To make a three-dimensional form by modelling.
2 To create the appearance of a solid form in a painted or drawn image. **modelled** *adj.*

modelling *n*

1 The process of making a sculpture by shaping a form in a malleable material. It is an additive process: a small form may be made by manipulating pieces of the material into the required shape; larger works are generally built up over a rigid skeletal structure by gradual addition of the modelling material. Clay and wax are the materials most commonly used because they can be kept plastic over an extended period of work, but fluid and paste-like substances, eg wet plaster, concrete or resin, can also be modelled by various techniques though their natural hardening processes limit the scope of the work.
2 The effect of manipulating a malleable material, eg as seen in the volumes and surface textures of a sculpture made by modelling.
3 The method of representing three-dimensional form in a two-dimensional image using tonal gradation and contrast of light and shade to suggest the solidity and depth of a figure or object.
4 The effect of tonal gradation or contrast used to represent solid form on a flat surface.

modelling clay *n*

1 Any form of natural clay or mixture of clays used as a modelling material.
2 The term is also used of some synthetic compounds marketed as modelling materials which have a reasonable period of plasticity and harden without firing.

modelling paste *n*

A thick polymer medium added to acrylic paints to provide a heavy, malleable consistency for IMPASTO effects.

modelling stand *n*

A turntable mounted on a tripod, which supports a modelled sculpture while it is being worked. The turntable allows easy access to any part of the work and the stand can usually be adjusted in height.

modelling tool *n*

Any of a number of wooden, plastic or metal tools used to shape a modelling material. Common forms include spatulas, knives, narrow-shafted tools with square, pointed or serrated tips, and loops of wire in various shapes set in wooden handles.

modello *n* (*It* model, pattern)

A small painting or sculpture made as the proposed model for a large work to be commissioned. It is shown to the prospective client or patron for approval before work begins on the full-scale version.

modular *adj*
A term used to describe a construction or design which is built up from a number of identical or similar components.

Monastral colours *n pl*
See PHTHALOCYANINE COLOURS.

monochrome[1] *n*
1 A work, particularly a drawing, painting or print, in a single colour or tones of one colour. See also CAMAIEU, GRISAILLE.
2 The range of tones of a single colour, from the palest tint to the darkest shade.
3 Black and white and the range of dark, medium and light greys between the two.

monochrome[2] *adj*
The description of an image worked in a single colour or tones of one colour. Compare POLYCHROME.

monolith *n*
A statue, architectural column or freestanding pillar carved from a single block of stone.

monoprint *n*
1 See MONOTYPE.
2 More broadly, any single, unique image taken by impressing one surface on another which has been treated with ink, paint or dye.

monotype *n*
A single impression taken from a painting or design worked in oil colour or printing ink on a flat metal plate or glass sheet. With a metal plate, the image can be transferred by placing a sheet of paper over the plate and running both through a press. Alternatively, or if glass is used, the paper can be burnished on the back or pressed down evenly with a roller. As the plate itself is not treated in any way that defines a specific image and the ink or paint is transferred directly to the paper, it is impossible to repeat the impression precisely. Also called monoprint.

montage *n* (*Ge* fixing up)
1 The technique of forming a composite design or image by mounting a collection of objects or images on a common background.
2 An individual work made in this way. See also PHOTOMONTAGE.

monumental *adj*
In the context of art history and theory, a term used to describe

any work which, regardless of scale, has qualities of stability and intrinsic significance which can be judged to transcend the immediate preoccupations of a particular style or period.

mordant *n*
1 The acid solution used in ETCHING.
2 The adhesive ground on which gold leaf is laid in GILDING.

mosaic *n*
1 The technique of decorating a surface with small pieces of coloured stone, glass or ceramic material (tesserae) set in a layer of cement. This is typically a form of architectural decoration – on walls, floors, ceilings and also on less expansive features – and the design may form a picture or purely decorative pattern.
2 A picture or design formed in this way.
3 By extension, any basically flat picture or design created by piecing together small sections of material on an adhesive ground, eg paper, wood chips, shells etc.

motif *n*
1 A distinctive, dominant element in a composition.
2 A unit of design which is repeated to form a pattern or emphasize a theme.
3 The principal theme or subject matter of a work of art.

mould^1 *n*
1 A hollow or open form made by applying a liquid or plastic material to the surface of an object and allowing it to harden, then removing the object from the hardened shell. The interior of the mould is thus the reversed, or negative, form of the original object, ie recessed where the original form projects and vice versa. See also CASTING.
2 A hollow construction designed to have a specific interior form in which a solid shape can be cast by filling the construction with a liquid or plastic material which subsequently hardens.

mould^2 *vb*
To shape a material using a mould. **moulded** *adj.*

moulding *n*
1 The process of applying a plastic material to the interior form of a mould.
2 A decorative strip or edging forming ornamentation or finishing to an architectural feature, eg a length of carved wood or stone surrounding a door or window frame, or a section of modelled plaster fitting the angle between a wall and ceiling.
3 A length of wood decoratively shaped or carved on two sides,

which may be cut into sections forming the component parts of a picture FRAME.

mould-made paper *n*
A term used to categorize certain types of rag pulp. MACHINE-MADE PAPER.

mould making *n*
Any technique or process of making a MOULD. Commonly plaster, refractory compounds or synthetic resin or rubber materials are used to take a negative impression from a master form. See also COLD CURE RUBBER COMPOUND, LATEX, LOST PATTERN CASTING, LOST WAX PROCESS, SAND CASTING, SILICONE RUBBER, VINYL MOULDING COMPOUND.

mount[1] *n*
A sheet of inflexible material, usually a high quality paper board, used as a protective backing or surround for a picture. Mounts are used as a means of presentation and preservation of works on paper. The paper may be attached directly to the surface of the board, by means of a suitable adhesive, or attached to the back of the board behind a window opening cut to fit the image. A mount is cut larger than the picture to provide blank margins against which the image is clearly displayed, except in the case of DRY MOUNTING when the pictures adheres firmly and evenly to the board and can be trimmed down to the exact image area. A mount may be cut to size from a sheet of board or bought ready-cut to a standard size. Also called mat.

mount[2] *vb*
To attach a picture to a mount. **mounted** *adj*.

mount board *n*
A stiff, relatively thick paper board used to make a picture mount, commonly consisting of laminated paper sheets forming the basic thickness, faced with a high-quality white or coloured paper. See also MUSEUM BOARD.

muffle *n*
An internal chamber in a kiln, made from a refractory material and designed to protect the ware being fired from direct contact with the source of heat or the gases produced in the kiln.

muller *n*
A heavy stone or glass implement used for grinding pigments and oils on a correspondingly heavy flat stone or glass slab. The muller is bulbous in shape, with a flat or slightly convex base which forms the grinding face. The upper section swells slightly above a tapered neck, providing a hand grip.

multiple *n*
A work produced as art but designed in materials and processes suitable for mass reproduction, which can therefore potentially be reproduced in exactly the same form in unlimited numbers.

multiple line graver *n*
An engraving tool designed to cut fine, close parallel lines. It is shaped like a BURIN, but the straight underside of the shaft is grooved, ending in a cutting edge divided into a number of separate sharp teeth. Also called lining tool.

mural *n*
1 A painting or pictorial image executed directly on the surface of a wall.
2 A large-scale painting on canvas or panel designed to be fixed permanently to a wall.

museum board *n*
A board made from rag pulp used for mounting and preservation of drawings, prints, or other works on paper. Wood-pulp board contains acid which causes deterioration of paper kept in close contact with it: the rag pulp board is acid-free.

n

narrative painting *n*
1 The category of figurative paintings in which the image describes a particular scene or incident or tells a story. The picture may describe an invented incident, a literary text, a well-known public event or a traditional myth or legend.
2 An individual painting of this type.

natch *n*
See KEY.

naturalism *n*
The realistic representation of objects, figures and natural forms as they actually appear, without theoretical or symbolic interpretation.

nature morte *n (Fr)*
STILL LIFE.

needle *n*
1 A drawing instrument used in intaglio printing processes. See DRYPOINT NEEDLE, ETCHING NEEDLE.
2 A component of an AIRBRUSH, a narrow, finely pointed rod of metal set inside the shaft of the tool, which conducts the liquid medium from the reservoir to the tip of the airbrush.

needle file *n*
A fine, narrow file used for delicate shaping and finishing in various types of carving and metalwork. There are a number of different shapes, eg flat or rounded, triangular, lozenge-shaped or domed in section.

negative *n*
A MOULD taken from a fully-rounded or relief sculpture or decoration, which contains the reversed form of the original model.

negative space *n*
An area in a composition, either painting or sculpture, that surrounds or penetrates the main forms and thus contributes to the overall image without itself having positive form.

netsuke *n*
A miniature sculpture, carved in ivory, horn or wood, of an animal or figure. It is a traditional form of Japanese art serving as a personal ornament, eg a fastening attached to a belt, pouch or sash.

neutral colour *n*
1 As a general term, this describes any of a range of mixed greys and beiges which have no distinctive tendency towards a particular hue. Black and white are also sometimes described as neutral colours.
2 A colour in a painting which serves as a middle tone setting off the more active visual impression of adjacent or superimposed colours.

newsprint *n*
An inexpensive, lightweight paper made from wood pulp, useful for rough sketches or proofs but not suitable for finished work.

niello *n* (*It* from *Lat nigellus* = black)
1 A metalwork technique for decorating gold or silver plate. A design is engraved on the metal and the incised lines are filled with a black alloy compounded of silver, lead, copper and sulphur. The piece is heated to melt and fuse the alloy in the lines. The surface is then polished so the design shows clearly against the burnished metal surface.

2 The black alloy used to fill the incisions in work of this kind.
3 A metal object bearing this type of decoration.

nimbus *n* (*Lat* cloud)
See HALO.

non-figurative *adj*
See NON-OBJECTIVE.

non-objective *adj*
The description of art which makes no reference to actual things seen, used of purely abstract and self-referential forms of art. The terms non-figurative and non-representational also refer to abstract forms and images, but may be used in a less restricted sense, ie of motifs or compositions abstracted from existing or observed forms.

non-representational *adj*
See NON-OBJECTIVE.

not *n*
A category of papers with a relatively coarse or open surface texture. The term is a trade abbreviation for 'not hot-pressed'.

O

objective *adj*
The description of an image contrived as an accurate representation of something directly observed, with no comment, elaboration or selectivity.

objet trouvé *n* (*Fr*)
FOUND OBJECT.

ochre *n*
Commonly called yellow ochre, a natural earth or soft rock coloured with iron oxides, processed into pigments of the colour range yellow, light brown and red-brown. These are reliable and permanent pigments, relatively opaque and suitable for all painting media.

oeuvre *n* (*Fr*)
All the works executed by an individual artist, ie all major works and sketches, prints, models etc produced during the artist's working life.

offset *n*
The term for any method of transferring an image from one surface to another via a third, intermediary surface. This is the basic principle by which a COUNTERPROOF is taken, but its main use is in OFFSET LITHOGRAPHY, a process applied to making artists' original prints and extensively used as a commercial reproduction process.

offset lithography *n*
The method of printing from a prepared lithographic plate on a specially designed press equipped with a heavy cylinder coated with a thick layer of rubber, which mechanically travels the full length of a flat metal bed. The inked plate is secured on one half of the bed and a sheet of paper on the other half. The cylinder travels over the plate, the rubber coating picking up an impression of the inked image: it then travels back across the bed and lays down the image on the paper as it passes. In this way the print on paper is the same way round as the image on the plate rather than reversed, as is the case when the impression is made by direct contact between plate and paper.

oil-based *adj*
The description of a paint made with an oil VEHICLE, which is mixed and diluted with oil or spirit.

oiling out *n*
The process of rubbing a small amount of linseed oil into areas of an oil painting that have become dull in drying. This may be done to add a temporary sheen to the colours or to moisten the surface for a further application of paint. At one time it was practised as an alternative to varnishing, but excessive use of oil in this way tends to accelerate darkening and discolouring of the picture surface.

oil paint *n*
Paint consisting of pigment evenly dispersed in a drying oil, commonly linseed oil. The oil is the VEHICLE and BINDER for the pigments and the paint dries to a tough, flexible film adhering firmly to the support, in which the colours retain their richness. Oil paints are available commercially in a wide range of colours, packaged in tubes or tins.

oil pastel *n*
A drawing medium consisting of pigment mixed with an oil binder and compressed into stick form. An oil pastel is moist and more adhesive than a PASTEL made with gum binder and the colours can be spread and blended with a brush soaked in turpentine.

oils *n pl*
abb OIL PAINTS.

oilstone *n*
A stone block used for sharpening and honing metal cutting tools, called oilstone because a layer of oil is laid on the stone to offset the friction caused by rubbing the tool on its surface. Various materials are used to make oilstones, including natural stones with high silica content and artificially produced blocks of SILICON CARBIDE.

oleograph *n*
A reproduction print simulating an oil painting, usually printed by lithography in oil colours on a textured support meant to imitate the appearance of canvas weave.

oleoresin *n*
1 A viscous liquid mixture of resin and essential oil exuded naturally from certain trees, particularly conifers. Oleoresins are not soluble in water but can be mixed with the various oils and solvents used commonly in painting. They are used as ingredients of mediums and varnishes. Their own oil content evaporates as they dry and it is mainly the resin content which remains in the paint or varnish film.
2 A liquid mixture of oil and resin produced as a synthetic combination.

once-fired *adj*
1 The term describing ceramic ware which has had only one firing to produce chemical changes in both body and glaze at the same time.
2 The term also describes the glaze applied to the unfired ceramic ware. See also RAW GLAZE.

one-piece mould *n*
A mould taken from a simple shape, having an interior form which is sufficiently smooth and open to allow both the original model and the subsequent cast to be easily and directly withdrawn.

on-glaze decoration *n*
Decoration applied to ceramic ware that has already been glazed and fired. A glaze mixture containing colouring agent and flux is painted over the existing glaze and fired at a low temperature to fuse it to the surface. Also called enamelling or over-glaze decoration.

opacity *n*
The condition or characteristic of a material which is opaque.

opaque *adj*
The description of a material which reflects rather than transmits light, ie is not transparent or translucent.

open bite *n*
A deep or shallow recess in the surface of an etching plate where a relatively broad area of the metal has been exposed to acid. Such an area holds less ink than a single line or hatched texture and prints as a grey tone. If the bite is deep, the edges hold more ink and print as a black line surrounding a grey area. See also RELIEF ETCHING.

opener, opening material *n*
A non-plastic material added to a clay body to improve its working qualities, speed drying and reduce shrinkage in drying. The material must be finely ground: grog and sand are commonly used.

open form *n*
A sculpture designed with extended forms which project into the surrounding space, or incorporating a considerable proportion of internal space penetrating the whole structure.
Compare CLOSED FORM.

optical mixing *n*
An effect produced by a technique of painting with small dabs of pure colour. Viewed from a distance, the colours merge into hues of different values, according to basic principles of colour mixing. Thus an area painted with red and yellow dabs appears orange; one painted with blue and yellow appears green. By adding appropriate colours in different proportions a complete range of hues can be obtained from only a few colours: theoretically only red, yellow and blue, the PRIMARY COLOURS are needed. Mixed hues of this type can appear more intense and pure than those obtained by mixing the paints before application, because there is no devaluation of the colours due to the interaction of the pigments and mediums used in the paint.

organic pigments *n pl*
The classification of the range of pigments derived from animal or vegetable sources, including natural extractions and synthetic organic materials manufactured from coal-tar and petroleum derivatives.

original print *n*
A print for which the artist has prepared the image directly in terms of the materials and processes of the particular printmaking technique, ie has etched the plate, cut the wood block etc, though the mechanical work of printing the image may be undertaken by

someone else. This is distinct from a print created entirely by a professional printer on behalf of the artist, after an original drawing or painting by the artist.

outline *n*
1 A line which defines quite simply the exterior shape of an object or form, without regard to its total volume or internal structure.
2 A drawing or sketch describing only the outlines of forms within the composition, ie showing the basic plan of the composition.

over-glaze decoration *n*
See ON-GLAZE DECORATION.

overpainting *n*
1 The practice of applying coloured glazes, SCUMBLES and additional detail over an UNDERPAINTING.
2 The paint layers applied over an underpainting.
3 More generally, any practice of applying fresh layers of colour over paint previously applied.

overprinting *n*
The process of printing one colour over another, eg from separate blocks or plates, to build up the image in a COLOUR PRINT. An overprinted colour may completely obliterate parts of the previous printing, or the ink may be mixed as relatively thin, transparent colour which allows the overprinting to create a third colour, effectively a mixture of the two actually printed.

oxgall *n*
A WETTING AGENT for watercolours, originally processed from animal gall bladders, now replaced by synthetic equivalents.

oxyacetylene torch *n*
An item of equipment designed to produce a narrow, intense flame which can be used in processes of FLAME-CUTTING, BRAZING or WELDING. Oxygen and acetylene are fed into the torch via separate hoses from sealed gas cylinders: they are combined by valve controls within the torch and directed through a narrow nozzle. The gas jet is ignited by means of a flint, never a naked flame, to produce a narrow jet of flame which can be precisely directed. In brazing, the flame is used to melt the alloy which joins two sections of metal, in welding to melt the metal components and facilitate direct fusion. A torch designed to cut sheet metal has a lever control which increases the oxygen jet, which cuts through the molten path made by the flame.

p

p, **pinx** *abb* **pinxit** *vb* (*Lat* has painted it)
1 Lettering which appears on a print accompanying the name of the artist who created the original image from which the print was derived.
2 On a painting, the term simply indicates that the name accompanying it is that of the painter.

pack *vb*
To fill a mould with casting material.

paddle *n*
A flat section of wood used to beat a mass of modelling clay, to remove air pockets and give the material a compact, workable texture.

paint[1] *n*
A substance consisting of pigment evenly dispersed in a liquid vehicle, which is applied to a surface as a fluid coating and dries to form a continuous film of colour. See ACRYLIC PAINT, ENCAUSTIC, GOUACHE, OIL PAINT, TEMPERA, WATERCOLOUR.

paint[2] *vb*
1 To use or apply a paint.
2 To create an image or design on a surface using paint. **painted** *adj*.

painter *n*
1 An artist skilled in any of the techniques of painting and whose main body of work consists of paintings.
2 The person responsible for execution of a particular painting.

painterly *adj*
1 A term used to describe any type of painting in which the image is broadly defined by masses of colour and tone, not sharply defined by line or contour. This quality was originally identified by the term *malerisch* (*Ge*). See also LINEAR.
2 The description of painting in which the painter's interest in the actual substance of the materials is evident, eg the colour and texture of the paint are exploited in their own right, not strictly as a means of conveying a particular image.

painting *n*
1 Any technique or process of applying paint to a surface to produce an image.
2 An image formed by the application of paint to a surface.

painting knife *n*
A short, flexible metal blade on an angled shank set in a wooden handle. It is used for applying paint directly to a support or scraping the paint surface. The angled shank keeps the handle clear of the paint when the blade is resting on the support. Painting knives are made in a variety of shapes, eg with a rounded or lozenge-shaped blade, and sizes. The smaller the blade, the less flexible it is.

paint quality *n*
The character of a finished painting in terms of the surface effect produced by the artist's skill in applying and manipulating the paint. The term refers to the technical quality of use of the materials and is distinct from the style or content of the image and from the actual substance of the materials themselves.

palette *n*
1 Any object or surface on which paints are laid out and mixed in the course of painting with any medium. The traditional form of oil painter's palette is an oval or rectangular wooden board with a finger and thumb grip cut in one side. The range of palettes available includes different forms made of metal, plastic, ceramic material and paper, and some artists prefer to use simply a flat slab of glass or stone. See also DISPOSABLE PALETTES, WELL PALETTE.
2 The range of colours used in a single painting, ie as laid out on the palette.
3 The range of colours typically used by a particular artist or school of artists.

palette cup *n*
See DIPPER.

palette knife *n*
A flexible, spatulate metal blade set in a wooden handle, used for mixing paints on the palette and scraping paint from the palette or support. Palette knives are made in different sizes, with blades of different lengths and flexibility, some being relatively rigid while others are springy and resilient.

palimpsest *n*
A piece of parchment or vellum from which a hand-written text has been erased to make way for a new text. The surface is

scraped to remove the original writing and POUNCED to return it to a suitable condition for use.

panel *n*
Any rigid support for painting, traditionally a thick piece of seasoned timber but now including various types of composition board, eg chipboard or hardboard, properly strengthened as necessary. A panel, like canvas, requires an appropriate ground to give the surface suitable qualities for application of paint. The term also broadly includes other rigid materials, eg sheet metal or plastic, when used as painting supports.

panorama *n*
1 A large-scale painting, usually a landscape or townscape, arranged around the interior of a room, so the spectator is surrounded by the painting and can see it as a continuous view. **2** A large- or smaller-scale painting of this type curved around a cylindrical drum, so the spectator follows a continuous view around the drum.

pantograph *n*
A drawing aid used for copying, enlarging or reducing a drawing on a consistent scale. It consists of hinged arms of wood or plastic crossed to form a parallelogram at the centre. The framework can be extended or contracted and fixed in a particular arrangement. The bottom end of one arm is extended and forms a pivotal point. The bottom corner of the parallelogram and a second extended arm can be fitted with either a tracing point or a pencil. When the tracing point is moved over the original image, the pencil repeats the drawing on a smaller or larger scale, according to whether the inner or outer arm carries the pencil.

paper *n*
A range of materials in thin sheet form made from the cellulose fibres found in plant material. In simple terms, paper is made by shredding wood, linen rags or other suitable fibrous vegetable matter and mixing the fibres with water to make a liquid pulp, which is then spread on a wire mesh screen, drained and pressed. There are various ways of processing the pulp or the pressed material to create different qualities of weight, thickness, texture, colour and surface finish. See also BOARD, CARTRIDGE PAPER, HANDMADE PAPER, INGRES PAPER, LAID PAPER, MACHINE-MADE PAPER, PASTEL PAPER, RAG PAPER, WATERCOLOUR PAPER, WOVE PAPER.

paper sculpture *n*
1 The technique of creating a three-dimensional form using only paper, which may be cut, curled, curved, folded or rolled into various forms.

2 An individual sculpture made entirely of paper.

papier mâché *n* (*Fr* chewed paper)
A material used for making small sculptures and ornamental objects, basically consisting of shredded paper soaked in a liquid glue or paste. The composition can be varied, depending upon requirements, by the addition of chalk, sand or other filler to give tone and bulk. The wet paper pulp is pressed into or around a mould or used as a modelling material. It dries hard and an object made from it is relatively lightweight and durable. The surface can be sanded, painted and varnished.

papiers collés *n pl* (*Fr* glued papers)
1 A composition made entirely of torn or cut pieces of paper – plain, coloured, textured, printed with images or text – glued to a support. It is a form of COLLAGE but, specifically, only paper is used to form the image.
2 The papers used to make such a composition.

parchment *n*
A writing material prepared from the inner layer of a split sheepskin, a traditional support for hand-written manuscripts and illuminated texts. The skin is soaked in lime, scraped, stretched and dried. It is then degreased and shaved to produce a suitable writing surface. As compared to calfskin VELLUM, parchment is tougher and has a more resistant surface, though it is thinner because made from a split skin.

parergon *n*
An area of detail in a painting showing a subject subordinate to the main theme of the work, eg a still life on a table or a glimpse of landscape seen through a window. It may be included to enliven the image, to provide a demonstration of technical skill, or as an oblique commentary, symbolically expressed, on the main focus of interest.

parting agent *n*
A substance applied to the surface of one material to prevent another material from adhering to it, eg a coating painted over the interior of a mould so the material cast into it can be easily removed when it has hardened. Substances commonly used are soft soap, clay wash, shellac, wax; dry agents such as talc or graphite; or specially formulated agents such as those produced for use with casting resins.
Also called release agent or separator.

passage *n*
1 A distinctive area in a work of art, particularly a painting,

notable for the subject matter, technique or a formal element such as tone or colour.
2 An area of transition in a painting between one colour or tone and another.

paste¹ *n*
1 A water-based starch adhesive of a thick, fluid consistency. The simplest form is a basic flour and water mixture, but various ingredients are used and there are a number of proprietary brands. Paste can be used as an adhesive to bond materials such as paper and board and also as a medium for water-based paints.
2 More generally, any moist, viscous fluid or malleable material that can be used as a binder or adhesive.
3 The term is also used specifically of clay bodies prepared for manufacture of porcelain and bone china. In fact, a paste is differentiated from other bodies by its relatively low clay content, 40 per cent or less. See HARD PASTE, SOFT PASTE.

paste² *vb*
1 To apply a paste.
2 To bond materials using a paste.

pasteboard *n*
A stiff board made from two or more layers of paper pasted together. The sheets may be compressed while still damp and pulpy or put together in a dry state. The material has various uses, eg as the basic component of ACADEMY BOARD.

pastel *n*
A drawing medium consisting of pigment mixed with a gum binder, rolled or compressed into stick form. When applied to a support the pastel crumbles, depositing powdery colour on the surface. The pigment is unstable in this form and a finished work in pastel must be sealed with a fixative or protected under glass. The colours can be very brilliant but it is difficult to control tonal gradation by blending, so pastels are available in a wide range of pure hues, tints and shades, and in hard, medium and soft grades. Some pastels are water-soluble and can be worked into washes with a brush wetted with clean water.

pastel painting *n*
The term conventionally used for a work executed in pastel or the technique of working in pastels. Although a drawing medium in respect of its stick form and dry application, pastel has traditionally been associated with painting because of the rich colour effects and the dependence on mass as well as line in composition.

pastel paper *n*
A category of papers suitable as supports for work in chalk, crayon or pastel, generally made with a high content of rag pulp and a noticeable surface tooth. The papers are available in white and a range of colours.

pastel pencil *n*
A thin stick of pastel encased in wood.

pastiche *n*
1 A work by one artist composed of typical motifs borrowed from the work of another, usually well-known, artist and correspondingly carried out in the appropriate style and technique. It may be made merely as an imitation of the original artist's work or as a fake, with intent to pass it off as authentic.
2 A work by one artist in the style of another artist, acknowledged as such.

pastoral *n*
A type of landscape painting in which the landscape is represented in an idealized view and populated with mythical or idealized figures. Such a work is often based on a literary source, eg a poem or fable.

pastose *adj*
The description of paint which is thickly applied. See IMPASTO.

pâte dure *n* (*Fr*)
HARD PASTE.

pâte sur pâte *n* (*Fr* paste on paste)
A method of building up low relief decoration on ceramic ware by applying successive coatings of slip with a brush to model a shallow form. This technique can also be applied to making a FLATTENED RELIEF.

pâte tendre *n* (*Fr*)
SOFT PASTE.

patina *n*
1 A surface coating that forms on copper and bronze, also other alloys of copper, due to age and exposure to varying atmospheric conditions, including dampness above or below ground. The coating, which may be a thin film or thick incrustation, is caused by oxidation of the metal. It is usually green or brown, the colour being dependent on the proportion of other metals combined with copper in the alloy. A patina is considered to enhance the aesthetic value of certain types of metal sculpture and may be artificially induced. See also PATINATION.

2 By extension, variations of colour and texture in any surface, due to ageing or weathering of the material.

patination *n*
A general term referring to various techniques of creating a patina by artificial means. Commonly these consist of applying corrosive chemicals to a metal surface, but in the broadest sense the term may refer to any means of simulating a patina, eg by painting a surface.

pattern *n*
1 An arrangement of lines, shapes, colours or motifs.
2 A solid, hollow or flat shape used to determine the form of an object, which may allow any number of objects to be shaped in the same form by a repeated process.

pedestal *n*
1 A solid block of material or sturdy construction forming a base which supports a sculpture or decorative object.
2 The base of a COLUMN.

pegmatite *n*
See CHINA STONE.

peinture à l'essence *n* (*Fr* painting with a diluent)
A technique of oil painting in which much of the oil medium is extracted from the paint, soaked up on blotting paper or a similar absorbent material, and the colours are then heavily diluted with turpentine.

pellicle *n*
A fine skin or surface film, a term used of the skin that forms on oil paint as it dries.

pen *n*
A tool used for writing or drawing with a liquid medium, usually ink. The drawing tip is shaped to produce a characteristic line or stroke in use and the tool incorporates somewhere a reservoir capable of retaining a certain amount of medium which is smoothly conducted to the tip. Traditionally, natural materials such as quills and reeds have been used to make pens. Modern pens commonly have the form of a specially shaped metal tip set in a wooden or plastic shaft which forms the handle, and the term also covers plastic casings fitted with a sealed reservoir of ink which is conducted to a felt or synthetic fibre tip.

pen and wash *n*
See LINE AND WASH.

pencil *n*
A drawing tool or instrument, conventionally a thin rod of graphite and clay mixture encased in wood. Pencils are graded according to hardness or softness; from 9H (hard) to 6B (soft). The softest grades are almost pure graphite: in harder grades an increasing proportion of clay controls the texture. The actual drawing material is commonly known as 'lead', from black lead, an alternative name for graphite. The term pencil covers a variety of drawing instruments in which the lead may be housed in an adjustable metal or plastic casing, as well as the common wood form. See also CHARCOAL PENCIL, COLOURED PENCIL, PASTEL PENCIL.

pendant *n*
One of a pair of paintings or sculptures conceived and executed as related works and intended to be displayed together.

pentimento *n* **pentimenti** *pl* (*It* repentance)
Part of an original image that was subsequently overpainted which later begins to show through the surface layers of paint. This sometimes occurs in oil paintings when the paint becomes transparent due to a physical change in the linseed oil film as it ages. Pentimento is evidence of a deliberate alteration made by the artist in the course of the work, hence the idea of repentance, or second thoughts.

performance art *n*
A form of art in which an activity personally performed or organized and directed by the artist constitutes the work of art, often subsequently represented by photographs, film or videotape of the actual event. This covers a wide range of activities both simple and complex, some spontaneously improvised, others highly planned and theatrical.

permanence *n*
The quality of a permanent pigment.

permanent pigment *n*
A pigment which, in practical terms, shows no deterioration of colour under exposure to normal light and atmospheric conditions, in combination with other materials in a paint or ink, or in interaction with other colours.

perspective *n*
A system of representing three-dimensional form, space and distance on a flat surface. The basic principle of various forms of linear perspective, ie geometric frameworks for depicting forms, is that receding parallel lines appear to converge. In practical terms, the framework is established with a horizon line running

across the width of the picture surface and a vertical line crossing it, often centrally placed, which represent the artist's viewpoint. From a central viewpoint, the intersection of these lines acts as the vanishing point at which all lines running parallel and at right angles to the picture plane are made to converge. Further development of this basic arrangement may include other vanishing points on the horizon, governing different areas of the image, or, with increasing complexity, other points which do not fall on the horizon line itself. Certain forms of technical drawing demand highly structured perspectival systems which cover different ways of logically presenting a depiction of three-dimensional form: in pictorial composition, artists may employ any of a number of variations on the simple, basic principle of convergence. See also ATMOSPHERIC PERSPECTIVE.

Perspex *n*
A tradename often used as a general term for synthetic plastics in solid block or sheet form, especially clear, colourless plastic.

petuntse, petuntze *n*
The anglicized form of the Chinese name for CHINA STONE, an ingredient of porcelain.

photomontage *n*
1 The technique of creating a pictorial image by cutting out figures, objects, background features etc from different photographs and assembling them on a single sheet of paper or board. The technique is often used to create a fantasy image or pictorial message and a seamless image can be achieved by photographing the assembled composition and reproducing it as a single print.
2 An individual work made in this way.

phthalocyanine colours *n pl*
Synthetic organic pigments in the colour range blue, blue-green and green, manufactured from complex chemical compounds. The colours are permanent, relatively transparent but extremely intense. Certain colours in the range are also marketed under the name of Monastral colours.

pick *n*
A stone-carving hammer with an elongated metal head shaped to a point on either side, used to split away broad sections of stone from the block.

pictogram, pictograph n
1 A simple pictorial element representing a particular object or activity.

2 A symbol of this type used as an element of language, eg as a form of picture writing.

pictorial *adj*
The descriptive term for something which is visually expressed as an image, motif or symbol in two dimensions. The term extends to various forms of relief sculpture in which elements of the composition are arranged within a shallow range of actual depth.

picture *n*
A painting, drawing or other representation in two-dimensions. The term is more commonly used of figurative than abstract works, but is not strictly limited in this way.

picture plane *n*
The assumed vertical plane in relation to which the various elements of a painting are assembled. It corresponds to the actual surface of the support, but is conceptual rather than actual, being central to the principles of PERSPECTIVE. In illusionistic painting, for example, figures can be judged to recede from the picture plane or stand within the plane, sometimes seeming to gesture from it towards the viewer.

picturesque¹ *n*
A form of landscape painting in which elements of landscape and architecture are deliberately arranged in an irregular and apparently disordered composition.

picturesque² *adj*
A descriptive term generally applied to styles of painting in which a subject is presented in a particularly colourful and attractive form.

picture varnish *n*
A varnish used as the final protective surface coating for a finished painting.

piece mould *n*
A mould made up in several sections so it can be taken apart without damage to the form inside, reassembled for casting and then taken apart again, so a number of casts can be made from the mould. It can be formed from any suitable medium that can be applied as a liquid or paste and left to set hard: commonly the material is plaster of Paris. The plaster is applied to one section of the model and allowed to set: the edges are trimmed and a KEY is cut in the seam edge, which is coated with a PARTING AGENT before a second section is cast against it. This process continues until the model is completely encased in the mould. An outer case is usually also made in which the pieces of the mould can be

reassembled for subsequent castings. A complex form can be cast in a piece mould because the sections can be designed to accomodate UNDERCUTS in the original model.
Compare ONE-PIECE MOULD, WASTE MOULD.

pietà *n* (*It* pity)
A traditional image of Christian art in both painting and sculpture; a mourning figure of the Virgin Mary holding the crucified Christ in her lap.

pigment *n*
A finely ground, coloured powder that may be mixed with a liquid vehicle to make paint. A pigment is insoluble and is dispersed or suspended in the vehicle, though in some cases the substance is so fine that it appears to be dissolved. The term covers a range of natural and synthetic materials of various qualities: the important properties of a pigment are that the particles are of uniform size for even suspension, the capacity of its tinting strength, ie the amount of colour it imparts to the paint, its degree of permanence and inherent quality of opacity, translucence or transparency. Pigments are basic colouring agents also used to colour a variety of materials other than paint. See also INERT PIGMENT, INORGANIC PIGMENTS, ORGANIC PIGMENTS.

pinching *n*
A pottery technique for shaping a pot by hand. A ball of clay is held in one hand and the thumb of the other hand is pressed into the centre to form a hollow within the shape, thus making a small, crudely formed pot. The clay is then rhythmically turned and pinched to thin the walls and refine the shape of the pot.

pinch pot *n*
A ceramic pot formed by the technique of pinching. Also called thumb pot.

pinholing *n*
1 A defect in a ceramic glaze caused by gases escaping during firing, when tiny air pockets break and leave holes in the glaze surface.
2 More generally, a similar defect in any liquid coating intended to dry completely smooth, eg tiny holes in a GESSO ground caused by dust on the support.

pitcher *n*
A heavy stone carving chisel with a broad, bevelled edge, used in the early stages of roughing out a block.

plane *n*
1 A flat or level surface, eg of an object or material.

2 An apparent or imaginary surface within a two-dimensional image, on which any two points indicated at random can be joined by a straight line lying within the supposed surface.
3 A tool for shaving and smoothing the surface of wood. It has a flat base with an inset, angled blade and is pushed levelly across the material to shave off the surface layer.

plank-grain block *n*
A wood block used for making a WOODCUT, which is cut from plankwood timber so the grain of the wood runs along the surface used for printing. Also called side-grain block. See also END-GRAIN BLOCK.

plankwood *n*
A length of timber sawn from the trunk of a tree along the grain, ie in line with the natural direction of the fibres.

planography *n*
A term generally referring to methods of printing from a flat surface, as compared to INTAGLIO or RELIEF PRINTING. LITHOGRAPHY is the major process of this type. **planographic** *adj*.

plaster *n*
1 *abb* PLASTER OF PARIS.
2 The term is used generally for substances based on or similar in composition and behaviour to plaster of Paris.

plaster of Paris *n*
A sculpture material used for modelling, casting and mould making. It is made from gypsum, which is roasted to drive off moisture and ground into a fine white powder. For use, the plaster is dispersed in water to form a creamy liquid which subsequently sets hard. The name derives from the fact that gypsum was at one time extensively quarried in a particular area of Paris, but plaster is made from gypsum deposits worldwide.

plastic[1] *adj*
1 The term used to describe a malleable and relatively soft material which can be shaped into a particular form and will retain the shape, whether or not the material ultimately hardens and becomes rigid, in which case it is no longer described as plastic.
2 The descriptive term for a sculpture which is modelled rather than carved. See also GLYPTIC.

plastic[2] *n*
Any of a number of synthetic THERMOSETTING or THERMOPLASTIC materials which may be soft or rigid, generally

of dense, smooth and even texture, capable of being shaped and formed in a variety of ways. See ACRYLIC PLASTICS, EPOXY RESIN, EXPANDED POLYSTYRENE, POLYESTER RESIN, POLYSTYRENE, POLYVINYL ACETATE, POLYVINYL CHLORIDE.

plastic earth *n*
An alternative term which may be used in referring to any of the natural clays used in sculpture and ceramics.

plasticity *n*
1 The property of a material which is plastic.
2 The apparent quality of a painted image contrived to give an impression of solid form. See also MODELLING.

plasticizer *n*
1 Generally, any of a number of substances which may be added to a specific material, eg a synthetic plastic or rubber compound, to impart greater flexibility.
2 Specifically, any of various substances added to a paint or varnish to improve handling qualities or eliminate brittleness in the dried surface film. The particular character of the substance depends upon the composition of the paint.

plate *n*
1 In INTAGLIO PRINTING processes, a flat, rigid sheet of metal, typically copper, steel or zinc, with a smooth, polished upper surface which is engraved, etched or scratched to produce a recessed image which can be inked and printed.
2 A flat sheet of relatively thin zinc or aluminium on which a drawing is made in lithographic crayon and ink for printing by the process of LITHOGRAPHY. The upper surface is treated with a fine abrasive to produce an even, delicately grainy texture.

plate mark *n*
The outline of an etching or engraving plate indented in the paper on which an impression is taken. It is a particular feature of intaglio prints, as they are pulled on damp paper which is moulded over the plate as it passes through the press.

platen press *n*
A mechanical printing press for RELIEF PRINTING from wood or linoleum blocks. There are various kinds: all operate on the basic principle that the block is placed on a flat surface and covered with paper, which is then pressed firmly down over the block by another flat surface exerting pressure from above. In a typical form, the block and paper are arranged on a flat metal bed which is pushed underneath a heavy plate of thick metal, and this is pressed down by means of a screw or lever action.

plate oil *n*
A thickened linseed oil which is mixed with dry pigment to make ink used in INTAGLIO PRINTING.

plein air *n* (*Fr*)
See EN PLEIN AIR.

plinth *n*
1 A stone block or similarly solid structure on which a statue or other form of sculpture is displayed, particularly when associated with architecture.
2 The base of a COLUMN.

plique à jour *n* (*Fr* openwork fold)
An enamelling process in which wires or fine strips of metal are soldered together to form a design in outline. This is placed on a base of a material resistant to high temperatures: coloured enamels are dropped into the sections of the design and the whole piece is fired. The enamels fuse to the wires, but when cooled the whole piece can be lifted away from the base and is designed to be seen against the light, giving a stained-glass effect on a small scale.
Compare CLOISONNÉ ENAMELLING.

plug *n*
1 A small section of wood inserted in a hole cut in the surface of a wood block, to correct an error made in cutting the image for a WOODCUT or WOOD ENGRAVING. It is trimmed and finished level with the original surface.
2 See PLUG AND FEATHERS.

plug and feathers *n pl*
A device used to split a stone block, to remove a large section prior to carving or to trim the size of the block. The plug is a conical piece of metal which is inserted in a hole drilled in the block. A feather is a slender, tapered wedge of metal hooked at the top: two of these are inserted, one on either side of the plug. When driven into the stone they form an expanding wedge which splits the material down the grain. Several are placed in a row along the line where the stone is to be split.

plywood *n*
A laminated wooden board consisting of two or more thin sheets of wood glued together. The grain of each successive layer is set at right angles to that of the previous sheet.

pochade *n* (*Fr*)
A sketch in oils made out of doors as the model for a larger painting to be executed in the studio.

pochoir *n (Fr)*
STENCIL.

podium *n*
1 A raised platform constructed for a particular purpose, eg as a base for displaying a sculpture.
2 A continuous base supporting a line of architectural COLUMNS.

point *n*
A metal cutting tool used in stone carving. The cutting tip is faceted, roughly pyramidal in shape and ground to a sharp or slightly blunted point. It is used for roughing out a form to a stage where chisels can be used to refine the shapes. A heavy point is used initially to remove large pieces from the stone block, giving way to lighter tools as the cutting progresses towards the final shape.
Also called punch.

pointing *n*
A mechanical method of copying a modelled or carved sculpture by transferring measurements of its exact dimensions and proportions to a block of carving material which is cut into the form of the original, on the same or an enlarged scale. This is done by locating fixed points on the model corresponding to the major projections and recesses, then marking and drilling points on the block in precisely the same relation. The transitions of form between the points are assessed, measured and copied: the pointing procedure is continuously repeated as the carving is roughed out and gradually shaped in detail. This is an indirect carving process used primarily in stone carving to copy a MAQUETTE on a larger scale. It is no longer commonly used as techniques of DIRECT CARVING are generally preferred by modern sculptors.

polychrome *adj*
The description of any type of work executed in a variety of colours.

polychrome sculpture *n*
A sculpture in any material which is multi-coloured, whether through use of coloured materials or from surface colour applied to components or the completed sculpture. Early classical sculptures, such as carvings and casts, were traditionally painted in bright colours but gradually the convention arose of exploiting the surface qualities and colours of natural materials. More recently, the use of synthetic materials and paint finishes has revived interest in artificial colour as an element of sculptural form.

polyester resin *n*
A synthetic THERMOSETTING plastic resin commonly used as a sculpture material. It is obtained in liquid form and for use in CASTING and LAMINATION processes is mixed with chemical agents, an accelerator and a catalyst, which cause it to harden gradually. Various different types of resin are manufactured for particular purposes: fillers are added to the basic material to provide opacity and colour. When cured the material is relatively brittle and it is used in conjunction with GLASS FIBRE reinforcement.

polymer *n*
1 A synthetic compound consisting of large molecules formed by chemical combination of smaller molecular units in a repeated pattern.
2 A binder or emulsion used in paint manufacture which is a compound of this type.

polymer emulsion, polymer medium *n*
A synthetic emulsion used as a binder in ACRYLIC PAINT, as a diluent or medium added to the paint, or as a SIZE preparation applied to a support, depending upon the specific properties of the emulsion. A common type is a milky, slightly adhesive fluid which thins the paint and imparts a particular surface quality to the dried paint film.

polymer paint *n*
A paint manufactured with a binder which is chemically constructed as a polymer. See also ACRYLIC PAINT, POLYVINYL ACETATE.

polyptych *n*
A painting or relief sculpture worked on two or more panels, presented as a single unit or as companion pieces hinged together or mounted in a frame. As the terms DIPTYCH and TRIPTYCH are used specifically to refer to works of two and three panels respectively, it is often the case that the term polyptych is used to describe a work of more than three sections.

polystyrene *n*
A rigid, synthetic thermoplastic material available in sheet form, in various colours and thicknesses.

polyvinyl acetate *n*
A colourless, odourless, synthetic resin used in the manufacture of adhesives and paints. For artists' use it occurs as a binder in a certain form of polymer paints and is separately obtainable as a viscous, white, adhesive fluid which can be thinned with water and dries to a tough, flexible, transparent film. This is used as a

medium in polymer paints, as an adhesive or as a protective surface coating.
Commonly known by the abbreviation PVA.

polyvinyl chloride *n*
A synthetic thermoplastic material, widely used in the form of a flexible, coloured, transparent or opaque plastic sheeting. It is a useful covering material and is applied to the making of inflatable or soft sculptural constructions. Individual pieces can be joined by sewing, welding under heat or by the use of special adhesives.
Commonly known by the abbreviation PVC.

poppy oil *n*
A natural drying oil, very pale yellow in colour, pressed from the seed of the opium poppy (*Papaver somniferum*), used principally as a vehicle for light-coloured pigments. It has a slower drying rate than linseed oil but less tendency to yellow with age, though it may crack more easily.

porcelain *n*
Highly refined ceramic ware, originally produced in China. It is made from a mixture of china clay, china stone and flint and is fired at a high temperature. The finished material is hard, impermeable, white and translucent.

porphyry *n*
A form of granite which is dark in colour but coarse-grained and heavily embedded with large, light-coloured felspar crystals. It is used as a material for stone carving because the natural composition provides a characteristically decorative piebald surface which takes a high polish.

portcrayon *n (Fr)*
A hollow cylindrical holder, now usually made of plastic, in which a fragile drawing material such as chalk, charcoal, crayon or pastel, can be inserted to prevent it from crumbling and breaking in use. It may be a simple casing designed to fit a proprietary brand of crayon or fitted with an adjustable device at the tip which can be expanded or contracted to accommodate different materials.

portfolio *n*
1 A portable, flat case or other container in which works on paper or board, eg drawings, illustrations, prints, can be stored or transported. There are a number of different types, made of soft or rigid plastic, card or heavy board, secured with string ties, tapes or a zip. Some types contain clear plastic folders in which individual works can be stored and displayed. The range of sizes corresponds to standard paper sizes.

2 A selection of work representative of an artist's style and technical ability, ie a number of works which can be conveniently stored, transported and displayed in a portfolio.

Portland cement *n*
A heavy, grey cement, relatively slow-drying, which when cured resembles the texture and appearance of Portland stone.

Portland stone *n*
A granular limestone named for the area of south-west England where it is quarried. It can vary in colour, texture and resistance to weathering. There is a grey, close-grained type that is durable and responsive to carving processes and a buff-coloured type that is softer, coarser and rather less durable.

portrait *n*
1 An image in two or three dimensions representing an actual person, ie a likeness of a person. It may depict the head only or the head and any part of the body down to its full length. In paintings and drawings the face or figure is typically seen in a relatively close view, but the composition can be of any form decided by the artist.
2 The format of any picture in which the dimension of height exceeds width. The term derives from the fact that portrait paintings are commonly arranged within a vertical format. See also LANDSCAPE.

portrait bust *n*
A sculpture representing an actual person showing only the head and shoulders.

portrait head *n*
A sculpture representing an actual person, showing only the head.

portraiture *n*
The broad category, or genre, of works executed in any medium which are portraits.

positive *n*
A fully rounded or relief sculpture, whether carved, modelled, cast or constructed, used as the model from which a mould is made to reproduce the form as a cast.

poster paint *n*
A type of inexpensive GOUACHE, not generally used for work intended to be permanent. The paints consist of pigments cut with a relatively high proportion of filler, mixed with a gum binder. The colours are sold in fluid form in jars or as dry tablets.

potter *n*
A person skilled in the techniques of making POTTERY.

potter's wheel *n*
A circular platform mounted on a vertical shaft, designed to revolve consistently at any speed. It is either attached to a mechanical system which allows it to be foot-operated by the potter, or is powered by an electric motor. A mass of clay centred on the wheel can be shaped and hollowed into a perfectly symmetrical form. See also CENTRING, KICK WHEEL, THROWING.

pottery *n*
1 A general term for objects made of clay and fired to induce chemical changes which render the material hard and durable. The classification includes earthenware and stoneware, but porcelain is usually treated as a separate category. Commonly, the term is used to refer specifically to objects of a utilitarian nature, eg pots, cups, tiles, and is thus differentiated from the more general term ceramics, which includes clay sculptures and purely decorative items.
2 The techniques of shaping, decorating and firing such objects.
3 The place in which such objects are made, whether an individual artist's studio or a large-scale industrial complex.

pounce[1] *n*
1 A finely powdered material, eg chalk, charcoal, earth colour, used to make the outlines of a drawing in pouncing.
2 A finely powdered substance, eg pumice, sandarac, talc, used to prepare the surface of parchment or vellum.

pounce[2] *vb*
To carry out a process of pouncing. **pounced** *adj*.

pouncing *n*
1 The method of transferring the outline of a drawing or CARTOON to a fresh support by pricking holes along the drawn lines, laying the original drawing over the clean surface and forcing a fine coloured powder through the holes to mark the support beneath. Any pointed instrument can be used to prick the outlines: for large-scale cartoons a ROULETTE is a convenient tool. The powder can be applied directly to the paper and rubbed into the holes, or placed in a bag of fine fabric which is dabbed over the pricked lines, allowing a certain amount of the colour to pass through.
2 The method of preparing parchment or vellum to receive ink by rubbing the surface with a finely powdered substance which removes traces of grease from the material and leaves the surface smooth and evenly textured.

pouring *n*
A method of applying a ceramic glaze by pouring it over the outer surface of the ware to leave an even coating. The inside of a ceramic vessel can also be treated in this way: the glaze is poured in, swilled around the inner surface and poured out.

pouring gate *n*
The opening in a mould or INVESTMENT through which a casting material is poured, giving direct access to the RUNNER channels conducting the material into the interior of the mould. In the LOST WAX PROCESS of casting this is prepared by attaching a cup of wax to the wax rods forming the runners, all of which melt out when the mould is baked prior to casting.
Also called sprue.

pouring ring *n*
A circular band of metal attached to a long handle, used to carry a crucible full of molten metal in order to pour the metal into a mould.

powder colours *n pl*
Inexpensive paints in dry powder form consisting of pigment and filler, sometimes including powdered gum as a binder. They are mixed with water to form a fluid or paste medium, but are not generally of a standard useful in work intended to be permanent. See also DRY COLOUR.

powder gold *n*
A small cake of gold made by mixing real gold ground to a fine powder with a gum or gelatin binder. It is moistened with distilled water and can be applied with a brush or quill. Also called shell gold, because originally supplied in mussel shell containers. See also GILDING.

precious metal *n*
The term used of gold, platinum or silver, as distinct from all other metals which are known as base metals.

precious stone *n*
Any of the rare crystalline minerals – diamond, emerald, sapphire and ruby – highly valued for use in jewellery and other forms of highly crafted ornamentation. Semi-precious stones, eg amethyst, aquamarine, opal, topaz, are also highly prized but generally have a lesser value.

predella *n*
The bottom panel or base of an ALTARPIECE, typically wide but not high and painted or carved in a manner in keeping with the decoration applied to the main sections of the work.

press mould *n*
A plaster mould in which soft clay is compressed and formed into a specific shape. Strictly, it is a mould of two pieces and the plastic clay is squeezed between them to shape a profile on either side, but the term is also used to refer to open moulds in which clay is pressed and smoothed to produce FLATWARE.

press moulding, pressing *n*
The method of shaping clay in a PRESS MOULD.

primary clay *n*
Clay found naturally in its place of origin, in association with the rocks from which it is derived. China clay and some fireclays are of this type. Primary clays are characteristically refractory, lacking plasticity and light-coloured when fired. Also called residual clay.
Compare SECONDARY CLAY.

primary colours *n pl*
In colour theory as applied to painting, red, blue and yellow, which are theoretically pure colours. They cannot themselves be mixed from others but can be used in various combinations to mix all other hues. See also COLOUR CIRCLE, SECONDARY COLOURS.

prime *vb*
To apply a PRIMER. **primed** *adj*.

primer *n*
1 A fluid coating applied to a canvas or panel in preparation for painting, which dries to form a hard, even ground on which the paint is laid. The material used depends upon the type of paint to be applied: oil-based primer is used for oil painting, applied over a coating of SIZE which has sealed the surface of the support: proprietary acrylic primers are produced for use with acrylic paints. The primer supplies the required properties of the surface, eg brilliant whiteness, the right degree of absorbency and an even texture.
2 More generally, any coating applied to a surface which makes it receptive to a topcoat of paint or varnish.

priming *n*
1 The process of applying a primer.
2 The coating of primer laid over a canvas, panel or other material.

print[1] *n*
1 An image made indirectly by any process in which a surface

prepared to retain or transfer ink is pressed against another surface, usually paper, which receives the ink.
2 An image made by any mechanical process of transfer or reproduction, which can be repeated in the same form a number of times.

print[2] *vb*
To produce a print, by any method.

printing *n*
1 Any mechanical method of preparing an image on one surface and transferring it to another, eg by pressing paper against a plate, block, stone which bears an inked image.
2 The activity of producing a print from a prepared surface. See INTAGLIO PRINTING, PLANOGRAPHY, RELIEF PRINTING.

printmaking *n*
The term referring to techniques and processes of producing prints, when applied to original images created by artists rather than to commercial methods of reproduction. See DRYPOINT, ENGRAVING, ETCHING, LINOCUT, LITHOGRAPHY, MEZZOTINT, SCREENPRINTING, WOODCUT, WOOD ENGRAVING.

profile *n*
1 The shape of a MOULDING as seen in cross-section.
2 The outline or contour of a form, following the whole shape or representing one side of a perfectly symmetrical form.
3 In portraiture, a depiction of a head seen from a side view, showing the line of forehead, nose and chin.

profile perdu *n* (*Fr* lost profile)
The depiction of a head turned away from the viewer so it is seen almost from the back, with the face described only by the contour of cheek and jaw.

progressive proof *n*
One of a number of proofs pulled at different stages of work on a plate or block, which show the artist how the image has developed. Collectively, the proofs form a record of each different STATE.

proof[1] *n*
A print made at any stage of a printmaking process, enabling the artist to check progress of the image and plan the next stage of work, or try out a combination of ink, paper and printing method to test their suitability for printing of the final image. Proofs are basically taken for the artist's or printer's reference and are records of work in progress. The term is not strictly synonymous with the terms PRINT or IMPRESSION, although

prints designated ARTIST'S PROOF are a special case. See also PROGRESSIVE PROOF, TOUCHED PROOF, TRIAL PROOF, WORKING PROOF.

proof[2] *vb*
To pull a print at any stage of a printmaking process before the final stage of printing an EDITION. **proofed** *adj.*

proportion *n*
The dimensions and scale of various parts or components of an image or object in relation to each other and to the thing as a whole. **proportional, proportionate** *adj.*

provenance *n*
The documentary record of all known owners of a work of art, attributions given to an unsigned work, locations where the work has been kept, and so on. It is as far as possible a complete history of a single work, which can authenticate its value.

puddling *n*
A method of compacting wet concrete and eliminating air bubbles from the mixture by inserting a thick wooden rod vertically in the material and moving it up and down steadily until the mass is dense and evenly textured.

pugging *n*
The process of compacting clay in a pugmill.

pugmill *n*
A machine which processes clay to an even, compact consistency suitable for ceramics and pottery techniques. In the first section of the machine, blades chop and shred the clay, which is then passed through a vacuum chamber where air pockets are eliminated. Finally it is compressed and extruded as a continuous roll of material. Large machines are used industrially to process massive quantities of clay, but there are smaller versions of the pugmill suitable for studio use.

pull *vb*
1 To take a print from an inked block, plate or stone.
2 To shape a piece of clay by PULLING.

pulling *n*
1 The process of printing from an inked block, plate or stone, ie the actual manipulation of the press to produce the printed image.
2 A method of shaping clay by hand into an elongated form, eg a handle for a cup or jug. The clay is roughly pressed into a cylindrical or conical shape and one end is pulled gently between fingers and thumb, with a stroking motion that stretches the clay

into a narrow strip and models it with convex or concave faces. The strip is cut to the required length, bent into the shape of the handle and left to dry until leather-hard before it is attached to the object. See also LUTING.

pumice *n*
A porous volcanic rock used in block form as an ABRASIVE, or ground to powder as an abrasive, FILLER or POUNCE.

punch *n*
1 See POINT.
2 A hand tool with a shaped or textured tip used to emboss the surface of a material by the impact of the tool being driven against the surface.

putto *n* **putti** *pl* (*It* little boy)
A plump, usually naked and sometimes winged infant, often included as a symbolic or decorative element in Renaissance paintings and sculptures.

putty rubber *n*
See KNEADED ERASER.

PVA *n*
abb POLYVINYL ACETATE.

PVC *n*
abb POLYVINYL CHLORIDE.

pyramidal composition *n*
A form of composition in which the objects or figures represented as the main subject are arranged within a structure of triangular planes rising to a common apex. The basic format of the composition is roughly triangular.

pyrometer *n*
An instrument which measures the temperature within a kiln, recording the rise and fall during the firing process. It depends upon use of a thermocouple, two different metals joined together which produce an electric current when exposed to heat. The current activates a gauge on which the electrical activity is converted into a temperature scale.

pyrometric cone *n*
A cone made of ceramic material which is known to collapse at a given temperature. A group of cones, each with a different melting point, is used to indicate kiln temperatures at different stages of firing. The cones are positioned where they can be observed by means of a spyhole in the kiln and are seen to bend and collapse in sequence as the temperature rises.

q

quadratura *n* (*It*)
Illusionistic painting of interior architecture designed to give the impression that the space is open and continuous rather than enclosed by solid walls and ceiling. It typically depicts architectural features, figures and landscape with exaggerated foreshortening and perspective.

quadro-riportato *n* (*It* transferred picture)
A painting used as a ceiling decoration which is executed in the perspective that would be used if it were to be hung vertically on a wall, though in place it is necessarily angled or horizontal and seen from below.
Compare SOTTO IN SÙ.

quartz *n*
A hard, crystalline natural mineral, a constituent of many igneous and metamorphic rocks.

quenching *n*
The process of cooling a hot metal rapidly by immersing it in water, oil or brine. See also TEMPERING.

quill *n*
An implement for writing and drawing made from the large wing-feather of a bird, commonly taken from a goose, swan or turkey. The feather is stripped of its barbs, laying bare the hollow, slightly curved, tapering shaft. The thicker end of the shaft is trimmed and shaved at an oblique angle to form a pointed or squared tip. It is then a natural pen, with the hollow shaft acting as reservoir for the ink. The tip is split vertically to conduct ink freely to the point. The quill is the traditional tool for CALLIGRAPHY in western cultures.

quill brush *n*
A brush made by fitting hairs into the hollow tip of a QUILL, usually designed to form a flexible, pointed shape for fine writing and drawing.

quinacridone pigments *n pl*
Synthetic organic pigments in the colour range red, red-violet and violet, which are brilliant and lightfast in use.

quire *n*
The name given to a standard number of paper sheets, usually 25, but strictly a quire is one-twentieth of a REAM.

r

rabbitskin glue *n*
A glue made by boiling the skins of rabbits, available in solid form as tablet, granules or powder. The material is dissolved in hot water to render it into liquid glue, used as an adhesive or SIZE.

radial easel *n*
A sturdy wooden easel used mainly for studio work, consisting of vertical struts mounted on a low tripod of thick wood and crossed by a moveable horizontal section on which the painting rests. All parts of the easel are fastened with wing nuts and are adjustable to give various heights and angles, and the whole unit can be folded around the main vertical section for temporary storage when not in use.

rag paper *n*
A category of various types of paper made with pulp processed from linen rags, sometimes including a percentage of cotton fibres. A pure rag paper is stronger and more durable than one made from any other fibre. Some papers are made with a percentage of rag content, mixed with wood pulp or other vegetable fibres.

raised gold *n*
A traditional form of illumination, especially in manuscripts on vellum, in which layers of GESSO are applied to a letterform or ornament to model the shape in low relief and the gesso is then covered with gold leaf. The pattern of light and shade on the raised form enhances the brilliance of the gold.

raising *n*
The process of drawing up the walls of a clay pot being thrown on a wheel. When the form has been partially hollowed, the potter places one hand inside the pot and the other on the outside, then gently squeezes the clay and coaxes it upwards as the wheel rotates evenly.

raku *n*
A type of coarse, soft-glazed ceramic ware originally developed in Japan. The main characteristic of raku ware is that the glaze, usually a lead and borax mixture, is low-fired in a pre-heated kiln and cooled quickly, therefore the clay body used in making the ware contains a relatively high proportion of grog to make it coarse and open, with less tendency to shrink in firing and able to withstand the shock of sudden temperature changes.

rasp *n*
A coarse abrasive tool in the form of a flat metal bar covered with sharp, pyramidal teeth. The bar is shaped with a smooth shoulder at one end tapering into a handle.

raw clay *n*
Clay which has not been fired, also called green clay.

raw glaze *n*
1 A glaze applied to an unfired clay object so that only one firing effects the necessary changes in both body and glaze. Also called green glaze or once-fired glaze.
2 A glaze which contains no FRIT, ie no material which is already a compound of raw ingredients.

ready-made *n*
An everyday, manufactured item chosen by an artist for exhibition as a work of art. In effect, it is a comment on the role of the artist's intentions in making art, as distinct from the manipulative skill applied to traditional forms.

realism *n*
A term used of art which represents a subject with accuracy as regards appearances but also, particularly, implying that the subject matter is concerned with everyday events and social conditions rather than grand traditional or literary themes.

ream *n*
The name given to a standard number of paper sheets, usually 500 but sometimes 480 (short ream) or 516 (printer's ream).

rebate *n*
A narrow groove or recess cut along one edge of a wooden MOULDING used to make picture frames. In assembling a frame, the rebate forms the inner edge of the back of the frame and the glass, mount, picture and backing board fit within the recess and can be secured against the main thickness of the moulding.

recession *n*
In a figurative or illusionistic painting, the apparent depth, space and distance within the image, created by various devices of

FORESHORTENING or PERSPECTIVE, eg the diminished size of objects or figures apparently further away from the viewer, the loss of clarity or detail in a distant view, the contraction of forms depicted as at right angles to the picture plane.

red-figure *n*
A style of decoration applied to early Greek pottery, superseding BLACK-FIGURE painting, in which an image was painted in outline on a natural red clay object and the background area coloured solidly in black, interior details of the forms being added with finely painted black lines.

reduction firing *n*
The firing of ceramic ware in an atmosphere where the level of oxygen is deliberately reduced. This is used in the firing of certain types of stoneware to produce calculated effects on the surface of a clay body or glaze by returning a metal oxide in the material to a colour characteristic of the original metal.

reed pen *n*
A tool for drawing or writing made from a hollow reed or natural cane. The cylindrical reed is cut at an oblique angle to form a broad tip which is trimmed and shaved into a pointed or square-cut edge. The hollow material forms a natural reservoir for a small amount of ink which flows down to the drawing tip.

reflected colour *n*
See ACCIDENTAL COLOUR.

refractory *adj*
The description of a material that is capable of withstanding high temperatures without altering its physical composition.

register *n*
1 In any form of printing, the accurate alignment and overprinting of different elements or colours in the image when these are printed separately and successively.
2 In a pictorial composition or relief sculpture, a single section or tier of the image which is contained between two parallel GROUND LINES.

register marks *n pl*
Small marks, commonly fine crosses, drawn on the margins of each printing plate used to print a colour image. These marks are inked and printed with the image and form a check on accurate overprinting and alignment of colours; ie if the register marks correspond in successive printings, the whole image is accurately aligned.

registration *n*
Any method of ensuring that a printed image composed of separate and successive elements, eg the different colours combined to form a colour print, are accurately aligned and overprinted. This generally involves marking the position of a plate or block on the bed of a press and accurately positioning paper in relation to this for each print, then ensuring that subsequent blocks or plates are set in the precise position and again correspond to positioning of the paper. There are various processes of registration suited to different methods and working processes. In silkscreen, for example, guides are placed on the bed underneath the screen to show the position of the paper, and the silkscreen frame is locked into a particular position. In lithography, REGISTER MARKS are commonly used to check alignment.

release agent *n*
See PARTING AGENT.

relief *n*
1 An image which in some degree projects from a background plane, otherwise described as having a partly or wholly raised surface. See RELIEF PRINTING, RELIEF SCULPTURE.
2 The characteristic of an image in which there is an apparent rather than real projection, eg in a figurative painting in which tonal contrasts are used to imitate three-dimensional form, the image is said to be modelled in relief.

relief etching *n*
1 The process of RELIEF PRINTING from an etched plate, to take an impression of the raised surface area of the print, as opposed to the usual method of INTAGLIO PRINTING. An image is painted directly on the plate with STOPPING OUT VARNISH and the remaining exposed areas are deeply etched to leave a clearly defined relief image. The surface is then inked and printed. Also called ANASTATIC PRINTING.
2 A printed image obtained by this process.

relief printing *n*
The process of taking an inked impression from a design or image upstanding from a block of solid material, in which the areas not to be printed have been cut back to a lower level. The raised image corresponds to the original surface of the block. A print is taken by applying an even layer of ink to the raised surface, with a roller or dabber, covering the block with a sheet of paper and applying even pressure to the whole image area to transfer the ink from block to paper. See LINOCUT, WOODCUT,

WOOD ENGRAVING. See also CYLINDER PRESS, PLATEN PRESS, RELIEF ETCHING.

relief sculpture *n*
1 All types of sculpture in which the forms are developed in or on a flat plane surface. They are in some degree fixed to a background and can only be seen from certain viewpoints. In most types of relief sculpture, the forms project from the background and are categorized by the degree of projection. In figurative work there is a strong pictorial element which requires a complex ordering of spatial relationships to deal with the combination of illusionistic and actual depth. The forms may be carved, modelled or constructed: therefore the image may be achieved by cutting into a fixed plane surface or building up forms by the application of plastic or rigid materials. See FLATTENED RELIEF, HIGH RELIEF, LOW RELIEF, MEDIUM RELIEF, SUNKEN RELIEF.
2 An individual sculpture of this type.

relining *n*
The process of mounting a fragile or damaged canvas on a fresh fabric support. This is strictly more accurately referred to as LINING.

remarque *n*
A sketch made close to the edge of an etching plate to test the strength of the acid's action on the plate or to try out an idea for the final image. These tests may be proofed, but are trimmed off or burnished out before final printing of the plate.

rendering *n*
1 The manner in which an image is presented, ie the style and technique adopted by the artist in a particular work.
2 Specifically, a drawing or painting based on architectural plans, which shows how a building will look when completed, including the effect of its immediate surroundings.

replica *n*
Strictly, an exact imitation of a painting or sculpture made by or under supervision of the original artist. The term COPY is sometimes used with this meaning.
Compare FACSIMILE, REPRODUCTION, VARIANT.

repoussage *n* (*Fr* pushing back)
The technique of smoothing out an indentation in an intaglio printing plate, the result of scraping out an error or of accidental damage, by hammering the metal plate from behind to push the depression up to a level with the plate surface.

repoussé *n* (*Fr* pushed back)
A technique of forming a relief pattern or image in sheet metal by beating it from the back with hammers or punches, making concave shapes which emerge as projections on the right side of the sheet. Traditionally, the metal is supported on a thick layer of tarry compound which cushions the impact but yields as the projections are formed under the movement of the tools.

repoussoir *n* (from *Fr repousser* = to push back)
A figure or object in the foreground of a pictorial image, arranged in a form or position that leads the viewer's eye towards the centre of the picture. See also COULISSE.

representational *adj*
The description of an image or motif which is a realistic or recognizable depiction of the physical appearance of its subject.

reproduction *n*
A copy of a work of art made by a mechanical technique, such as casting, photography or printing. The term COPY is often loosely used to denote a reproduction rather than a handmade imitation.

reredos *n*
An ornamental screen placed above or behind the altar of a Christian church. It may be carved or painted, a tapestry or embroidered hanging, or metalwork decoration. The term is sometimes used as a synonym for ALTARPIECE.

reservoir *n*
In any tool designed for use with a liquid medium, eg pen, airbrush, spraygun, a receptacle or recess built into the tool which holds a quantity of liquid.

residual clay *n*
See PRIMARY CLAY.

resin *n*
1 A natural, transparent, solid substance which is a hardened secretion from any of various types of trees. A resin is insoluble in water but can be dissolved in alcohol, oil or turpentine. See also DAMAR, MASTIC.
2 Any of a number of synthetic polymers or thermosetting plastics variously used as ingredients of paints or varnishes or in various forms as sculpture materials. See also EPOXY RESIN, POLYESTER RESIN.

resist *n*
1 A wax or varnish material applied to parts of a surface to protect these areas when a liquid is applied to the whole surface. See ACID-RESIST, WAX RESIST.

2 A substance or material applied to a surface as a MASK, which can be removed without damage to the surface.
3 A method of using such a material in any appropriate process of creating an image.

restorer *n*
A person skilled in any of the techniques of restoring works of art.

restoring, restoration *n*
A particular aspect of the field of conservation of works of art, referring specifically to the techniques and processes involved in repairing or reconstructing works which have undergone deterioration of the original materials or have suffered actual damage. This includes processes such as repair of the support and ground of a painting, repainting a surface to fill gaps in an image, cleaning of a discoloured or darkened painting or remodelling of some part of a damaged sculpture.

restricted palette *n*
A relatively small range of paint colours chosen either to set the colour KEY of a painting or as the minimum useful range providing versatility in colour mixing.

retable *n*
1 A single decorated panel or a fixed frame in which a group of panels is mounted, set above or behind the altar of a Christian church.
2 A raised shelf behind an altar where ornaments are displayed.

retarder *n*
A substance added to paint to delay drying. Specially formulated liquids are available for use with proprietary brands of acrylic paint: in oil painting, oil of cloves traditionally serves this function.

retouching *n*
Any method or process of applying fresh paint to an existing painted image to enliven a dulled surface, repair damage to the paint film or modify the image in some way.

retouching varnish *n*
A varnish preparation used in oil painting, formulated to be applied in thin layers. It is used for moistening the surface of a painting before a further application of paint, or as a temporary protective varnish.

retreating colour *n*
A colour which the viewer perceives as apparently receding from a picture surface, by comparison with other hues and tones in the

painting. In general, cool, devalued and neutral colours tend to retreat by comparison with pure, intense or warm colours. This property can be used to contribute to an illusion of spatial depth in a painting. See also ADVANCING COLOUR, COOL COLOUR.

retrospective *n*
An exhibition showing an artist's life's work or a representative selection of it, or a body of work done over a period of years which shows progressive developments in style and form.

retroussage *n*
The technique of lifting ink in the lines and recesses of an intaglio printing plate to enrich the quality of the printed image. When the plate has been thoroughly inked and wiped, a piece of fine muslin is trailed lightly across the surface and this has the effect of drawing the ink fractionally over the edges of the intaglio, so the image is softened and darkened in the subsequent print.

riffler *n*
A metal abrasive tool consisting of a flat, round or faceted shaft shaped at either end into a small filing surface. The shaped ends may be curved, pointed, rounded, spatulate or squared and are covered in fine metal teeth. It is used for delicate shaping and finishing of a carving or similar work.

rilievo stiacciato *n* (*It*)
FLATTENED RELIEF.

ripsaw *n*
A long-bladed, hand-held saw with relatively broad, straight teeth, used to cut along the grain of wood.

riser *n*
An open channel through the thickness of a mould which allows gases to escape from the interior as a casting material is poured in. In the LOST WAX PROCESS of casting, a riser is made by attaching a wax rod to the original wax model. Risers are set at various points, clear of the RUNNERS and POURING GATE, and melt out when the fully prepared mould is baked prior to casting.

rocker *n*
A hand tool with a sturdy metal blade fashioned into a curved and serrated cutting edge, used to prepare a MEZZOTINT plate. The tool is held vertically with the centre of the cutting edge resting on the plate surface: it is then rocked to and fro on the curve of the blade to mark the plate. It is worked in many different directions across the plate to create a dense and uniform texture.

rodding *n*
The process of attaching wax rods to a wax model in preparation

for the LOST WAX PROCESS of casting, to form RUNNERS and RISERS within the mould.

rolling up *n*
The process of preparing a relief block or plate for printing, using a roller to lay an even coating of ink over the surface.

rollover *n*
The application of a second colour to an intaglio plate. When the intaglio has been inked and wiped, a roller is used to lay a coating of a different-coloured ink on the relief surface of the plate.

rosin *n*
A natural resin which is the residue left by the distillation of TURPENTINE from oleoresins extracted from pine trees. It is unsuitable as an ingredient of painting mediums and varnishes, but has various other uses, eg as an ingredient of etching grounds.
Also called colophony.

rough *n*
A category of papers which are not pressed in the finishing processes of manufacture and have a relatively coarse, open surface texture.

rough aquatint *n*
An etching technique which differs from the usual AQUATINT process in that resin is shaken onto the metal plate from a muslin bag or pepper-pot device so that it falls unevenly. When processed, areas of rough aquatint print as irregular tones and textures.

roughcast *adj*
The description of a layer of coarse plaster applied to a wall over the basic construction material, given a rough surface texture to provide a tooth for the adhesion of subsequent plaster layers. See FRESCO.

roughing out *n*
The process of cutting a block of carving material with relatively heavy, imprecise tools, gradually reducing the mass of material until it has the rough shape of the intended form and can be more precisely developed with finer tools.

roulette *n*
1 A hand-tool used in various intaglio printing processes to produce a regular pattern of dots in the surface of a metal plate. It consists of a small, toothed metal wheel or drum attached to a shaft in such a way that when the tool is pushed across the plate, the wheel rotates freely and the teeth impress regular indentations

in the metal. In etching, the tool is used to mark the etching ground rather than the plate itself.
2 A larger version of this tool used in POUNCING.

round *n*
A brush with long hairs or bristles arranged in a tight cluster and forming a pointed or bluntly curved tip.

roving *n*
A lightweight, loosely spun rope made of bonded glass fibres, used as reinforcement for synthetic resins used in CASTING and LAMINATION processes.

rubbing *n*
See FROTTAGE.

rubrication *n* (from *Lat rubrica* = red ochre)
The practice of writing important features in a hand-written manuscript with red ink, eg initial letters, dates, names, opening phrases or paragraphs, to differentiate from the main text written in black.

runner *n*
An open channel through the thickness of a mould by which the casting material flows into the interior of the mould. In the LOST WAX PROCESS of casting, a runner is made by attaching a wax rod to the original wax model. Runners are set at various points, gathered together into a POURING GATE, and melt out when the fully prepared mould is baked prior to casting. The same principle may be used in making a mould from a clay original, ie a cylinder of clay is attached to the model before a mould is constructed around it.

S

sable *n*
1 Red or black hairs taken from the tail fur of any of various small mammals, eg mink or marten, used to make high quality brushes.
2 A brush made of sable, used especially for watercolour painting.

safflower oil *n*
A natural drying oil, light yellow in colour, pressed from the seed

of the safflower plant (*Carthamus tinctorius*), used as a vehicle in oil paints.

saggar, sagger *n*
A box made of refractory clay in which ceramic ware being fired can be placed within the kiln for protection from direct contact with the source of heat, eg the flames of a gas-fired or solid-fuel kiln. This is particularly for use in a kiln which is not fitted with a MUFFLE.

salt glaze *n*
A glaze applied to ceramic ware by the simple method of throwing common salt into the kiln at the point in firing when the clay is reaching its maturing temperature. The salt is vaporized and its sodium combines with alumina and silica in the clay to form a glassy coating on the surface of the ware. The glaze gives an enriched, speckled appearance to the natural colour of the clay.

sandarac *n*
A brittle, yellow, natural resin extracted from a tree of the pine family (*Calitris quadrivalis*) native to north Africa. It has been variously used as an ingredient of oil mediums and varnishes but in commercial manufacture has been largely superseded by natural and synthetic equivalents.

sandbag *n*
1 A small leather cushion filled with sand on which a metal plate or wood block is supported while it is being engraved. The cushion, circular with firm, convex upper and lower faces, acts as a turntable on which the engraver can rotate the plate or block in cutting curved lines. Also called engraver's cushion.
2 A bag made of strong fabric and filled with sand, used as a prop or base to cushion a stone block during carving.

sand blasting *n*
A method of abrading the surface of a rigid material, eg glass, stone, by bombarding it with a pressurized spray of sand, or other fine abrasive. This is done by machine in order to achieve the necessary density and pressure and may be used as a cleaning or shaping process. Parts of the surface can be masked while others are abraded, to form an image in relief.

sand box *n*
A shallow box filled with a thick layer of sand on which a small stone is placed for carving. The sand base cushions the stone so it can absorb the impact of the cutting tools.

sand casting, sand moulding *n*
A method of casting in metal from a plaster original, using a mould of damp sand. Adjustable metal frames are used to contain the sand and the mould is built up in layers around the original model. The first frame is placed on a flat surface and filled with sand: the model is pressed into this bed and more sand is added, TAMPED firmly around the model and levelled with the top of the frame. The surface is dusted with a powder PARTING AGENT and a second frame is placed on top of the first and the process is repeated. When the layers of sand enclose half the form it is turned upside down, the completed section of the mould is removed and the other half of the form is treated in the same way. The original model is then removed and the mould is fully assembled: channels are cut through the sand to act as RUNNERS and RISERS and the molten metal is poured in. To make a hollow cast from a sand mould, a core of sand is made up and suspended within the open form at the centre of the mould.

sandstone *n*
A porous stone, sedimentary in origin, consisting primarily of fine silica and quartz grains bound together in a natural cementing material. Sandstones are durable, ranging from extremely hard stones with a high quartz content which tend to fracture in carving to softer, granular substances which can be freely carved. They vary in colour from grey, yellow or buff to red, brown, green or black.

sanguine *n*
1 A natural chalk with a rich, red-brown colour, derived from iron oxide in its composition, used as a drawing material.
2 The red-brown colour associated with this material.

saturation *n*
The vividness of a colour, ie its degree of intensity or purity.

saw *n*
1 A hand-held cutting tool consisting basically of a toothed metal blade set in a handle, used with a back-and-forth or up-and-down motion to cut through a solid material. See COPING SAW, CROSSCUT SAW, HACKSAW, RIPSAW.
2 A mechanical power-driven cutting tool consisting basically of a toothed metal blade set in heavy machinery. The machinery operates the blade in the particular motion required to cut through a solid material. See BANDSAW, CIRCULAR SAW, JIGSAW.

sc, sculp *abb* **sculpsit** *vb* (*Lat* has carved it)
1 Lettering which appears on a print accompanying the name of

the engraver, as distinct from the artist responsible for the original image.
2 On a sculpture, the term indicates that the name accompanying it is that of the sculptor, and may also signify that the work is an original carving, not a cast or copy.

scale¹ *n*
The dimensions and proportions of an image or object, ie its actual measurements, such as height, depth, width, and their relations to each other.

scale² *vb*
To plot or determine the scale of an image or object. **scaled** *adj.*

scaling *n*
See FLAKING.

scauper *n*
Alternative spelling of SCORPER.

schema *n*
1 A diagram or simple, stylized line drawing showing the basic structure of an object or figure, which can be used as a model for developing a drawn, painted or sculpted form.
2 A diagram or simple drawing showing the basic structure of a full-scale composition, eg grouping of figures, directional lines, balance of masses etc.

school *n*
The term applied to a group of artists who have some identifiable similarity, eg were trained in the same studio, share particular aims and ideals, show stylistic affinities in their work or belong to a specific region or location.

score *vb*
To mark a material with a sharp instrument such as a needle, fine knife blade or stylus, to scratch or groove the surface but not cut through the material. This action is variously used to provide guidelines for folding or cutting a sheet material, to mark the surface of a rigid substance, or to make a basic layout, eg on vellum for a hand-written manuscript, without actually drawing on the surface.

scorper *n*
A cutting tool used in engraving on wood and metal. It has a metal shaft, set in a wooden handle, with straight sides and an oblique cutting tip which may be square or rectangular in section, or slightly rounded at the cutting edge. It is used to clear broad

areas from the surface of a wood block or to create textures by stippling and HATCHING.

scraper *n*
1 A metal tool with a three-sided cutting tip which tapers to a sharp point. The three faces are convex and have extremely sharp edges. The tool is used to shear off the burr raised by an engraver's BURIN or to scrape down the surface of an etching or engraving plate to remove an error. The shaft of the tool is set in a wooden handle.
2 A metal tool with a flat, pointed or curved tip used to wear down the surface texture of a MEZZOTINT or AQUATINT plate, to create light tones and white areas in the finished print.

scraperboard *n*
A drawing material consisting of a good quality paper board coated with a chalky white ground, similar in composition to GESSO, and finished with a layer of dense black drawing ink. Fine knives and pointed metal tools are used to scrape into the black layer, producing a broadly or finely drawn black and white image which can resemble the effect of a WOODCUT or WOOD ENGRAVING. Prepared boards are available, or a board can be made up with the necessary materials. Also called scratchboard (*US*).

scratchboard *n* (*US*)
See SCRAPERBOARD.

screen *n*
A rectangular framework of wood or metal across which a fine woven fabric is tautly and evenly stretched. Also called silkscreen. See SCREENPRINTING.

screenprint *n*
A printed image obtained by the SCREENPRINTING process. Also called silkscreen.

screenprinting *n*
A method of printing a flat image through a screen of fine, woven fabric stretched on a rectangular frame of wood or metal. An image is made on the fabric by any of various processes which have the effect of blocking parts of the mesh, leaving other open areas which a thick, fluid ink can pass through. The frame is laid on paper with the mesh downwards and ink is poured along the top edge inside the frame, then pulled down the entire length and width of the mesh with a rubber blade (squeegee) so it is forced through the open parts of the mesh onto the paper below. In this way the image on paper is the same way round as that on the screen. Blended and textured colours can be produced by mixing

inks on one screen, but cannot be fully controlled: precise printing of a colour image is achieved using a separate screen for each colour. Also called silkscreen printing and serigraphy. See also DIRECT STENCIL, INDIRECT STENCIL.

scribe *n*
1 The term used for a highly skilled or professionally practising CALLIGRAPHER.
2 See SCRIBER.

scriber *n*
A finely pointed tool of tough metal used for marking out dimensions and guidelines on metals and rigid plastics.
Also called scribe.

scrim *n*
1 (*sculpture*) A coarsely woven, openwork fabric made of jute, used as a flexible framework by which liquid plaster can be made to adhere to an armature. It is subsequently used to reinforce successive layers of plaster as a form is modelled.
2 (*intaglio printing*) A light but stiff open-weave cotton fabric, available in different grades of fineness, used primarily for wiping surplus ink from the surface of a metal printing plate.

scrimshaw *n*
1 The art of decorating fine materials such as ivory, bone or shells with carved or incised images or decorative patterns, originally a form of FOLK ART practised by sailors as a pastime.
2 An object decorated in this way.

sculpt *vb*
To shape a sculpture, by whatever technique. **sculpted** *adj*.

sculptor *n*
1 An artist skilled in any of the techniques of sculpture and whose main body of work consists of sculptures.
2 The person responsible for execution of a particular work of sculpture.

sculpture *n*
1 The techniques and processes of creating three-dimensional forms and images, by CARVING, CASTING, CONSTRUCTION or MODELLING. See also ASSEMBLAGE, KINETIC SCULPTURE, RELIEF SCULPTURE, SOFT SCULPTURE.
2 An individual work of art which is partly or fully three-dimensional.
3 The term is also used broadly to cover activities and effects that deal with real space and three-dimensional form, though not necessarily resulting in a tangible or lasting end product. See

ENVIRONMENTAL ART, LAND ART, LIGHT SCULPTURE, LIVING SCULPTURE.

sculpture in the round *n*
The category of sculptures which are freestanding and show the progressive development and relationships of individual component forms from all points of view.

scumble[1] *n*
A thin layer of opaque colour created by SCUMBLING.

scumble[2] *vb*
To apply paint by scumbling. **scumbled** *adj*

scumbling *n*
The technique of working a thin layer of opaque colour over a previously applied colour in such a way that the underlayer is not completely obliterated, particularly when working light over dark. There are various ways of applying the paint, eg with feathered or scrubbed brushstrokes, by rubbing the colour with fingertips etc. The scumble may be a broken, textured area of paint through which the underlying colour is seen in patches, or may be a thin film of colour which does not completely mask the previous colour, though overlaid across the whole surface.

seam *n*
1 The division between two sections of a PIECE MOULD.
2 A mark left on the surface of a cast sculpture where the casting material has penetrated the line of a mould seam.
3 A joint between sections of a COMPOSITE FORM.

seascape *n*
1 A painting or other representation of the sea, possibly including a view of the coastline and local features such as small boats, seabirds etc.
2 The broad category, or genre, of works of this type. See also MARINE PAINTING.

seasoning *n*
The process of drying out the natural moisture in wood, to reduce the weight of the material and make it more stable. Wood seasoned naturally is allowed to stand in a free circulation of air for several months: the length of time depends upon its weight and moisture content. Industrially, the process is speeded up by drying the timber in a kiln. Wood must be seasoned for use in carving or construction, or for making panels used as painting supports, so it is less susceptible to movement and less likely to split under different conditions.

secco *adj* (*It* dry)
abb FRESCO SECCO.

secondary clay *n*
Clay which has been carried in water from the original site in which it was formed and deposited elsewhere, having picked up additional minerals and other impurities along the way. Ball clay is of this type. Secondary clays are of varying degrees of plasticity and are found in a range of colours from blue-grey and buff to red. Also called sedimentary clay.
Compare PRIMARY CLAY.

secondary colours *n pl*
The three colours obtained by mixing pairs of PRIMARY COLOURS in equal proportions. They are orange (red and yellow), green (yellow and blue) and violet (blue and red). See also COLOUR CIRCLE, COLOURED GREY, TERTIARY COLOUR.

sedimentary clay *n*
See SECONDARY CLAY.

sedimentary rock *n*
Rock formed from eroded fragments of other rocks carried away by water from their original sites and deposited elsewhere as natural sediments, which over time consolidate into new rock masses. The category includes sandstones and limestones, both materials commonly used in stone carving.

separator *n*
See PARTING AGENT.

sepia *n*
1 A semi-transparent, dark brown pigment prepared from the natural inky secretion of the cuttlefish. At one time it was widely used in ink and watercolour, but because of its tendency to fade under strong light, synthetic equivalents are preferred.
2 The dark brown colour associated with this pigment.

serial imagery *n*
The use of a single, recurring motif, figurative or abstract, to form a composition. Minor variations may occur in each repeat or on a random basis, but the overall effect is of a coherent sequence or rhythmic pattern and texture, depending upon the complexity of the basic unit.

serigraphy *n*
An alternative term for the SCREENPRINTING process, often specifically denoting its use in making artists' original prints, rather than as a method of commercial reproduction printing.

setting *n*
1 The process by which a material in moist or liquid form becomes solid. See also CURING, HARDENING.
2 The process of packing a kiln with ceramic ware in preparation for firing.

sfregazzi *n* (*It* rubbing)
A technique in oil painting for creating subtle shadows on flesh colours by applying a thin, dark glaze rubbed in with the fingertips.

sfumato *n* (from *It fumo* = smoke)
A painting technique in which areas of paint are blended and softened to create gentle, hazy transitions between light and dark tones or from one colour to another.

sgraffito *n* (*It* scratching)
1 The technique of scratching a design or image into a layer of material to reveal a different-coloured layer or ground beneath. This method is applied to painting, enamelling, slip coatings on ceramic ware, plaster decoration of architectural forms and paint applied over gold leaf. The scratching can be done with any suitable pointed or tipped tool, usually while the upper layer of material is moist or malleable and easily scratched without damage to the underlying surface. Also called graffito.
2 An image or design created by this technique.

shade^1 *n*
1 A dark tone of a colour, as made by mixing a pure hue with black. Compare TINT.
2 A dark mass or area in a picture, eg a form or element which appears to be in shadow.

shade^2 *vb*
1 To darken a colour by adding black.
2 To create an area of tone in a drawing or painting, eg by applying a film of paint or wash of ink, or by HATCHING with a pencil.

shank *n*
The shaft of a tool, eg a painting knife or chisel, which is not in itself the directly functional part of the object but is vital to its efficient operation.

shaped canvas *n*
A painting on canvas stretched over a specially constructed frame of any shape other than rectangular.

shellac *n*
A varnish material processed from the resinous secretion of the

lac insect. It is generally light brown in colour, though it can be bleached after refining, and in use can be thinned with alcohol. It is primarily used as a sealant for porous materials such as wood or plaster. It is not suitable as a picture varnish.

shell gold *n*
See POWDER GOLD.

shim *n*
A lightweight, flat brass strip, used as a fencing material to section off different parts of a modelled form during casting of a PIECE MOULD.

short clay *n*
The term for a clay body which is not fully plastic and tends to break when shaped or stretched. Also called lean clay.

shuttering *n*
A construction used as a mould for casting a heavy material, eg concrete, in the location where the finished sculpture will stand. The structure is often of wood, but may be of any material that can be fitted up in the required hollow shape and sealed for as long as it takes to make the cast. Shuttering can be used for casting a particular form, or to make a block of material which can be cut or abraded into shape or added to a constructed sculpture.

siccative *n*
See DRIER.

side-grain block *n*
See PLANK-GRAIN BLOCK.

sienna *n*
A natural earth clay containing iron and manganese processed from its original condition as the dark yellow pigment raw sienna and roasted to produce the rich, red-brown pigment burnt sienna. Both colours are reliable and permanent.

silhouette *n*
1 The overall shape of a form as it appears against a brightly-lit background, when the shape is outlined against the light and detail of the form is in shadow.
2 A cutout paper image mounted on a light-coloured background, which shows the form as a flat, dark shape without interior detail.
3 A painting or drawing in which the image is presented as flat shapes against a contrasting flatly-coloured background.

silica *n*
Silicon dioxide, occurring naturally as quartz and recognized as a number of common natural materials, eg flint and sand, which are hard, refractory and insoluble. It is used in various forms as an abrasive, extender or filler and as an ingredient of ceramic bodies, enamels and other vitreous substances.

silicon carbide *n*
A hard, grey-black, crystalline compound made by combining carbon and sand under high temperatures, used in block or powder form as an abrasive and as a refractory ingredient of various compound substances.

silicone rubber *n*
A synthetic plastic material used for making flexible moulds. It consists of two basic ingredients, a rubber solution and a catalyst which causes the solution to harden: these are mixed together into a liquid which sets to form a thick, flexible skin. It is used in the same way as VINYL MOULDING COMPOUND, except that the fluid is cold when poured and can therefore be used to make a mould from a small, detailed wax model which would melt if exposed to a hot or heat-producing material.

silkscreen *n*
1 See SCREEN.
2 See SCREENPRINT.

silkscreen printing *n*
See SCREENPRINTING.

silverpoint *n*
See METALPOINT.

simultaneous contrast *n*
The mutual effect of two colours seen together, when tone and colour contrasts seem intensified. A bright and dark colour may seem respectively brighter and darker when seen together than they would if separated: complementary colours of equal strength seem more vivid in juxtaposition; a bright, pure hue on a neutral grey ground seems to tinge the grey with its complementary colour.

simultaneous representation *n*
A method of composition in which a figure or object is shown from several different viewpoints within a single image. This may consist of a simple, stylized form in which each element is seen flatly from a single view, eg the figure typical of early Egyptian art in which head and legs are seen in profile, torso and arms in frontal view. It may otherwise involve interlocked and

superimposed views built into a complex image intended to analyse three-dimensional structure.

sinking *n*
The drying process of oil paint which becomes ABSORBED.

sinopia *n* (*It*)
1 The full-scale composition of a FRESCO painting sketched out on the base coat of coarse plaster. See ARRICCIO.
2 Originally, a red-brown pigment made from iron oxide, commonly the material used to sketch out the composition of a fresco.

size¹ *n*
Any of various adhesive substances diluted with water to form a liquid glue solution, used to stiffen or seal a porous material, eg canvas or paper, or as a binder for a non-adhesive substance. Casein, bone glue and rabbitskin glue are examples of materials commonly used in size preparations.

size² *vb*
To use or apply a size. **sized** *adj*.

sizing *n*
1 The process of applying size to a canvas or panel to fill the pores of the material and seal the fibres. Sizing is the first stage of preparing a GROUND for painting and is followed by PRIMING.
2 Any process of applying size to an absorbent material or surface to make it less absorbent or provide an adhesive quality receptive to application of another material.

sketch¹ *n*
1 A preliminary drawing or painting made as preparation for a larger, more finished work. It may establish the general plan of the composition or some basic feature of the work, eg relationship between line and mass, distribution of tone, colour etc.
2 A preliminary model made as preparation for a full-scale sculpture, showing the basic form or proposed character of the work.
3 Any roughly made drawing, painting or model used as a form of visual notation to record something directly observed.

sketch² *vb*
To make a sketch.

sketch box *n*
A sturdy wooden box divided into compartments for carrying paints, brushes, palettes, boards, paper etc, designed for

convenient use in sketching out of doors, or any location other than the artist's own studio.

sketching *n*
The process or activity of making a sketch, generally used of drawing and painting but not commonly of sculpture processes.

sketching easel *n*
A lightweight wood or metal easel consisting of three narrow, adjustable legs arranged as a tripod, topped by a vertical strut and horizontal crosspiece on which a painting is supported. All sections of the easel are adjustable and it can be folded up into a compact and easily portable unit.

skew chisel *n*
A wood carving chisel with the cutting edge trimmed at an angle, rather than squared across the tip of the shaft.

skewing *n*
The process of cleaning the surplus edges of gold leaf from an area of gilding. These are brushed away once the leaf has fully adhered to the MORDANT on which it is laid.

skin glue *n*
Any type of glue manufactured from animal skins.

slabbing *n*
A process of hand-building hollow ceramic forms, particularly pottery, from pieces cut out of thick sheets of clay. The basic shapes are cut and may be left to dry until leather-hard. The faces to be joined are scored and made adhesive with SLIP, then pressed together and locked in place. The form can then be trimmed and refined, and the seam marks cleaned.

slab pot *n*
A ceramic vessel formed by the technique of slabbing.

slaked plaster *n*
Plaster of Paris which has been submerged in a considerable quantity of water over a period of time, eg twelve hours or more, so that it loses its active setting property. In this inert form it has traditionally been used as an ingredient of GESSO, although chalk or whiting can be substituted to avoid the lengthy process of slaking.

slip *n*
Liquid clay of an even, creamy consistency, used for SLIP CASTING or as surface colouring or decoration for a clay form. It also serves as an adhesive for joining sections of a composite form

while the clay is still in a plastic or leather-hard condition. Compare SLURRY.

slip casting *n*
The process of casting a hollow ceramic form from liquid clay (slip). A porous mould, usually made of plaster, is made from a modelled master. It is filled with the slip and allowed to stand until the plaster has absorbed enough moisture to turn the slip to a solid clay coating on the inner face of the mould. The excess slip is poured off and the cast form is left to harden. When it is removed from the mould, it can be cleaned and refined in shape, eg to remove seam marks, before it is dried out and fired.

slip glaze *n*
1 A ceramic glaze containing a high proportion of plastic clay. It is applied to unfired ceramic ware and melts in firing to form a glassy coating.
2 A slip containing a FLUX or FRIT, used in the same way.

slipstone *n*
A small, narrow sharpening stone, tapering to a rounded or angled edge on one side, used to hone the inner face of the cutting edge of a gouge or V-tool. The composition of the stone is like that of an OILSTONE.

slurry *n*
Thick liquid clay, similar to slip, but of a heavier and less even consistency. Like slip it is used as a surface coating for clay forms and as an adhesive for joining clay pieces, but its consistency is not suitable for casting.

smoking *n*
The process of blackening a hard ground laid on an etching plate with a sooty deposit from burning wax tapers. The grounded plate is held upside down and the tapers passed underneath in continuous motion until the ground turns black and shiny. The darkened ground shows up the lines made with the etching needle more clearly.

smooch *n*
An area of a chalk, charcoal, pastel or pencil drawing which has been deliberately smudged to soften the tones.

soaking *n*
A stage in the process of firing ceramic ware when there is no further rise in the temperature within the kiln but it is maintained at a steady heat which penetrates the ware to effect the required changes.

soapstone *n*
A soft stone, metamorphic in origin, used as a material for stone carving because its light, soapy consistency is easily worked. It is found naturally in a range of green and grey tones which may be mottled or lightly veined. It can be polished to a smooth, bright finish but because of its softness is not suitable for sculpture to be located outdoors.

soft glaze *n*
A ceramic glaze fired at a low temperature.

soft ground *n*
An acid-resistant coating applied to the surface of an etching plate. It is basically HARD GROUND with a greasy element added to render it soft and non-drying. Like hard ground, it is resistant and durable in acid, but it lifts more easily under pressure from a drawing tool or textured material, so the etched effects it provides are characteristically different. See also ETCHING GROUND, SOFT GROUND ETCHING.

soft ground etching *n*
A method of ETCHING using a soft, acid-resistant ground to produce characteristic effects of line and texture. It may be used to create the whole image, or to add textural detail when combined with other etching techniques. The conventional method of drawing an image in soft ground is to place a sheet of paper over the grounded plate and draw on the paper with a pencil or other pointed drawing tool. The soft ground sticks to the underside of the paper where pressure is applied and is lifted with it, leaving soft lines and hatched areas exposed on the plate for etching. Thus the technique can be used to simulate the effect of pencil or crayon drawing. The other exploitable feature of soft ground is that it will take a clear impression of texture, eg coarse fabric or thin wood veneer, a leaf or feather, and the full detail of the impression is reproduced when the plate is etched.

soft paste *n*
The now obsolete term for materials originally made in imitation of the HARD PASTE used to make true porcelain, commonly a mixture of light-coloured clay and a glassy FRIT which could be fired at a relatively low temperature.
Also called *pâte tendre* (*Fr*).

soft sculpture *n*
The general term for sculptures made from soft or flexible materials, eg canvas, felt and other types of fabric; polythene, PVC and other soft plastics. Soft sculptures may have well-defined but not completely fixed forms, eg hanging, stuffed

or inflated components, or may be temporary and changeable in form.

softwood *n*
A general classification of the woods obtained from coniferous trees with narrow or needle-shaped leaves. The term does not refer to physical softness, which varies across the range of materials; eg there are both hard and soft grades of wood from various species of pine, but all are technically termed softwoods. They are typically open-grained and less resistant in carving than hardwoods.

solder¹ *n*
A fine rod of metal used in the process of soldering. Commonly an alloy of lead and tin is used, called soft solder, but if the joint must withstand considerable stress a more durable alloy based on copper or silver can be applied, called a hard solder.

solder² *vb*
To join metal components by soldering. **soldered** *adj*.

soldering *n*
A method of joining pieces of metal using an alloy (solder) as an adhesive in the joint. The pieces are brought together in the correct relationship and the solder is applied and heated directly so it melts into the joint and attaches to both components as it hardens. A process involving use of an alloy with a high melting point is known as hard soldering. Where a solder with a low melting point is used, which gives less strength in the joint, the process is called soft soldering. See also BRAZING.

solid casting *n*
CASTING by any method in which a solid form is made by completely filling a mould with casting material.

solvent *n*
A liquid capable of dissolving a particular substance. In painting, a solvent is used to clean brushes and palette and may also be used as a diluent for the paint, which evaporates leaving the pigment and binder on the support. Appropriate solvents are used with a wide range of artists' materials, eg paints, resins, varnishes.

sopraporta *n* (*It* over the door)
A painting fitted to the space above a doorway.

sotto in sù *adv* (*It* from below upwards)
A technique of pictorial composition in which figures and architectural details are depicted with exaggerated foreshortening and perspective, so they are viewed as from below and appear to

be soaring upwards, though actually painted on a flat surface. This device has been used in painted decoration of interior architecture, eg on ceilings, to give an impression of extra height, sometimes creating the illusion that the ceiling is open to the sky.

spackling *n*
The process of repairing a damaged plaster surface by cutting out the flaw and making good the depression with fresh plaster or a suitable filling compound.

spall *n*
A fragment of stone, whether deliberately chipped from a block during carving or accidentally broken from a finished sculpture.

spatter[1] *vb*
To create a painted texture by SPATTERING. **spattered** *adj.*

spatter[2] *n*
The effect created by spattering.

spattering *n*
1 A technique of laying paint or ink in an irregular, mottled texture by loading a stiff brush with colour and drawing one finger or the edge of a ruler sharply across the brush tip, causing the bristles to flick colour onto the support.
2 The effect created by this technique, also called spatter.
3 A similar effect created by lowering the pressure of air passing through an AIRBRUSH, causing the spray of liquid medium to become coarse and uneven.

spatula *n*
A simple modelling tool of wood or metal, basically a flat strip of material with a rounded end, which may be used to smooth, press or scrape a malleable material, eg clay, wax, wet plaster.

spectrum palette *n*
A range of colours used for painting, consisting only of the colours of the spectrum – red, orange, yellow, green, blue, indigo, violet – and white. An important feature is that black is omitted, so shadows and low tones must be conveyed by mixing pure colours, rather than by devaluing the hues with the addition of black.

spiral wedging *n*
See WEDGING.

spitsticker *n*
A cutting tool used in wood engraving, similar to a BURIN, but elliptical in section, so the obliquely angled cutting tip narrows to

a point or sharp curve. It is used for cutting curved and swelling lines and hatched textures.

spokeshave *n*
A small version of a DRAWKNIFE, consisting of a short metal blade with a handle at either end, used to shave or strip the surface of a piece of wood, particularly useful for curved surfaces.

spolvero *n*
A copy of a CARTOON used for POUNCING, so the original can be preserved without marks or perforations.

spraygun *n*
A heavy-duty tool for spraying liquid paint, resembling a gun in construction and worked by a trigger action which releases the flow of paint through a narrow nozzle. It operates on the same basic principle as the AIRBRUSH, the liquid medium being contained in a receptacle screwed to the top of the tool. A supply of pressurized air is fed into the tool from a COMPRESSOR and this converts the flow of medium into a broad spray of fine paint particles.

sprig *n*
A preformed motif applied to ceramic ware as a low relief ornament or surface decoration. A press mould is used to shape the plastic clay and the motif is applied directly to the damp surface of the ware.

sprue *n*
See POURING GATE.

squaring up *n*
A method for enlarging a drawing, eg for copying a drawing on paper at a larger scale on canvas. A grid is ruled over the original drawing to divide it into equal squares. A proportionately larger grid is ruled on the new support and each section of the drawing is copied square by square. Because there are a large number of fixed points of reference created by the grid lines, it is possible to enlarge the drawing accurately. The same principle can be applied to reducing an image, by copying on a smaller grid.

squeegee *n*
A thick rubber blade set in a heavy strip of wood, used in SCREENPRINTING to force ink across the screen and through the fabric mesh. The length of the squeegee should be almost equal to the width of the screen, so it can be pulled across the whole mesh in a single, fluid action.

stabile *n*
A term invented to describe a constructed sculpture similar in

form to a MOBILE, but which is immobile as its components are fixed in relation to each other and to the position of the whole piece.

stabilizer *n*
An ingredient of oil paint which prevents separation of the pigment and oil vehicle and determines the consistency of the paint. Various substances can be used, eg a waxy material, aqueous solution or inert pigment. If the pigment and oil are of good quality, the stabilizer should be only a very small percentage of the total paint composition.

staffage *n*
Small figures painted into a landscape or townscape which have no narrative function but serve to emphasize the sense of scale and perspective or are intended simply to enliven the composition.

stain[1] *n*
An area of colour soaked into a ground or support, created by an application of dilute paint to a relatively absorbent surface.

stain[2] *vb*
To apply paint in a manner which creates a stain on the support.

stained glass *n*
1 A picture or design set in a window, formed of flat sections of coloured glass held together in a framework of soft metal strip, traditionally lead. There are three basic methods of colouring the glass: the addition of colouring agents during manufacture; the practice of covering clear glass with enamel colours and fusing them to the surface; painting on the glass as the design is assembled. The image is carefully worked out on paper as a full-scale CARTOON and the construction of the metal framework and cutting of glass pieces follows the exact form of the drawn composition.
2 The process of creating a picture or design in coloured glass.

stand oil *n*
Linseed oil which has been heated in oxygen-free conditions. It is more viscous and slow-drying than cold-pressed or refined linseed oil and is usually used as a medium added to oil paint rather than a vehicle for the pigments.

state *n*
A particular stage in the development of a print, as shown in a proof pulled to check progress of the image. Thus different states are identifiable by the alterations and additions made to a plate, block or stone between one proof and the next. There may be any

number of states, depending on how often the artist has wanted to see the image in printed form, leading up to the final state which is that of the finished print as seen in an EDITION.

statue *n*
A carved, cast or modelled sculpture representing a human figure or animal. It is typically a realistic representation, close to life-size or scaled up in proportion.

statuette *n*
A small statue, on a scale no more than half life-size.

steel facing *n*
A process of coating an engraved or etched copper plate with a thin layer of steel to make it more durable in printing. See ELECTROPLATING.

stele *n* (*Gr* standing stone)
A stone slab designed to stand upright, bearing incised lettering, a carved relief image or painted decoration. The origin of this form was in the use of such objects as grave markers.

stencil[1] *n*
1 A thin sheet material, such as metal, plastic, board or paper, bearing the cutout shape of a motif or image. The stencil acts as a MASK: it is placed on a support and paint is brushed or sprayed into the cutout areas to reproduce the motif in colour on the flat support.
2 An image applied by any of various methods to the fabric mesh of a screen used in the SCREENPRINTING process. It may be drawn or painted with a crayon or adhesive liquid; or may consist of a thin film of paper or plastic cut to shape and used to cover the screen mesh; or it can be photographically made by exposing an image on a light-sensitive liquid coating applied to the screen. See also DIRECT STENCIL, INDIRECT STENCIL.

stencil[2] *vb*
To apply an image or motif to a surface using a stencil. **stencilled** *adj*.

stencil brush *n*
A thick brush with short, stiff hairs clustered together to form a rounded head with a flattened tip. It is used with a vertical dabbing motion to press paint into the cutout area of a stencil.

stencilling *n*
Any method of painting a motif, image or pattern using a stencil, particularly when the stencil is a means of forming a repeated pattern of identical shapes.

stereochromy *n*
See WATER-GLASS PAINTING.

stiacciato *adj* (*It* flattened)
abb RILIEVO STIACCIATO. See FLATTENED RELIEF.

stick ink *n*
A drawing ink in the form of a rectangular-sectioned stick of pigment compressed in a gum binder. It is made liquid for use by rubbing the tip of the stick in a shallow dish of water to dissolve the colour.

still life *n*
1 A painting or other representation of a group of inanimate objects. Traditionally the subject matter is flowers, fruit, vegetables and other natural forms, and some manufactured objects such as household utensils and musical instruments. As a rule, still life compositions have reflected the range of everyday items in any particular period and these may now include mechanical and electrical items and packaged foodstuffs etc. Also called *nature morte* (*Fr*).
2 An arrangement of inanimate objects used as the model for such a representation.
3 The broad category, or genre, of works of this type.

stilts *n pl*
Small tripods of refractory material used to support glazed ceramic ware during firing.

stipple[1] *vb*
To mark a surface by the technique of STIPPLING.

stipple[2] *n*
An area of tone or colour created by stippling.

stipple engraving *n*
1 A method of INTAGLIO PRINTING intended to imitate the grainy effect of a chalk drawing by marking a metal plate with masses of small dots and ticks contrived to produce a tonal image when printed. It is a combination of etching and engraving processes: initially, the basic image is established by working into an ETCHING GROUND on the plate with a needle or roulette. The marks made by these tools are bitten into the plate and the ground is cleaned off. The image is then further developed directly in the metal using engraving, drypoint or mezzotint tools. The size, depth and spacing of the dots determines the range of tones in the finished print. The process is sometimes also combined with SOFT GROUND ETCHING. Also called crayon engraving.

2 A printed image obtained by this method.

stippling *n*
1 A technique used in drawing, painting and INTAGLIO PRINTING processes of creating an area of tone or mixed colour by dabbing with a brush or drawing tool to produce a mass of tiny dots.
2 The effect created by this technique.

stone *n*
A fragment, section or mass of natural rock broken or cut away from the site of its original formation.

stone carving *n*
1 The process of making a sculpture in stone by cutting and shaping a solid mass of material.
2 A stone sculpture made by carving.

stoneware *n*
Ceramic ware fired at a high temperature, usually above 1200° C (2192° F) to vitrify the body, which is then hard, dense and either non-porous or having a very low degree of porosity. The ware may be opaque or slightly translucent, depending upon the composition of the clay body. If a glaze is applied it is also high-fired and fuses with the body in an integrated layer. Compare EARTHENWARE.

stopping *n*
The process in conservation of paintings in which a hole or depression in the ground of a painting is repaired and levelled with the original surface. This is done using a substance appropriate to the composition of the original materials and if there is actual damage to the painting support, may involve patching from behind.

stopping out *n*
The process of coating areas of an etching plate with acid-resistant varnish, to protect the metal when the plate is immersed in acid solution. This is done to stop biting of certain areas which have already been exposed to the acid, to cover errors in drawing or seal faults in the ground. The varnish is also used to paint a design directly on the plate in order to create areas of OPEN BITE. It is also applied to protect the back and edges of the plate while the design is being etched.

stopping out varnish *n*
A liquid varnish which dries to a tough, shiny acid-resistant coating when painted on an etching plate. It is usually a mixture of bitumen and turpentine, forming a brownish-black, glossy

liquid with the consistency of pouring cream, which dries relatively quickly when spread as an even layer.

straight-edge *n*
A heavy, flat strip of metal or wood with perfectly straight edges, which can be used as a guide for drawing or cutting straight lines.

strainer *n*
A wooden frame over which canvas is stretched to form a support for painting. It differs from a STRETCHER in that the corner joints are fixed and no adjustment can be made to tauten the canvas when it is first stretched or if it subsequently slackens.

Strasbourg turpentine *n*
A thick, liquid OLEORESIN, a natural product of the Tyrolean silver fir tree, used as an ingredient of painting emulsions, mediums and varnishes. It is a clear, viscous liquid which when dry has little tendency to discolour.

stretched canvas *n*
A section of canvas pulled taut over a STRETCHER or STRAINER and stapled or tacked to the back of the frame.

stretched paper *n*
A piece of paper which has been thoroughly soaked in water, taped with gumstrip to a drawing board and allowed to dry out naturally. When the paper is subsequently wetted, eg if used for watercolour painting, it will expand and swell over the surface of the board, but because the edges are taped in place and the material has already been stretched and dried, it flattens out perfectly as it dries.

stretcher *n*
A wooden frame over which canvas is stretched to form a support for painting. Stretchers are usually sold as sets of straight wood sections which are assembled by fitting together pre-cut tongue-and-groove corner joints. The corners are cut with slots on the inner edges into which small wooden wedges can be fitted. These are knocked in tightly after the canvas is stretched to expand the corners of the stretcher, thus tautening the canvas.

striking *n*
The process of forming a RELIEF image in a temporarily soft material by stamping the material with a die bearing an INTAGLIO image. This leaves a reversed impression which is retained as the material hardens. The traditional method of striking a coin or medal is by stamping a softened metal blank with a different die image on either side.

stucco *n*
A quick-drying, malleable material resembling plaster, capable of being modelled or moulded into sculptured forms and used for internal or external architectural decoration. The traditional composition of this material is lime mixed with ground marble bonded with glue size, but the term broadly covers various mixtures which may include cement or gypsum as the chief binding material. In some forms of stucco decoration, pigments are added to the basic material and the forms are directly modelled in different colours.

studio *n*
1 The room in which an artist works.
2 A workshop equipped for work in a particular discipline, eg painting, printmaking, sculpture.

studio easel *n*
A heavy, upright wooden easel used for supporting a large canvas or panel. It consists of a rectangular framework mounted vertically on a sturdy base, with a central vertical strut and adjustable horizontal crosspiece on which the painting rests. This type of easel forms a permanent fixture in the studio: it may be set on castors to make it moveable and is slightly adjustable in height and angle, but it is not designed to be folded away or dismantled when not in use.

studio of ———— *n*
A term used in cataloguing and art historical reference followed by the name of an artist, to indicate that the work it describes was carried out under supervision of that artist, probably by trained studio assistants, but that the artist had little or no hand in actual execution of the work.

study *n*
1 A detailed drawing or painting made as preparation for a proposed work, representing accurate investigation of a particular form or element to be used in the composition, eg part of a figure, a detail of landscape. It may otherwise be a preliminary version of the whole composition.
2 A model, similarly accurately worked out, made in preparation for a proposed sculpture. Again, it may be a detail of the form or a preliminary version of the whole work.

stump *n*
A narrow cylinder of tightly rolled paper fashioned into a round point at one end, used to rub and spread a powdery drawing medium, eg chalk or pastel, to blend colours and create mixed tones. Also called tortillon.

stun *vb*
To strike stone with a carving tool in such a way that the structure of the material is shattered around the point of impact but not cut. This generally implies a faulty stroke when the tool is applied at the wrong angle to the surface.

style *n*
The distinctive or characteristic manner of working identifiable to a particular artist, school or period in art. This includes the type of imagery or motifs employed, the objects produced, the way in which techniques and materials are applied and the distribution of formal elements such as colour, tone and texture.

stylized *adj*
The description of a composition, image or motif which is planned and executed according to particular conventions of representation. It implies an image which is recognizable but not essentially realistic. FRONTALITY and SIMULTANEOUS REPRESENTATION are examples of stylized approaches to composition.

stylus *n*
A metal drawing instrument with a fine but slightly blunted point used for scoring guidelines on the surface of canvas, vellum or paper.

sugar aquatint *n*
An image created on an etching plate by the LIFT GROUND method and treated with AQUATINT to create tonal areas.

sugar lift *n*
See LIFT GROUND.

suite *n*
The collective term for a group of paintings, drawings or prints linked by their subject matter, particularly when designed as continuous illustration of a theme or narrative.

sumi ink *n*
A name borrowed from the Japanese for the type of drawing ink known as INDIA INK.

sunken relief *n*
1 A category of relief sculptures in which forms are recessed from the plane surface of a block of material. In effect, the surface of the block acts as a background to the image but the forms have a degree of projection within the block, the highest point of any form being on a level with the original surface.
Also called cavo-rilievo, coelanaglyphic relief and intaglio relief.

2 An individual sculpture conforming to this principle of composition.

support *n*
The basic material that forms the physical surface on which a painting or drawing medium is applied, commonly canvas, panel, paper or board but also possibly ivory, metal, plaster or other suitable material. See also GROUND, PRIMER.

surface quality *n*
The immediate visual and tactile qualities of a work of art, dependent upon the inherent properties of the materials, eg density, colour, texture, and their effects when applied or shaped in particular ways. See also PAINT QUALITY.

surform *n*
A metal abrasive tool with a pierced, toothed surface which allows particles of the abraded material to pass through the pierced holes, so they do not clog the cutting teeth. The blade may be flat, curved or rounded and the tool is used for shaping relatively soft sculpture materials, eg damp plaster.

suspension *n*
A liquid compound consisting of particles of a solid substance dispersed but not dissolved in a liquid vehicle.

swag *n*
See FESTOON.

symbol *n*
1 A drawing, motif or sign which stands for an object, figure or abstract idea, representing it in a simplified version of the actual form or conventionally recognized by an association of ideas between the motif and the thing it represents.
2 An abstract element, eg colour or pattern, intended to represent a particular idea or association. **symbolic** *adj.*

symbolism *n*
The use of symbols in an individual image or collection of images to represent actual objects or abstract ideas.

symmetrical *adj*
The description of a form or composition which, assuming a vertical axis through the form, displays a balanced arrangement of similar components around or on either side of the axis. Compare ASYMMETRICAL.

synthetic pigment *n*
Any pigment prepared entirely by artificial, chemical means, as compared to one processed directly from a natural substance.

t

table easel *n*
A lightweight wooden easel designed to be set up on a table or desk to support a drawing board or small painting. The simplest form consists of two rectangular frames hinged together, one being set flat on the tabletop to form the base and the other raised to support the painting and secured on the base frame by means of hinged props on either side.

tack, **tackiness** *n*
The adhesive quality of a material, ie its propensity to stick to a surface or feel sticky to the touch.

tactile values *n pl*
The term applied to the characteristics of a painting in which three-dimensional form is represented with an illusion of solidity and texture that stimulates a sense of tangibility.

taille directe *n* (*Fr*)
DIRECT CARVING.

talc *n*
A natural mineral, a form of magnesium silicate, found in metamorphic rocks. It may be white, grey or green and has a slightly greasy texture. Processed into the form of a soft white powder, it has various uses in the manufacture of artists' materials, eg as an inert pigment or filler, and as an agent in a number of processes, eg as a PARTING AGENT. The powder form is also commonly known as French chalk.

tamp *vb*
To consolidate a material by TAMPING.

tamping *n*
The method of consolidating a moist, fibrous or granular material packed into a mould, to remove air pockets and firm the consistency. It basically consists of pressing or beating the surface of the material with a flat or rounded instrument. **tamped** *adj*

tap drill *n*
A metal shaft, set in a handle, with a projecting THREAD spiralled

around the tip and vertically split to form a cutting edge. This is used to cut a corresponding channelled thread inside a drilled hole.

tapestry *n*
A woven fabric bearing a pictorial design which is woven in as the fabric is made.

tapping *n*
The process of using a TAP DRILL and DIE to cut THREADS in two matched components, enabling them to be screwed together.

technical illustration *n*
A field of ILLUSTRATION originally concerned with accurate representations of machinery and parts for printing in technical manuals, now broadly defined as dealing with technology and manufactured items of various kinds across a wide range. It can involve highly detailed drawings to scale, showing existing items or projecting the appearance of an object from preliminary plans and specifications.

technique *n*
1 The collective processes of working in any medium, eg oil painting, stone carving, pottery, to produce a particular result by skilful manipulation of materials, tools and equipment.
2 The individual method pursued by an artist working in a particular medium.
3 An individual method of applying or manipulating a material, eg HATCHING as a method of drawing, SCUMBLING as a method of painting.

temper¹ *vb*
1 To alter the hardness of metal by TEMPERING.
2 In a sense no longer commonly used, the term also means to convert a non-plastic substance into a useable form by mixing it with another substance, eg mixing dry pigment in a binder to make paint. This is the likely derivation of the term TEMPERA.
tempered *adj*

temper² *n*
The condition of a metal at any stage of the tempering process.

tempera *n*
1 A paint consisting of pigments bound in a water-miscible EMULSION. Traditionally, the emulsion used is egg yolk and this produces a paint which is translucent and quick-drying; the dried paint film is tough, durable and waterproof and the colours retain their brilliance. Because of the paint's drying speed it is difficult to blend and diffuse colours on the support, so hatching, cross

hatching and stippling are employed to create gradations of tone and colour. Opacity and full intensity of colour are achieved by overlaying successive applications of thin paint. The egg yolk binder is quite stable when dry but if the liquid paint is stored it deteriorates quickly and it is usual practice to mix colours in relatively small quantities as they are needed. The traditional support for painting in tempera is a panel coated with a brilliantly white ground of GESSO.

2 More broadly, the term is used of various water-based paints, eg with a gum or CASEIN binder. Originally the term distinguished paints containing a binder from FRESCO colours of pigments ground in water only.

temper colours *n pl*
A range of colours from pale yellow to dark blue which appear successively on the surface of a metal as it is heated during the tempering process. They correspond to the range of temperature changes and are directly indicative of the hardness of the metal at any stage.

tempering *n*
The process of regulating the hardness of metal, eg for toughening a metal cutting tool. The metal is heated to red-heat and rapidly quenched in oil or water. In this process it becomes harder but also more brittle; the brittleness is taken out by subjecting the material to a further stage of controlled heating and cooling. The process can be scientifically monitored through changes in the surface colour of the metal showing temperature changes which directly relate to the hardness of the metal at any stage of heating.

template *n*
A shape cut in sheet metal, wood or plastic which serves as the pattern for the outline or profile of a form, allowing accurate repetition of the shape.

tensile strength *n*
The strength of a material in terms of its ability to withstand physical stress, usually expressed as the degree to which it can be stretched without breaking. In sculpture, this is reflected in the suitability of a material to be shaped into extended forms able to support their own weight.

terracotta *n* (*It* baked earth)
1 Adhering to its literal meaning, this term refers to any object made of clay which is finished by firing, but not glazed. It is often used to mean unglazed ware made from coloured clays and, more specifically, naturally red or red-brown clays and objects made from them.

2 By extension, the red-brown colour associated with certain types of clay.

terre verte *n* (*Fr* green earth)
A grey-green pigment derived from a natural green earth, traditionally used as the colour for underpainting of flesh tones, to establish shadow areas subsequently overlaid with flesh tints and glazes of warm colour.

tertiary colour *n*
A colour produced by mixing two SECONDARY COLOURS in any proportions. Depending upon the original colours and the proportions of the mix, tertiary colours constitute a range of browns, greys and blacks.

tesselate *vb*
To decorate a surface with tesserae. **tesselated** *adj*.

tessera *n* **tesserae** *pl*
The individual unit of material used in making a MOSAIC, typically a small cube of ceramic, glass or stone, though it may be of any suitable shape or material, depending on the form of the mosaic.

thermoplastic *adj*
The description of a material which becomes soft when heated and hardens as it cools, but without changing its basic properties, so the process can be repeated.

thermosetting *adj*
The description of a liquid or gel material which hardens under the application of heat and is then permanently rigid and cannot be returned to its original form.

thinner *n*
A DILUENT added to a paint, varnish or printing ink to create a more fluid consistency. A thinner is not necessarily a SOLVENT for the medium.

thixotropic *adj*
The description of a fluid substance or GEL which loses viscosity when disturbed, eg a gel medium added to paint which becomes more fluid when spread with a brush.

thread *n*
1 A projecting spiral ridge on the outside of a form or component, or a corresponding spiralled groove or channel on the inside of a form, which enables two items to lock securely when screwed together.
2 A fine, needle-shaped piece of ENAMEL. A thread flattens and

spreads slightly when fired and may be used for basically linear decoration on a flat base coat of enamel.

threesquare *n*
A file with a triangular-sectioned blade, used in working metal.

throw *vb*
To make a clay form by THROWING. **thrown** *adj*.

throwing *n*
The process of shaping clay on a potter's wheel. There are various aspects of this craft, but typically it is applied to making hollow, symmetrical, rounded forms. The basic stages in the process are CENTRING, HOLLOWING OUT and RAISING. See also COLLARING, TURNING.

tin glaze *n*
A ceramic glaze containing tin oxide, which makes it characteristically light-coloured and opaque.

tint[1] *n*
1 A light tone of a colour, as made by mixing a pure hue with white or diluting paint to reduce the colour strength. Compare SHADE.
2 The term is also more broadly used to refer to the colour of a material, or colour which has been added or applied.
3 In artwork, illustration and layout, an area of flat colour printed as background or colour detail in a design or image.

tint[2] *vb*
1 To lighten a colour by adding white.
2 The term is also used more generally to mean mixing one colour into another to tinge the basic hue.

tinting strength *n*
The capacity of a pigment to impart its colour to a paint medium or other substance. In paint manufacture, the strength of a pigment is quantified by standardized testing methods.

tint tool *n*
A cutting tool used in wood and metal engraving, less broad than a BURIN and tapered in section so the obliquely angled tip has a narrow, flat cutting edge. It is used for cutting fine lines of equal width to create tonal areas by HATCHING.

tip *n*
A broad, flat brush of badger, sable or squirrel hair, used to lift and lay gold leaf in gilding. The fine, clingy material attaches to the tips of the hairs.

titanium white *n*
A synthetic inorganic pigment derived from titanium dioxide which is dense, opaque, brilliantly white and permanent. It is used in grounds and paints and has an extremely high tinting strength.

thumb pot *n*
See PINCH POT.

tinting medium *n*
A viscous fluid with no colouring property which is mixed with a printing ink to give it greater transparency or reduce the strength of the ink colour without devaluing the hue.

tondo *n* (*It* round)
A circular painting or relief sculpture.

tone *n*
1 A term applied to black, white and any of the range of greys between them, thus meaning a quality of relative lightness or darkness.
2 A light or dark variation of a hue. See also SHADE, TINT.
3 The relative lightness or darkness of any particular element in a composition. **tonal** *adj*.

tooth *n*
The slightly coarse or rough quality of a surface which supplies a grip for a substance or material applied to it, eg the surface texture of canvas due to the fabric weave, which assists adherence of ground and paint applied to the canvas.

toreutics *n pl*
The art of making a decorative relief design, especially on metal, by carving, chasing, embossing or incising the material.

tortillon *n*
See STUMP.

touched proof *n*
A WORKING PROOF showing evidence of drawing or manual correction by the artist.

townscape *n*
1 A painting or other representation of a town, city or general view of urban architecture.
2 The broad category, or genre, of works of this type.

tracery *n*
Ornamental stonework or wood carving forming basically linear patterns, typically used as architectural decoration to fill window areas or create screening rather than solid walls. Blind tracery is

decoration of this type set against a wall or panel to form a pattern in relief.

traction *n*
A defect in a film of paint or varnish when the material cracks and the edges of the cracks recede, leaving relatively large fissures in the surface.

trailing *n*
1 (*ceramics*) A method of applying SLIP as surface decoration of ceramic ware. It is similar to icing a cake: the thick slip is squeezed from a forcing bag or syringe to form a raised linear pattern of heavy slip trails over the surface of the form.
2 (*enamelling*) A decorative effect achieved by heating enamel in the form of lumps, powder or threads on a metal or enamel base and using a pointed steel instrument to draw fine trails of molten enamel across the surface.

transfer paper *n*
A thin paper coated on one side with a fine layer of coloured powder, used to transfer an outline drawing from the original support to a clean piece of paper or board. The original drawing is traced and the transfer paper laid between the tracing and the fresh support. When the lines are retraced they are faintly impressed in colour on the clean surface and the image can then be fully worked, eg in ink or paint, with the lines eventually being obliterated completely.

transitional medium, transitory medium *n*
A sculpture material, eg clay or wax, used for working a particular form from which a mould is taken to make a cast in a more durable material, or one with different tactile qualities.

transparency *n*
The quality of a substance which transmits rather than reflects light, ie can be seen through. As a property of a paint or pigment, the term means that the colour will not conceal or completely obliterate the surface to which it is applied.

trial proof *n*
A proof taken at any stage of work on a plate, block or stone so the artist can see the progress of the image and make the necessary adjustments towards printing the final state.

triptych *n*
A painting or relief sculpture worked on three separate panels which form a single unit in terms of composition or are conceived as companion pieces to be viewed together. The panels

may be hinged together or mounted in a single frame. See also DIPTYCH, POLYPTYCH.

trompe l'oeil *n* (*Fr* deceives the eye)
A style of painting in which the image is represented with such a degree of realistic detail as to deceive the viewer into thinking it is actually real and three-dimensional. It is particularly associated with relatively small-scale and highly detailed still life compositions, but the term is appropriate to a range of work of this type, including large-scale architectural decoration intended to alter the viewer's perception of the actual space. See also QUADRATURA.

trucage *n* (*Fr* rigging)
The process of creating a FAKE.

trullisatio *n* (*It*)
A roughcast coating of plaster providing the foundation layer for a FRESCO painting. The term is not commonly used. See also ARRICCIO, INTONACO.

tub-sized *adj*
The term describing paper which has been soaked in a solution of gelatin or glue after the main process of manufacture.

turning *n*
1 (*ceramics*) The process of shaping the base of a clay pot made by THROWING when the clay has dried to a leather-hard condition. The pot is placed upside down on the potter's wheel and secured with a roll of damp clay pressed around the form. The wheel is set in motion and as the pot rotates, a square, triangular or rounded cutting blade is held to the base which pares away the partly dried clay. This process can also be applied to the sides of the pot, to reduce the thickness of the clay and refine the overall shape.
2 The process of shaping material on a LATHE.
3 The process of shaping plaster in a TURNING BOX.

turning box *n*
A type of FORMER consisting of an open box with a central spindle set across the top and a template fixed along one edge. A mass of damp plaster is applied to the spindle and this is rotated so that as the plaster begins to set it scrapes against the template and is shaped into a particular form.

turntable *n*
A flat platform mounted on a base by means of a vertical shaft through the centre, which can revolve freely around the fixed central point.

turpentine *n*
1 A colourless, volatile, oily liquid distilled from natural OLEORESINS, used as a diluent and solvent for oil paints. See also WHITE SPIRIT.
2 A natural oleoresin from which this liquid is derived, typically taken from any one of various species of pine trees.

tusche *n* (*Ge*)
1 See LITHOGRAPHIC INK.
2 A dense, liquid drawing ink, such as INDIA INK.

tympan *n*
A metal frame attached to the bed of a PLATEN PRESS over which a piece of vellum or heavy fabric is stretched. The tympan is lowered over the bed when printing block and paper are in place and holds the paper firmly on the surface of the inked block.

tympanum *n*
An area of brickwork or stonework enclosed within an arch rising above a doorway, a feature often decorated with RELIEF SCULPTURE in a cathedral, church or architectural monument.

type *n*
1 Printed letterforms constructed, assembled and printed by any of a number of mechanical means.
2 Blocks of wood or metal each with a letterform cut in relief on the upper surface. This form of type is no longer used in commercial printing methods but old type blocks may be used in conjunction with LINOCUT, WOODCUT, or WOOD ENGRAVING blocks for individual designs.

type-height *n*
The depth of a piece of type, ie the level at which the relief surface stands above the bed of a press. When a lino or wood block is used to print an image in conjunction with type blocks, all the elements must be assembled at the same surface level.

typographic design *n*
The design of letterforms and alphabets for use as printed forms.

typography *n*
1 The process or activity of designing printed texts.
2 A design or layout composed of printed letterforms, eg individual letters, words and texts.
3 The mechanical techniques of assembling and printing such a design.

u

ultramarine *n*
1 A blue pigment of a rich, deep hue, originally made by grinding the semi-precious stone lapis lazuli, now manufactured from compounds which simulate the colour artificially. It is mainly known and used as a blue pigment, but can be the basis of a range of colours from green to violet.
2 The blue colour associated with this pigment.

umber *n*
A natural earth clay containing iron and manganese, processed from its original condition as the greenish-brown pigment raw umber and roasted to produce the dark reddish-brown pigment burnt umber. Both pigments are reliable and permanent.

undercut[1] *vb*
To shape a form by UNDERCUTTING. **undercut** *adj.*

undercut[2] *n*
The recess or angle passing around or behind a form shaped by undercutting.

undercutting *n*
A technical feature of a carved or modelled sculpture in which a detail of the form is cut or shaped in such a way as to be partly separated from the mass, so there is an angle or recess between them. Undercutting must be taken into account when making a mould from the sculpture, as a moulding material applied thickly to the surface will be trapped in the recess as it hardens and cannot be easily released. This is solved by passing the seam of a piece mould around the undercut form in a position which allows easy removal of each section of the mould.

underdrawing *n*
The process of sketching out a composition in line, using a brush and thinned paint or soft material such as charcoal, to establish the form of an UNDERPAINTING or to provide a guideline for direct application of colours.

under-glaze decoration *n*
Any form of decoration applied to an unfired clay body or biscuit ware, subsequently given a coating of glaze and fired.

underpainting *n*
1 The first stage of an oil painting in which the overall composition of the picture – outlines, masses, highlights and shadows – are worked out in monochrome, providing a basic image which is subsequently developed in colour and range of tone by the addition of further layers of paint. Traditionally the colours are overlaid as thin glazes and SCUMBLES, so the form of the underpainting is modified towards the final image, not covered completely.
2 The process of laying in a composition in monochrome.
3 More generally, any technique of applying the first rough form of a composition over which the full image is subsequently developed.
4 A layer of colour over which another colour is applied, intended to modify or show through the upper layer.

undertone *n*
The colour effect of a pigment when spread as a thin, transparent layer and affected by transmitted light, also seen when the pigment is used to tint white paint. It can have a different colour quality in this form from that of the full strength. See also MASS TONE.

v

vacuum forming *n*
A method of shaping hard sheet plastic over a solid relief shape or pattern, known as a former. This must be done in an airtight box from which the air can be drawn out to form a vacuum and is usually carried out in a machine specially designed for the purpose. The former is placed at the bottom of the box and the plastic sheet fitted across the top. Heat is applied to the plastic until it softens and the air is then rapidly extracted from the base of the box. The resultant vacuum pulls the plastic down onto the former and moulds it tightly over the shape. The plastic maintains the shape as it cools and can be lifted away from the former.

value *n*
1 The lightness or darkness of a tone, judged on a monochromatic range from black to white, through dark, mid-and light greys.

2 The inherent lightness or darkness of a chromatic colour judged by comparison with the range of tonal values, eg yellow as a light colour, violet as a typically dark colour.

vanishing point *n*
A fixed point in a system of PERSPECTIVE at which parallel lines receding from the picture plane are made to converge.

vanitas *n* (*Lat* vanity)
A form of still life composition in which the objects depicted are symbolic of the passage of time and human mortality, therefore representing the vanity of human desires.

variant *n*
A drawing, painting or sculpture which is a version of another work, very similar to the original but with minor variations in composition or technique of execution. It may be made by the artist responsible for the original work, by assistants under supervision, or by another, unconnected artist.

varnish[1] *n*
1 A liquid preparation that when applied to a surface dries to a more or less tough, glossy, transparent and flexible protective coating. There are many different types of varnish produced for different purposes, mainly compound liquids based on natural or synthetic resins. The types of varnish commonly used in oil painting are resin dissolved in a solvent, which dries by evaporation of the solvent, or resin cooked in a drying oil and thinned with turpentine or a similar solvent, which dries by a more complex process similar to the drying of oil paint.
2 A surface coating of this type of preparation. See also INTERMEDIATE VARNISH, MIXING VARNISH, PICTURE VARNISH, RETOUCHING VARNISH.

varnish[2] *vb*
To apply a varnish. **varnished** *adj*.

veduta *n* (*It*)
A painting or drawing showing a recognizable, realistic view of a particular town or city, rendered with extreme accuracy and detail.

veduta ideata *n* (*It*)
See CAPRICCIO.

vehicle *n*
The fluid constituent of a paint in which the pigment particles are suspended. The term is used interchangeably with the term MEDIUM, but strictly refers to the liquid used in paint

manufacture, rather than one added during the process of painting. The vehicle may also be the BINDER for the pigments.

veil *n*
1 A thin glaze of transparent colour applied over a white painting ground. See also IMPRIMATURA.
2 An area of colour in a painting applied as a stain or wash overlapping other colours.

veiner *n*
See V-TOOL.

vellum *n*
A writing material prepared from the skin of a calf, the traditional support for hand-written manuscripts and illuminated texts. The skins are soaked in lime solution, scraped to remove fur and flesh, stretched, dried and shaved to the required thickness. This procedure produces a flexible material with a slightly velvety texture in a creamy, yellow or light brown tone, depending upon the original fur and skin colour.
Compare PARCHMENT.

veneer *n*
1 A thin layer of wood used to give a decorative or superior finish to an object constructed from a lesser-quality wood.
2 Generally, a protective or decorative surface layer applied to an object or material of a different character.

Venice turpentine *n*
A thick, liquid OLEORESIN, a natural product of the Austrian larch, used as an ingredient of painting emulsions, mediums and varnishes. There are various grades of the substance and that preferred for painting is light-coloured, slightly cloudy and aromatic, and when dry has little tendency to yellowing.

vent *n*
A channel in a mould through which gases can escape when a casting material is poured into the mould. See RISER.

verdaccio *n*
A neutral brown or greenish-brown paint used for UNDERPAINTING or outlining a composition. It is a mixture of colours, not a pigment, therefore the actual colour varies from one painting to another.

verdigris *n*
1 A bright green or blue-green PATINA that forms on bronze, copper and other metals containing copper, due to chemical changes caused by exposure to the elements. Also called aerugo.

2 A blue-green pigment, now obsolete, of a similar composition, formed by the action of acetic acid on copper.

verism *n*
The concept that the purpose of art is to reproduce accurately and objectively the outward appearance of forms and objects, without selectivity or subjective interpretation.

vermilion *n*
1 A bright, opaque, pure red pigment, a form of mercuric sulphide produced artificially. Its permanence is not reliable and it has been largely superseded by lightfast colours such as cadmium red.
2 The red colour associated with this pigment.

vibration *n*
The agitation of a filled mould to compact or settle the casting material inside and allow escape of air bubbles.

vignette[1] *n*
1 A decorative motif consisting of intertwined leaves and tendrils, used as an ornament surrounding a letterform in a printed book or hand-written manuscript, or as an ornament filling a blank space on the page.
2 An image, painted drawn or printed, which fades off into the surrounding area without a clearly defined edge.
3 A dark background surrounding a figure or object in a drawing or illustration which fades to a light tone as it recedes from the focal point of the image.

vignette[2] *vb*
To make a vignette, by whatever technique. **vignetted** *adj.*

vignetting *n*
1 A technique used in airbrushing in which a solid background of colour surrounding a figure or object is faded out towards the edges by lightening the spray of paint.
2 More generally, any technique of fading the edges of a centralized image.

vinyl moulding compound *n*
Any of a number of compound substances based on the class of synthetic resins known as vinyl resins, used to make moulds from original forms in materials such as plaster, cement or resin. The rubbery compound is heated until molten and poured into the space created by surrounding an original model with an outer jacket or retaining wall. It solidifies as it cools but the finished mould is flexible. The material can reproduce fine detail and does

not deteriorate if stored. A mould made from it can be melted down and the material re-used.

viscosity *n*
The thickness and relative stickiness of a liquid or fluid substance, characterized by its degree of resistance to flowing freely when not confined. **viscous** *adj*.

vitreous *adj*
The descriptive adjective for glass, and by extension, for materials related to or resembling glass.

vitrification *n*
The process of turning to glass or becoming glassy. The term is used in connection with ceramic ware fired at high temperatures, when the components of the clay body fuse and it becomes hard, compact and non-porous.

volume *n*
The shape and mass of a three-dimensional form, as may be realized in terms of the actual space which it occupies. The term may be used in referring to the overall form of a sculpture or to an individual part or component which has a distinctive shape and mass.

V-tool *n*
A gouge which is narrow and V-shaped in section, used in WOODCUT printmaking and wood carving for cutting fine detail. Different sizes and weights are available for different types of work. Also called veiner.

w

walling wax *n*
Beeswax which is softened and used to build a low wall around the edges of an etching plate, so acid solution can be poured directly on the plate surface and is contained there by the hardened wax while exposed parts of the plate are etched. This is an alternative to immersing the plate in an acid bath.

walnut oil *n*
A natural drying oil, pale yellow in colour, pressed from walnut kernels. It is primarily used as an ingredient of oil painting

mediums, being generally regarded as inferior to linseed oil as a vehicle for pigments.

ware *n*
1 The collective term for manufactured items made of the same material, usually qualified by a prefix indicating the material, eg CERAMIC WARE, glassware, silverware, or the condition or type of the material, eg EARTHENWARE, GREEN WARE.
2 In context, objects made of the same material.

warm colour *n*
Any colour included in the range of red, red-purple, orange or orange-yellow hues, which can be said to have an apparent warmth. See also ADVANCING COLOUR.

wash *n*
An application of ink or watercolour heavily diluted with water to form a thin film of transparent colour on the support. Generally, the term can be applied to any dilute application of water-based paint, but is most commonly used of transparent media.

waste mould *n*
A plaster mould which is used only once for casting because it is shaped from an UNDERCUT form and must subsequently be broken to release the cast inside. The mould is usually made in two or more pieces over a soft clay model and when the plaster has hardened, the clay is cleaned out from the inside. The mould pieces are then reassembled and sealed before the casting material is poured in.

water-based *adj*
The description of a paint made with an aqueous vehicle, which can be mixed and diluted with water.

watercolour *n*
1 Paint consisting of finely ground pigments dispersed evenly in a water-soluble gum binder. So that the paint remains readily soluble in use, a small amount of moisture-attracting substance, eg honey or glycerin, or a wetting agent may be added in manufacture. Watercolour is thinned and mixed with water and is typically applied in a transparent film or WASH of colour, strong colours and tones being built up gradually by successive overlaid washes. The most suitable pigments are therefore those which have an inherent degree of transparency. Watercolours are available as dry cakes or semi-moist pans of colour, in fluid form packaged in tubes or liquid form in bottles.
2 A painting executed in this medium.
3 More broadly, the term is sometimes used as a general

reference for any type of paint that can be thinned and mixed with water, eg GOUACHE, TEMPERA.

watercolour paper *n*
A term used of various rag papers of different weights and textures suitable as supports for watercolour painting. Generally, the requirements of a watercolour paper are that it should be relatively heavy and stable, able to keep its shape under repeated wettings, not chemically treated and neither too smooth nor too rough in surface texture.

watercolour pencil *n*
A thin stick of coloured crayon encased in wood, the medium being water-soluble so that colour applied to a support can be wetted and spread with a brush.

water-glass painting *n*
A technique used for mural painting in which a mineral solution known as water glass is used as the medium and protective coating for water-based paints applied directly to a smoothly plastered wall. Reactions between pigments and the mineral solution tend to produce rapid deterioration and this method has been superseded by use of reliable acrylic paints and other media better suited to mural work.
Also called mineral painting and stereochromy.

watermark *n*
A motif or lettered design visible in a sheet of paper when it is held to the light, caused by a wire motif fastened to the mesh on which the paper is made. When the pulped fibres settle they form a thinner layer over the raised motif, which is more translucent than the surrounding paper in the sheet. The watermark is a manufacturer's identification.

water-tension breaker *n*
See WETTING AGENT.

wax^1 *n*
Any of a number of natural and synthetic substances that have in common properties of being viscous or solid in their original states, lustrous and translucent in appearance, sensitive to heat in that they soften and melt under rising temperatures, and insoluble in water. Natural waxes are of animal and vegetable origin: synthetic products are derived from oil and petroleum distillates. They have various uses as modelling materials, ingredients of paint mediums, surface coatings and grounds etc. See ENCAUSTIC, LOST WAX PROCESS.

wax[2] *vb*
To apply wax as a surface coating or polish. **waxed** *adj.*

waxing *n*
Any process of coating a surface, eg of bronze or stone, with a film of wax intended to act as a protective layer which seals pores in the material and imparts a lustrous finish.

wax resist *n*
1 A method of combining drawing and painting in an image using a wax crayon, candle or other waxy material to draw on paper, then coating the drawing with washes of watercolour paint which are repelled by the wax and settle on the paper in the areas around the drawn image.
2 A waxy material applied in this way.
3 An image or part of an image created by this method.

wedge[1] *n*
1 (*sculpture*) A piece of wood or metal thick at one end and tapered to a sharp edge at the other, which is hammered into a block of wood or soft stone to split the material down the grain.
2 (*painting*) A triangular piece of wood driven into a slot at the inner corner of a STRETCHER. Wedges are fitted into all four corners of a stretcher and by pressing on the joints they expand the corners slightly, thereby tautening the stretched canvas. Also called key.

wedge[2] *vb*
To prepare a mass of clay by WEDGING. **wedged** *adj.*

wedging *n*
The process of preparing clay which will eventually be fired, to give it an even, workable texture and to eliminate air pockets. There are two basic methods: spiral wedging involves twisting the clay mass upwards with one hand while pressing it down with the other, the action performed in a continuous motion in which the clay is stretched, turned and compressed. In the alternative method, the clay is pressed into a compact mass and cut in half laterally: the sections are smoothed and the top half is turned and thrown down heavily onto the bottom half. Both processes are performed repeatedly until the right texture is achieved.

weld[1] *vb*
To join pieces of metal by WELDING. **welded** *adj.*

weld[2] *n*
A joint between pieces of metal made by welding.

welding *n*
The process of joining two pieces of metal by heating the parts until the edges to be joined are molten and bringing them into direct contact so the molten sections fuse together.
Compare BRAZING, SOLDERING.

well palette *n*
A ceramic, metal or plastic palette used for mixing and thinning colours to be applied in liquid consistency. There are various types, the important feature being that the palette is moulded into a number of separate recesses that will hold quantities of fluid paint.

wet and dry *n*
Paper coated with a thin layer of silicon carbide granules or powder, used as an abrasive material for smoothing and polishing a hard surface, eg stone. The name derives from the fact that the paper is water-resistant and can be used wet or dry.

wet into wet *n*
The technique of working a fresh application of paint over paint layers which are still wet. The term is used especially of work in oils or watercolours.

wet over dry *n*
The technique of applying fresh paint over paint layers which have been given some time to dry. The term is used especially of work in oils or watercolours.

wetting agent *n*
A liquid formulated with the capacity to reduce the surface tension of water. It may be added in small quantities to a water-based paint, eg acrylic or watercolour, to improve the fluidity and adherence.
Also called water-tension breaker.

wetting down *n*
1 The practice of flooding the surface of a stone block with water during the carving process to bring out the colour and texture, enabling the sculptor either to identify veins and flaws in the material or to estimate the likely effect of polishing the stone.
2 The method of keeping a clay model moist and in a workable condition between periods of work by spraying the surface with water and wrapping the clay form in polythene or damp cloths.

white line engraving *n*
An impression taken from an engraved surface printed as relief, so the image appears as white lines on a black ground, as in wood engraving.

white spirit *n*
A colourless liquid distilled from petroleum, used as a diluent and solvent for oil paints and other materials. It is sometimes inaccurately called turpentine, because it has similar properties and is commonly used as an inexpensive substitute for turpentine.

whiting *n*
A fine white powder made by grinding and cleaning natural calcium carbonate (chalk), used as an extender or filler in paints and grounds.

window dipping *n*
A technique for decorating ceramic objects with glaze or SLIP by partially dipping the form into the liquid mixture. If the side of a pot, for example, is partially dipped, the surface picks up an even, clean-edged patch of glaze which is known as a window.

window mount *n*
A piece of board used to frame the image area of a work on paper, made by cutting an opening at the centre of the board to leave wide margins on all four sides. The picture is mounted on the back of the board by use of a suitable adhesive, the edges of the image aligned with those of the window opening. The window is usually cut with bevelled edges to reduce the abruptness of the framing and to avoid allowing the thickness of the board to cast a shadow into the image area.

wiping *n*
The process of cleaning the surface of an inked INTAGLIO plate, leaving ink only in the recessed lines and areas which have been engraved or etched for this purpose. A pad of SCRIM is used to wipe surplus ink from the plate and the surface is then polished with the side of the hand or a piece of soft tissue or fabric rubbed flatly on the plate surface. The purpose of wiping is not only to clean the surface to produce white areas in the print, but also to ensure an even distribution of ink in the intaglio so a run of identical prints can be taken by repeating a thorough wiping each time the plate is inked. To produce special effects of softened lines or reduced contrasts the plate may be only lightly wiped or the ink can be lifted by the technique of RETROUSSAGE.

wood *n*
The hard, fibrous mass of plant tissue formed in the trunk and branches of a tree.

wood block printing *n*
This term can be used as a synonym for WOODCUT, but more specifically refers to the technique of making colour prints using a separate wood block for each colour in the design.

wood carving *n*
1 The process of making a sculpture in wood by cutting and shaping a mass of material.
2 A wood sculpture made by carving.

woodcut *n*
1 A RELIEF PRINTING process in which the image or design is cut into the surface of a PLANK-GRAIN wood block. The cutting tools used are knives, gouges and chisels: since these must follow or cut across the wood grain, the design cannot be too complex or delicate because of the tendency to split the grain. The typical form of a woodcut when printed is black lines and masses on a white ground. To create a coloured image, a separate block is cut for each different colour.
2 A printed image obtained by this process.

wood engraving *n*
1 A RELIEF PRINTING process in which the design or image is achieved by engraving lines in a block of wood. It differs from a WOODCUT in that a BURIN is used to engrave on an END-GRAIN block of a hardwood such as boxwood. The compact surface is resistant but allows fine lines to be engraved in any direction without splintering the surface. The printed effect can be typified as white lines on a black ground, though sometimes broad areas are cleared to print white around black lines. It is because of the delicate linear qualities that the process is identified as engraving, but the block is inked and printed as a relief surface.
2 A printed image obtained by this process.

working proof *n*
A proof taken from a partly-worked block or plate and used to develop the image. The artist works on the proof with a pencil, ink or other drawing medium, to plan further stages of the work.

workshop *n*
1 A studio in which all the tools and materials for a particular process are assembled, particularly when this includes items of permanently fixed equipment, eg printing presses, heavy cutting machinery etc.
2 In medieval times, the studio of an artist in which work was carried out by assistants under supervision. This use of the term is still applicable to comparable situations.

wove paper *n*
A broad category of various types of paper made by hand or machine on a closely-woven wire mesh, which itself imparts no discernible surface texture or internal pattern to the paper sheet. The texture and surface finish of the paper are dependent on the

fibres and the particular processes of finishing. The majority of papers can be categorized under this term. See also LAID PAPER.

wrinkling *n*
A defect in oil painting, seen as wrinkling of the surface into irregular ridges and furrows, caused either by contraction of a paint layer as the medium dries out or by actual damage to the paint film, eg when a rigid support becomes warped or a canvas is rolled painted side inwards.

x

xylography *n*
A term now rarely used for methods of printing from wood blocks. See WOODCUT, WOOD ENGRAVING.

y

yellowing *n*
1 The discolouring of an oil painting as it ages, due to a natural tendency of the oil or varnish ingredients to turn yellow with age, excessive use of linseed oil or an accumulation of dirt on the varnish layer.
2 The discolouring of a particular material used in a painting, eg the medium or varnish.

z

zinc white *n*
A synthetic inorganic white pigment based on zinc oxide. It is permanent but has less tinting strength than titanium white and is

less opaque. It is suitable for use in oil and watercolour paints and as a watercolour is also marketed under the name Chinese white.

zinnober *n* (*Ge*)
VERMILION.

zones of recession *n pl*
In a system of LINEAR PERSPECTIVE, the successive vertical planes receding from the picture plane towards the horizon line or vanishing point, within which figures or objects in the composition become progressively smaller and angles of receding planes become more acute.

zoomorphic *adj*
A term used to describe stylized motifs and ornamentation based on animal forms.